D1500290

POPULATION CHANGE, LABOR MARKETS, AND SUSTAINABLE GROWTH

TOWARDS A NEW ECONOMIC PARADIGM

CONTRIBUTIONS
TO
ECONOMIC ANALYSIS

281

Honorary Editors:
D. W. JORGENSON
J. TINBERGEN†

Editors:
B. BALTAGI
E. SADKA
D. WILDASIN

ELSEVIER

Amsterdam – Boston – Heidelberg – London – New York – Oxford
Paris – San Diego – San Francisco – Singapore – Sydney – Tokyo

POPULATION CHANGE, LABOR MARKETS, AND SUSTAINABLE GROWTH

TOWARDS A NEW ECONOMIC PARADIGM

Edited by
Andrew Mason
University of Hawaii – Manoa and the East-West Center, USA

Mitoshi Yamaguchi
Kobe University, Japan

ELSEVIER

2007

Amsterdam – Boston – Heidelberg – London – New York – Oxford
Paris – San Diego – San Francisco – Singapore – Sydney – Tokyo

Elsevier
Radarweg 29, PO Box 211, 1000 AE Amsterdam, The Netherlands
The Boulevard, Langford Lane, Kidlington, Oxford OX5 1GB, UK

First edition 2007

Notice
No responsibility is assumed by the publisher for any injury and/or damage to persons
or property as a matter of products liability, negligence or otherwise, or from any use
or operation of any methods, products, instructions or ideas contained in the material
herein. Because of rapid advances in the medical sciences, in particular, independent
verification of diagnoses and drug dosages should be made

Library of Congress Cataloging-in-Publication Data
A catalog record for this book is available from the Library of Congress

British Library Cataloguing in Publication Data
A catalogue record for this book is available from the British Library

ISBN-13: 978-0-444-53051-6
ISBN-10: 0-444-53051-7

For information on all Elsevier publications
visit our website at books.elsevier.com

Printed and bound in The Netherlands

07 08 09 10 11   10 9 8 7 6 5 4 3 2 1

Working together to grow
libraries in developing countries

www.elsevier.com | www.bookaid.org | www.sabre.org

ELSEVIER   BOOK AID
International   Sabre Foundation

CONTENTS

List of Contributors   vii

Chapter 1   **Introduction**   1
Andrew Mason and Mitoshi Yamaguchi

Chapter 2   **Evolution of Recent Economic-Demographic Modeling: A Synthesis**   5
Allen C. Kelley and Robert M. Schmidt

Chapter 3   **A Century of Demographic Change and Economic Growth: The Asian Experience in Regional and Temporal Perspective**   39
Allen C. Kelley and Robert M. Schmidt

Chapter 4   **Demographic Dividends: The Past, the Present, and the Future**   75
Andrew Mason

Chapter 5   **Demographic Change and Regional Economic Growth: A Comparative Analysis of Japan and China**   99
Tomoko Kinugasa, Wei Huang, and Mitoshi Yamaguchi

Chapter 6   **Job Opportunities for Older Workers: When Are Jobs Filled with External Hires?**   133
Robert Hutchens

Chapter 7   **Skills, Wages, and the Employment of Older Workers**   161
Naoki Mitani

Chapter 8   **Work-Life Balance Measures and Gender Division of Labor**   189
Akira Kawaguchi

Chapter 9   **Optimal Education Policies Under an Equity–Efficiency Trade-Off**   211
Takashi Oshio

Chapter 10   **Why Are Japanese Refusing to Pay the National Pension Tax?: A Simultaneous Equation Analysis**   243
Mitoshi Yamaguchi and Noriko Aoki

Author Index   265
Subject Index   269

LIST OF CONTRIBUTORS

Andrew Mason is Professor of Economics, University of Hawaii at Manoa, and Senior Fellow, Population and Health Studies, East-West Center, Honolulu.

Mitoshi Yamaguchi is Professor of Economics, Graduate School of Economics, Kobe University.

Noriko Aoki is a graduate student, Graduate School of Economics, Kobe University.

Robert Hutchens is Professor of Economics, Department of Labor Economics, School of Industrial and Labor Relations, Cornell University.

Akira Kawaguchi is Professor of Economics, Faculty of Policy Studies, Doshisha University.

Allen C. Kelley is Professor of Economics, Duke University.

Tomoko Kinugasa is Associate Professor of Economics, Graduate School of Economics, Kobe University.

Naoki Mitani is Professor of Economics, Graduate School of Economics, Kobe University.

Takashi Oshio is Professor of Economics, Graduate School of Economics, Kobe University.

Robert M. Schmidt is Professor of Economics, University of Richmond.

Wei Huang is a Ph.D. candidate, Graduate School of Economics, Kobe University.

CHAPTER 1

Introduction

Andrew Mason and Mitoshi Yamaguchi

Population growth is in decline and populations are becoming older throughout the world. Low fertility is the common factor behind both of these trends. In many Asian and European countries, women are averaging fewer than two births over their reproductive span and, often, closer to one. With fertility so low, population decline is inevitable. Ever smaller cohorts of births are leading to ever smaller cohorts of children and young adults, and eventually to populations in which the old greatly outnumber the young. Reinforcing the effects of low fertility are continuing improvements in life expectancy. In the past, mortality gains were achieved by reducing death rates among infants and children. This is still true in the world's poorest countries, but elsewhere death rates among the young have reached very low levels. Further gains are being achieved by reducing death rates among the old, reinforcing the effects of fertility on population age structure. As a consequence, the most rapidly growing demographic groups in many countries are those in their 70s, 80s, and older.

The contributions to this volume are concerned primarily with the economic implications of and the policy responses to these demographic changes. The original papers were prepared as part of a Center of Excellence (COE) research initiative, funded by the government of Japan and carried out by the Graduate School of Economics Research Institute for Economics and Business Administration at Kobe University. Leading scholars from Japan and the United States were invited to prepare papers on this common theme and to present them at the 4th International Conference of the Japan Economic Policy Association, co-sponsored by the Kobe University Center of Excellence and held at the Awaji Yumebutai International Conference Center in Awaji, Hyogo, Japan, during 17–18 December, 2005. The papers were refereed and revised in accordance with the reviewers' suggestions prior to being copyedited.

The issues addressed here are of interest everywhere, but they are particularly salient in Japan. Japan has the highest life expectancy and

POPULATION CHANGE, LABOR MARKETS, AND SUSTAINABLE GROWTH
VOLUME 281   ISSN 0573-8555/DOI 10.1016/S0573-8555(07)81001-7

the oldest population of any country in the world. Its fertility rate has dropped steadily for decades and is currently just below 1.3 births per woman. Its population has peaked and is beginning to decline for the first time in modern history. Its working-age population has been in decline for a number of years. Like many other countries, Japan is struggling to understand the implications of these demographic changes for its economic strength. Generational issues are squarely on the front burner in important policy debates. How can couples be encouraged to marry and have children? Can educational reform lead to a more productive young labor force, helping to offset their meager numbers? Can labor market reform extend the working life of older workers without damaging the interests of others? How should the social safety net that supports the elderly evolve in ways that are both fair and sustainable? Of course, these very same issues are being debated in Europe, North America, and increasingly elsewhere around the world. The studies presented here rely on both Japanese and international experience to address these issues.

The first four chapters provide a macroeconomic perspective that frames the policy issues. In Chapter 2, Kelley and Schmidt provide a conceptual framework for modeling the economic effects of demographic change that builds on their own work and important studies by Barro; Bloom and Williamson; Bloom, Canning, and Mulaney; and others. Using a cross-country panel spanning the 1960–95 period, they show that demographic change in recent decades has played a pro-growth role accounting for about 20% of per capita output growth, on average. In Asia and Europe the positive contribution has been even greater.

In Chapter 3, Kelley and Schmidt build on the growth model presented in Chapter 2 and focus their attention more on the future than on the past. They provide important details about regional variation in the growth effects of demographic change, concluding that the effects will be favorable in Africa, Latin America, and South-Central Asia, but unfavorable in East Asia and the West. Of particular importance are the effects of age structure on saving and investment. They present evidence that declining youth dependency has had strong positive effects on saving and investment, but these favorable effects will be overwhelmed by the negative effects of rising old-age dependency in the near future. If Kelley and Schmidt prove to be correct, aging may lead to slower growth or even economic decline.

Mason's analysis presented in Chapter 4 builds on earlier work with Lee and recent empirical analysis with Kinugasa, providing an interesting contrast to Kelley and Schmidt's contribution. Mason relies on a simulation approach and long-term historical data to explore how demographic change influenced economic growth in India, Japan, and the United States. His results are consistent with Kelley and Schmidt's conclusion that demographic change had very favorable effects on per capita income growth during the second half of the twentieth century. With respect to capital accumulation and the future, his findings differ. He points to increases in life expectancy as the primary force that led to the rapid accumulation of wealth. Moreover, his analysis implies that, although saving rates may decline as populations age, wealth will increase relative to GDP. In the United States, demographic factors will continue to be moderately favorable. In Japan, however, labor productivity is likely to rise but per capita income will drop because the share of the population in the labor force will decline so rapidly.

Most research on population and development emphasizes the national level, but many of the most important issues related to aging are local. Many public services on which the elderly depend are provided by local governments. The ability of the private sector to provide services for the elderly depends on the resources that must be locally available. Moreover, the age distributions of populations vary enormously by region. The young flock to the cities, while the elderly remain in the countryside. In Chapter 5, Kinugasa, Huang, and Yamaguchi fill this void by analyzing the influences of demographic factors on economic growth at the prefectural level in Japan and the provincial level in China. Their most important finding is that population size has a strong positive effect on economic growth at the regional level. If so, population decline will have particularly severe effects on economic growth in regions where many of the elderly are living. This could greatly complicate efforts to formulate effective policy responses to population aging.

Retirement behavior and policy will inevitably play a vital role in determining the economic effects of population aging. The available evidence suggests that the elderly are not only living longer, but are healthier as well. By remaining in the labor force to a later age, older adults can reduce the financial burden they impose on younger generations—their adult children in some societies and taxpayers in other settings.

Chapter 6 by Hutchens and Chapter 7 by Mitani address two aspects of the employment of older workers. Hutchens considers a difficult aspect of the labor market for older workers: the transition into new jobs that are more suited to their (often declining) skills. Many workers are forced to retire from firms and seek new jobs. Many employers, however, are reluctant to fill jobs with "outside" rather than "inside" workers—that is, workers who are already employed by the firm. Using a survey of establishments with information on white-collar jobs, currently held by older workers, Hutchens provides new information about which types of jobs are likely to be filled by outside workers and which worker characteristics influence the decision to hire rather than to fill from within the firm.

Mitani explores two important issues that affect policy toward older workers. The first is whether the increase in wages received by workers as they age is matched by an increase in their skills. If not, employers will be reluctant to retain older workers. Mitani finds that in some occupations the match is close, but that in others it is not. The second issue, he investigates, is whether the firms that retain older workers reduce their hiring of younger workers. He finds that they do. If extending the working life of older workers leads to the displacement of younger workers, more flexible retirement policies are a less attractive response to population aging.

An entirely different approach to population aging is to increase the number or the "quality" of young workers. As fertility rates drop ever lower, many governments are adopting policies to encourage childbearing. In Chapter 8 Kawaguchi examines one set of such policies implemented in Japan. The government is encouraging private firms to adopt work-life balance programs that provide time off and other benefits to parents of newly born children. The rates of uptake by men are very low, however, and Kawaguchi explores why this is so and whether government subsidies should be provided to encourage greater participation by fathers in these programs.

The total productivity of each new generation of workers depends on both their numbers and their individual productivity. As the numbers shrink, the importance of education and other forms of human capital investment become all the more important. As Oshio points out in Chapter 9, however, public spending on education typically benefits the most talented—raising productivity but sacrificing equality. He shows how a mixed system of public and private education can be used to solve this dilemma. The emphasis of the public sector should be on offering public education to low-ability individuals, while high-ability individuals are best served by private education systems. To the extent that this has a regressive effect on income inequality, other distributive policies can be employed to achieve the desired distribution of income.

The final chapter in the volume, by Yamaguchi and Aoki, addresses a remarkable development in Japan's political economy, but one that may be repeated elsewhere: taxpayer revolt against the public pension system. As populations age, public pension systems will become increasingly unattractive to taxpayers. They face higher tax rates and reductions in pension benefits. Yamaguchi and Aoki analyze why pension compliance rates vary and conclude that low rates of compliance are found in areas with more university students, a higher birth rate, lower death rates, higher unemployment, and higher rates of investment in financial securities. These results identify some of the possible explanations for low compliance and also provide clear evidence that workers are substituting personal saving for participation in the public pension program.

CHAPTER 2

Evolution of Recent Economic-Demographic Modeling: A Synthesis

Allen C. Kelley and Robert M. Schmidt

Few issues in social history have attracted more attention than assessments of the economic consequences of rapid population growth. Debates have been vigorous and contentious. The primary evidence that has both stimulated and sustained these debates is cross-country regressions and simple correlations that expose the impacts of demographic variables on per capita output growth. A surprising result emerges: the overall impacts of population are generally found to be small, especially for the 1960s and the 1970s, although some negative impacts appear to emerge for the 1980s and possibly beyond (Kelley and Schmidt 1994). There are a number of reasons why the cross-country studies are inconclusive, not the least being their somewhat simple rendering of demographic processes.

Empirical analysis was enriched in the 1990s with the emergence of a theoretical framework by Robert J. Barro that incorporates population into convergence (or technology-gap) models. He and his collaborators concluded that high fertility, population growth, and mortality all exert negative impacts on per capita output growth (Barro 1991, 1997; Barro and Lee 1994). We (Kelley and Schmidt 1994) extended this list to include population density and size, which revealed positive impacts, although a net negative assessment of combined demographic trends represented the bottom line.

Convergence modeling of demographic trends evolved further in the late 1990s through a series of papers by several Harvard economists (e.g., Bloom and Williamson 1997, 1998; Bloom and Canning 2001, 2003; Bloom, Canning, and Malaney 2000; Radelet, Sachs, and Lee 2001). Building on the Barro setup (albeit with a different choice of core variables),

This chapter has been modified slightly from an article that appeared in 2005 in the *Journal of Population Economics* 18(2), 275–300. It has been included with the kind permission of Springer Science and Business Media.

POPULATION CHANGE, LABOR MARKETS, AND SUSTAINABLE GROWTH
VOLUME 281   ISSN 0573-8555/DOI 10.1016/S0573-8555(07)81002-9

the Harvard framework focused on population impacts that take place as a result of imbalanced age-structure changes over the demographic transition. Their modeling compactly captured these impacts by just two variables: population growth (N_{gr}) and working-age growth (WA_{gr}). Such a specification neatly "translates" a traditional neoclassical model formulated in per-worker output growth into a comparable model formulated in per capita output growth. While such a translation derives from an identity, it is nevertheless a useful framework that provides a way of exposing some shorter-period "population impacts" within the usual long-run neoclassical framework. Such "translation" impacts of population in numerous Harvard empirical studies are assessed to be sizable, especially in East Asia.

Important to appraising these empirical findings is an understanding of the nature of the highlighted impacts of demographic translations. Although N_{gr} and WA_{gr} are primarily introduced into these models to translate per-worker growth rates into per capita growth rates, they are often interpreted to play a role in the determination of the per-worker growth rate as well. Here, we build on the Harvard tradition by emphasizing the point that any per capita output growth rate can be separated into two components: an economic production (productivity) component and a translations component. We argue that these components are potentially separable and that clearer insights into the multifaceted role of population in economic growth can be gained by modeling them separately. In particular, such a rendering allows for the possibility that N_{gr} and WA_{gr} play little or no role in explaining productivity growth once the productivity component is modeled to include additional demographic variables. In this chapter we take a hard look at these potentially separable components in a framework that provides reasonably clear, consistent, and interpretable empirical results with interesting policy implications. Our approach makes several contributions.

First it enables us to formulate an economic growth paradigm that highlights the separability of production and translations components. We identify quite distinct roles that population may play within each component. We believe that this paradigm clarifies several specific ways in which economic and demographic change interconnect. We further believe that the modeling perspective developed in this chapter need not be restricted to the particular empirical renderings chosen for this study. Indeed, our paradigm provides a potential platform for introducing alternative treatments of population into the modeling of economic growth.

Second, we evaluate this framework empirically using the Barro core. The results show that translations demography has little or no impact on economic production per se, although the analysis of translations clarifies some welfare implications of demographic change. On net, demographic change elicits positive translations impacts over the full period in all regions. Such impacts, a by-product of the demographic transition in many countries, are not uniformly positive over time. Our results indicate that the positive impacts relatively early in the demographic transition tend to turn negative during a later phase.

Third, we show that population does matter within the productivity component, but primarily through linkages such as youth age structure, a variable highlighted in the literature of the 1950s–80s. These demographic impacts on economic production, while notable, are not remarkable. World-wide, demographic changes account for around 8% of the influences effecting change in output per laborer growth, an impact with substantial regional variance spanning 3% in Africa to 28% in Asia. Impacts of demographic translations are also sizable (13%), but with smaller variance spanning 11% in South America to 16% in Asia. Overall, the results place population's role as neither alarming nor benign. What has changed with the evolution of modeling in the 1990s is a clearer interpretation of the channels and sizes of demographic changes on the economy.

The remainder of the chapter has five sections. The first provides an organizing framework that highlights the separability of impacts of demographic change on per-worker output growth from those of per capita output growth. The second assesses alternative ways of incorporating demographic variables into the convergence model. The third defends our preferred empirical paradigm that meshes the Barro core, the Harvard translations structure, and our own demographic enrichments. The fourth examines the importance and alternative roles of population in this framework, compares these results with other models in the literature, and arrives at empirical assessments that qualify the recent literature. The final section summarizes our conclusions.

2.1. Productivity and translations as an organizing framework

We present in equation (2.1) an initial taxonomy for organizing an assessment of demographic change:

$$(Y/N)_{gr} \equiv \underbrace{Y/L_{gr}}_{\text{Productivity Component}} + \underbrace{(L_{gr} - N_{gr})}_{\text{Translations Component}} \tag{2.1}$$

It decomposes per capita output growth $[(Y/N)_{gr}]$ into two components: (1) a labor productivity component $[(Y/L)_{gr}]$ and (2) a translations component $[L_{gr} - N_{gr}]$ that converts output growth per labor hour into output growth per person. Equation (2.1) derives from the identity $Y/N \equiv (Y/L)(L/N)$ (see Bloom and Williamson 1998).

Equation (2.1) is deceptively simple—it is, after all, an identity. We would argue, however, that recasting the Harvard model into separable productivity and translations components not only serves to clarify inconsistent demographic results found in previous empirical studies, but also provides a framework upon which further advances can be based. In this regard, note that this framework remains agnostic with respect to the importance of both the two components to per capita GDP growth rates and the models chosen for either component. Our study builds upon, challenges, and enriches the modeling of the Harvard studies. As such, we consider it a bridge between past and future demographic modeling. We begin by considering several candidates for the translations component.

The translations component can take many forms. The one employed in most neoclassical theoretical modeling,

$$\text{Translation I} \qquad \left(L_{gr} - N_{gr}\right) = 0 \qquad\qquad (2.2)$$

results in a focus on labor productivity due to the simplifying assumption that $L_{gr} = N_{gr}$. Population growth has no impact on per capita economic growth per se unless it has a direct impact on $(Y/L)_{gr}$. Such a framework is most relevant in the longer run (e.g., at or near a demographic steady state) or during conditions of slowly evolving demographic change, and less relevant during conditions characterized by sizable variations in L_{gr} and N_{gr} due to major changes in mortality and fertility.

A second translation takes full advantage of the components of labor change:

$$\text{Translation II} \qquad \left(L_{gr} - N_{gr}\right) = (L/LF)_{gr} + (LF/WA)_{gr} \\ + WA_{gr} - N_{gr} \qquad (2.3)$$

where $L = $ total labor hours, $LF = $ laborers available for work, and $WA = $ working-age population. This expression reveals, in order, the impacts of changes in labor utilization rates (L/LF), labor force participation rates out of the working-age population (LF/WA), working ages (WA), and population (N). The last two terms represent population, driven by changes in fertility, mortality, and migration. The other terms evolve from labor market conditions and household choices. While beyond the scope of the chapter, this translation illuminates several potentially fruitful areas for future modeling, possibly within an endogenous framework. Consider the last three terms. While WA_{gr} is largely predetermined within our 10-year growth periods, changes in labor force participation out of the working ages $[(LF/WA)_{gr}]$ as well as fertility and mortality changes (N_{gr}) need not be. An endogenous treatment of the interplay between fertility and female labor force participation could be intriguing in this context. Such modeling might incorporate macroeconomic renderings of the labor–leisure tradeoff as well as changes in public family planning programs and family structure during development.

A third translation, advanced by the Harvard scholars, focuses on the working-age population (WA, say ages 15–64):

Translation III $(L_{gr} - N_{gr}) = \text{WA}_{gr} - N_{gr}$ (2.4)

This formulation abstracts from labor force participation and employment rates. Because changes in the age distribution can be large and account for much of the variation in L, WA is a potentially useful proxy for labor force effects that occur during the demographic transition. We adopt this translation for the empirical work in this chapter for two reasons. First, this translation provides a productive comparison between empirical results from the Harvard model and the extended model we propose. Second, and more important, within the 10-year growth periods employed in this chapter, WA_{gr} is exogenous to the model whereas LF_{gr} is not. An endogenous modeling of labor force growth—and in particular one highlighting female labor force participation—is well beyond the scope of the chapter, especially given the problematic quality of labor force estimates.

Common to each of these specifications is the overriding lesson that the translations variables might have no impact on $(Y/L)_{gr}$. If that were the case, then their role would be mechanical in the sense that no econometric estimation would be necessary to estimate their net impact on $(Y/N)_{gr}$; the net impact would be the unweighted difference between L_{gr} (however approximated) and N_{gr}. This does not imply that their quantitative impact need be small. Indeed, their difference can be quite large, positive or negative, at various points during the demographic transition. We would argue, however, that fuller modeling should include additional direct roles for demographic change on labor productivity growth, the variable highlighted in neoclassical growth theory. We expand on this distinction between direct "productivity" impacts and "translations" impacts in the following two sections. Additionally, the fourth section provides empirical tests for productivity impacts of the translations variables while the fifth section presents estimates of the productivity and translations components on changes in $(Y/N)_{gr}$.

2.2. Expanding the theory: Elaborating the roles of population

Prior to elaborating the roles of population, we provide background on the convergence framework. We then assess possible roles of population in the productivity component of equation (2.1). Finally, we discuss another possible translations role that is not included in equation (2.1), the translation of the convergence term itself from per-worker into per capita terms.

2.2.1. Expanding theory: The convergence framework for modeling productivity growth

The economic growth literature provides numerous ways to model productivity growth. We focus here on the "convergence" or "technology-gap" framework. Rooted in neoclassical growth theory, this paradigm explores the relationships between economic growth and the *level* of economic development. It focuses on the pace at which countries move from their current economic level to their long-run, or potential, or steady-state equilibrium level of output. (This section benefits from the presentations of Barro 1997 and Radelet, Sachs, and Lee 2001.)

The model begins by positing a convergence assumption:

$$Y/L_{\text{gr}_{it}} = c\left[\ln(Y/L_{it})^* - \ln(Y/L_{it})\right] \tag{2.5}$$

Here the rate of output growth per worker $[(Y/L)_{\text{gr}}]$ is proportional to the gap between the logs of the long-run, steady-state $(Y/L)^*$ and the current (Y/L) levels. The greater this gap, the greater is the gap separating physical capital, human capital, technical efficiency, or some combination of these three from their potential levels. Large gaps allow for "catching up" through (physical and human) capital accumulation and technology creation and diffusion across, and within, countries.

The rate of convergence, c, is assumed to be independent of time and place. By contrast, potential output per worker $(Y/L_{it})^*$ is specific to country (i) and time (t). This "conditional" convergence allows for the observed positive correlation between the level of development and economic growth rates. Were Y/L^* the same for all countries, the simple correlation would be negative. Were Y/L^* the same for all time periods, the world's economy would eventually stop growing. Potential productivity is, of course, unobservable and must be modeled. Its log is modeled as a linear function of a vector of country- and time-specific characteristics:

$$\ln(Y/L_{it})^* = a + b\,\mathbf{Z}_{it} \tag{2.6}$$

The actual specification of the determinants of long-run labor productivity (i.e., the selection of $\mathbf{Z}$'s) varies notably, but the basic model, which combines equations (2.5) and (2.6), is the same across scores of empirical studies:

$$Y/L_{\text{gr}_{it}} = a' + b'\,\mathbf{Z}_{it} - c\,\ln(Y/L_{it}) \tag{2.7}$$

where $a' = ac$ and $b' = bc$.

What types of **Z** variables should be included as determinants of long-run output per worker? Recognizing that a long-run, steady-state production function lies behind Y/L_{it}^{*}, one should consider factors that influence long-run physical and human capital stocks, technology, and natural resource stocks. Barro (1997, sect. I) additionally notes that endogenous growth theories that include the discovery and diffusion of new technologies suggest that Y/L_{it}^{*} depends upon "governmental actions such as taxation, maintenance of law and order, provision of infrastructure services, protection of intellectual property rights, and regulation of international trade, financial markets, and other aspects of the economy." Additionally, various authors have suggested climate, access to ports, education, health, and many other factors as possible influences.

More subtly, equation (2.5) provides additional insight. The invariance of the convergence parameter (c) across countries is consistent with a neoclassical view of efficient international capital markets. Simply stated, a neoclassical perspective models (physical and human) investment to flow fluidly within and across countries toward highest returns (e.g., to regions and countries with large gaps between potential and current Y/L). However, not all countries finance investment with equal ease. Thus, a second category of variables is added to the **Z** vector to "condition" the convergence rate, c. These variables include country- and time-specific factors that enhance or deter international capital flows, domestic saving, domestic investment, or migration. Included among these are, for example, restrictive licensing, the risk of expropriation, political conditions, the rule of law, and migration regulations.

Conspicuous by its absence from this list is the investment share in GDP. At first blush, investment might be the first variable one would think to include in a model of $(Y/L)_{gr}$. Indeed, Levine and Renelt (1992) surveyed numerous empirical growth studies to identify a common set of influential variables. They found investment rates to constitute the most robust variable. Rather than implying that the investment rate is a viable **Z** variable for predicting long-run capital-to-output ratios, however, its significance in a convergence model suggests an incomplete set of **Z** variables. If the convergence hypothesis is correct, the list of **Z** variables is complete, and factors enhancing or deterring the free flow of investment have been modeled, then the investment coefficient would be rendered largely moot. For a similar perspective, see Bloom, Canning, and Malaney (2000); Higgins and Williamson (1997); and Kelley and Schmidt (1994).

Finally, we consider another subtlety of the model. Long-run, steady-state productivity is specified as being time-specific. Indeed, Radelet, Sachs, and Lee (2001) develop the convergence model from an instantaneous growth perspective highlighting the idea that $(Y/L)_{it}^{*}$ changes for a country from one time to another. $(Y/L)^*_{it}$ might progress or regress as, for example, government tax policy changes. Since these models are estimated over a period of years, $\mathbf{Z}$ variables are typically calculated as period averages. (In some cases, beginning-of-period values are used as instruments for a variable, such as population size, which may be influenced by economic growth over a longer period.) For greater depth on the technical details of convergence modeling, see Radelet, Sachs, and Lee (2001).

2.2.2. Expanding theory: Modeling the productivity component to account for population

Are there roles for population among the $\mathbf{Z}$ variables in the convergence model; or, put differently, how does population influence the *labor productivity* component of definitional equation (2.1)? Consider first the translations variables themselves. Do N_{gr} and WA_{gr} influence productivity growth in addition to their role of translating productivity growth into per capita GDP growth? The potential for productivity effects of these variables has been advanced along several lines.

2.2.2.1. Measuring demographic impacts indirectly: $\mathbf{N}_{gr}$, $\mathbf{WA}_{gr}$

Within the neoclassical model, the steady-state levels of capital and output per worker depend upon the propensity to invest (or save in a closed economy), the growth rate of labor (or population if it is assumed to grow at the same rate), and the state of technology. In our context, this implies that WA_{gr} can play a role in the $\mathbf{Z}$ vector, holding the propensity to invest and technology constant. An economy can experience capital "deepening" when investment outpaces WA_{gr} or "shallowing" when WA_{gr} exceeds capital expansion. Can the economy attract sufficient investment to avoid capital shallowing in the face of a growing workforce? Some would argue that the answer to this question is driven largely by an institutional structure that facilitates entrepreneurial activity and the free flow of financial capital. For this reason, Barro's core of $\mathbf{Z}$ variables (discussed below) includes measures that represent his best efforts at proxying such impacts (government consumption, rate of inflation, a rule-of-law index, and a democracy index).

In a different vein, some analysts have justified the inclusion of N_{gr} and WA_{gr} to capture the impacts of "dependency" (the proportion of the population or work force in the youth or aged cohorts). Specifically, the impact of life-cycle consumption patterns on macroeconomic saving and investment levels can be large over the demographic transition due to swings in a country's age structure. Since the relative rates of N_{gr} and WA_{gr} influence dependency levels, which in turn influence savings and investment, which in turn influence the rate of an economy's productivity growth, N_{gr} and WA_{gr} can indeed exert an effect on labor productivity. While that is true, an issue arises whether these two variables best capture such dependency effects. We argue probably not. The savings literature posits that it is the current *level* of youth and aged dependency that influences savings and investment rather than their rates of change (see, for example, Kelley and Schmidt 1996 and Higgins and Williamson 1997). It would thus seem that while dependency effects are plausibly important, measuring their impacts *directly*, versus capturing them *indirectly* as correlates of the translations variables, represents a preferred empirical methodology, allowing, of course, for estimation of direct effects of the translations variables on labor productivity (if they exist) as well. This more direct approach to isolating the various impacts of population is the tack we present below.

Some authors (e.g., Bloom and Canning 2001) have justified the inclusion of WA_{gr} for another reason: rapid labor force growth may result in a deterioration of labor force quality as workers with lower than average skills and experience are hired. Again, while that is true, an issue arises whether WA_{gr} is the best variable for capturing these impacts. For example, the Barro core already includes life expectancy and post-primary educational attainment of males aged 25 and over as human-capital measures. Of course, it is arguable whether life expectancy primarily represents human capital. This issue is taken up in the next section, where we specify $\mathbf{Z}$s, data, and estimation.

In short, various authors have advanced arguments for the inclusion of WA_{gr} among the $\mathbf{Z}$ variables. In at least two cases, however, we would argue that other variables capture the posited effect more directly. We prefer to model those productivity effects explicitly and separately from the translations variables. Nevertheless, we agree with Bloom and Canning (2001) that the possibility that N_{gr}, WA_{gr}, or both exert an impact $(Y/L)_{gr}$ is a hypothesis that can and should be tested directly. A pure translations role predicts coefficients of $+1$ and -1 for WA_{gr} and N_{gr}, respectively. Deviations from those values imply either an incomplete set of $\mathbf{Z}$ variables or productivity impacts. For example, each of the above arguments posits a *negative* productivity impact for WA_{gr}, implying a coefficient WA_{gr} lower than $+1$. This is a testable hypothesis.

On the other hand, if WA_{gr} does not differ significantly from $+1$ and N_{gr} does not differ significantly from -1, we would prefer to constrain them to $+1$ and -1, respectively, since this approach introduces clarity into the modeling of population that has been absent from this literature. Indeed, a major contribution of the Harvard translations framework is to expose the "catch-all" nature of the N_{gr} variable included as the sole demographic measure in many studies. Introducing WA_{gr} (with N_{gr}) as a way of translating labor into per capita output growth provides a clearer meaning for this variable. However, to the extent that N_{gr} and WA_{gr} proxy additional demographic influences, the purity and usefulness of the framework are diminished. Such an outcome is minimized when those additional measures are explicitly included in the analysis. We next turn to some of these variables.

2.2.2.2. *Measuring demographic impacts directly:* D_1, D_2, N, *Density*

What demographic variables might have a direct (Z-variable) bearing on labor productivity growth? Of the various possibilities, two seem particularly promising.

The first has already been mentioned. To the extent that a population's age structure (proxied here by dependency ratios: $D_1 =$ ratio of population aged 0–14 to that of working ages 15–64 and $D_2 =$ ratio of population aged 65+ to that of working age) influences the rate of domestic saving (e.g., through life-cycle influences), then D_1 and D_2 can have both short- and long-run influences on productivity growth. The short-run influence is through facilitating or inhibiting the savings and investment necessary to close the gap of equation (2.5). The long-run influence is on Y/N^*. A basic lesson of the standard neoclassical growth model is that in long-run equilibrium, the savings level will affect the level of Y/N^* but not its rate of change. Modeling unobservable Y/N^* from currently observed variables is one challenge of convergence modeling, and dependency rates assist in this modeling.

The second possibility is that both the scale of production (population or labor force size) and density (population or labor force per unit of land) can exert an impact on long-run growth. It is in agriculture where the impacts of scale and density are most discussed. On the positive side, higher densities can decrease per unit costs and increase the efficiency of transportation, irrigation, extension services, markets, and communications. On the negative side, higher density may be associated with diminishing returns to land or deleterious effects of congestion. The predicted impact of rising population density on growth is ambiguous. We might note that the distribution of the population between urban and rural areas does not influence this density measure. Thus, the possibility of reverse causation, whereby rapid economic growth encourages urbanization, does not affect our density measure. With respect to population size, scale effects have been highlighted in earlier development studies, particularly with reference to specialization and diversification between firms. Recent endogenous growth models of technical change posit positive scale effects where an R&D industry produces a nonrival stock of knowledge. Holding density constant, we predict a positive impact of population size. Overall, evidence on scale and density effects is mixed and sparse.

2.2.2.3. Modeling a translations component for the convergence term

Equation (2.1) includes a component ($L_{gr} - N_{gr}$) that translates output growth from per-worker to per capita terms. Equation (2.5) indicates that, the higher is the initial level of labor productivity, the slower is economic growth. Although theory dictates the specification of this "convergence" term in output-per-worker terms [$\ln(Y/L_{it})$], nearly all empirical models prefer to specify it in per capita terms [$\ln(Y/N_{it})$]. To do so properly, however, the model should include another variable to translate the convergence term to per capita terms. When completed, equation (2.5) would appear as equation (2.8).

$$Y/L_{gr_{it}} = c\ \ln(Y/L_{it})^* - c\ \ln(Y/N_{it}) + c\ \ln(L/N_{it}) \qquad (2.8)$$

Thus, another translations term, $\ln(L/N_{it})$, must be included when the convergence term is specified in per capita units. Surprisingly few empirical studies include such a term. To our knowledge, the first study to do so was Bloom, Canning, and Malaney (2000).

Having said that, however, we prefer *not* to employ the per capita variant of equation (2.8) for our primary rendering, opting for the per-laborer variant of equation (2.5) instead. The two variants are equivalent unless $\ln(L/N_{it})$ plays a role beyond translations. While we can think of no compelling rationale for including $\ln(L/N_{it})$ in the productivity component of the model, we can for two of its correlates. Specifically, we argued previously that youth and aged dependency rates are plausible **Z** variables to the extent that they influence the domestic savings rate. Were equation (2.8) estimated without the dependency rates, the estimated coefficient for $\ln(L/N_{it})$ would include both translations and dependency impacts. Were we to include the dependency rates as well, we would introduce severe multicollinearity unnecessarily. (The simple correlations coefficient between WA/N, our variant of L/N, and D_1 or D_2 are -0.98 and 0.78, respectively.) Equation (2.5)'s rendering coupled with dependency rates as **Z** variables thus provides clean translations and labor productivity interpretations of age-structure effects. We will return to this issue when we examine the empirical results.

2.3. Toward an empirical rendering of population and growth

Our preferred theoretical model is presented as equation (2.9), derived by substituting equation (2.7) into definitional equation (2.1). This formulation highlights two sets of $\mathbf{Z}$ variables—an "economic" core ($\mathbf{Z}_e$) and a "demographic" core ($\mathbf{Z}_d$)—that determine output per worker (Y/WA) in the long run. The rationale for selecting specific $\mathbf{Z}_d$ variables was considered in the previous section, in which we elaborated the roles of population. Here we present the rationale for selecting specific $\mathbf{Z}_e$ variables, describe the data, set out estimation procedures, and present the results of alternative models that estimate the impacts of population on economic growth.

$$(Y/N)_{\text{gr}_{it}} = \underbrace{a' + b'\ (\mathbf{Z}_e + \mathbf{Z}_d)_{it} - c\ \ln(Y/L_{it})}_{Productivity\ Model} + \underbrace{L_{\text{gr}_{it}} - N_{\text{gr}_{it}}}_{Translations\ Model} + d\,\kappa_i + e\,\tau_t + \varepsilon_{it};$$

(2.9)

where κ_i provides for regional fixed effects, τ_t represents a period fixed effect allowing for exogenous shocks, and ε_{it} represents an error term following the classical assumptions.

2.3.1. Empirical rendering: Specifying Z_e variables, data, and estimation

Since the impact of population on the economy can be influenced by the choice of $\mathbf{Z}_e$ variables, we are cautious in selecting the $\mathbf{Z}_e$ variables. Furthermore, an extensive literature already exists in this area, including the pioneering work of Barro (1997), whose core economic variables we elect to adopt without notable modification. While one can easily imagine alternative variables, suffice it to say that Barro's empirical inquiries have been expansive.

2.3.1.1. The economic Z_e variables
A brief justification of the economic variables follows; see Barro (1991, 1997) for more detail. Growth in output per capita is held to be positively related to

1. A lower initial level of productivity [ln(Y/WA)]. This convergence is posited to be more rapid in countries with higher levels of schooling attainment [ln(Y/WA)•Ed].
2. Higher educational attainment for males of ages 25 and over [Male-Educ], which facilitates the absorption of new technologies.
3. Higher life expectancy [ln(e_0)], a proxy for better health and human capital in general (Barro 1997). Note that the mortality patterns underlying life-expectancy calculations can influence life-cycle saving; for example, rising e_0 can affect saving through the financing of earlier or later retirement in conjunction with an increasing life span (see Bloom, Canning, and Graham 2003 and Lee, Mason, and Miller 2001). Note

also that while life expectancy is a traditional demographic variable, it can still largely represent "health" if the demographic correlates of e_0 (e.g., N_{gr} versus WA_{gr}, youth and elderly dependency ratios) are held constant in the empirical modeling. We lean toward this *ceteris paribus* interpretation, but are open to reclassifying the impacts of e_0 between "economic" and "demographic" impacts in the section on the importance of population. Suffice it to say that much work remains in future research in decomposing the interpretation of e_0 between proxies for health, saving, and other factors. Recent work examining the influences of life expectancy on savings, productivity, and economic growth includes Kinugasa (2004), Kinugasa and Mason (2005), and Chapters 3 and 4 of this volume.

4. Improvement in terms of trade [TT% chg], posited to generate added employment and income.
5. A lower rate of inflation [Inflation], leading to a more stable investment climate and to better decisions with predictable price expectations.
6. A lower government consumption share netted of education and defense spending [Gcons/Y], posited to release resources for more productive private investment.
7. Stronger democratic institutions [Democracy] at low levels of democracy, which promote market activity by loosening autocratic controls. However, stronger democracies at high levels can dampen growth if the government exerts an increasingly active role in redistributing income. Democracy is thus entered in quadratic form, posited to rise and then fall.
8. A stronger rule of law [Rule Law], which stimulates investment by promoting sanctity of contracts, security of property rights, etc.

2.3.1.2. The demographic Z_d variables
As justified in the section above, in which we elaborated the roles of population, two demographic variables are posited as having negative impacts: $\ln(D_1)$ and $\ln(D_2)$, youth and aged dependency ratios, respectively. One [Density measured as 1000 population per square kilometer] has an uncertain impact, and the other, [Size measured as $\ln(N)$], a positive impact on output growth per worker.

2.3.1.3. The data
The data comprise 86 countries and four growth periods (1960–70, 1970–80, 1980–90, and 1990–95), resulting in a panel with 344 observations. Included countries have market economies, production structures that are not dominated by raw material exports, a population of at least one million

in 1970, and reasonably reliable data. Descriptive statistics, data sources, and a country listing are presented in the appendix.

2.3.1.4. Measuring L

We follow the Harvard studies and proxy L with WA (working-age population, ages 15–64). The rationale for this choice is provided above in the discussion of equations (2.3) and (2.4).

2.3.1.5. Estimation Procedures

Following Barro (1991, 1997), we employ two-stage least-squares estimation, running period-specific first-stage regressions for $\ln(Y/\text{WA})$, $\ln(Y/\text{WA})\bullet\text{Ed}$, Inflation, Gcons/$Y$, and Democracy. All rates of change are calculated as continuous rates over the period. Density, $\ln(Y/\text{WA})$, $\ln(Y/\text{WA})\bullet\text{Ed}$, MaleEduc, $\ln(e_0)$, and $\ln(N)$ are beginning-of-period values. Gcons/Y, Democracy, Rule Law, $\ln(D_1)$, and $\ln(D_2)$ are period averages. We include regional binaries for North and Central America, South America, Europe, Asia, and Oceania (with Africa in the intercept) to allow for possible cross-sectional fixed effects. A country listing by region is included in the appendix. Finally, we include period binaries for the 1970s, 1980s, and 1990s (i.e., period fixed effects with the 1960s in the intercept) to allow for exogenous shocks. Additional technical detail is provided in the appendix.

2.3.2. Empirical results: Choosing among alternative specifications

Table 2.1 presents five alternative regression models that account for per capita output growth. Each shares the Barro $\mathbf{Z}_e$ economic core, and each illustrates an alternative demographic setup designed to distinguish between $\mathbf{Z}_d$ variables (productivity impacts of population) and translations variables.

Model 1, termed *Simple Demography*, substitutes N_{gr} for the TFR (total fertility rate) in Barro's core. Using this model, we can ask, How do the impacts of population growth (N_{gr}) change with alternative modeling embellishments, and why?

Models 2 and 3, termed *Translations Demography*, append a translations component in the manner of Harvard. Both models include $\ln(\text{WA}/N)$ and $\ln(\text{WA}/N)\bullet\text{Ed}$ to translate the theoretical convergence terms, $\ln(Y/\text{WA})$ and $\ln(Y/\text{WA})\bullet\text{Ed}$, into the analogues typically used in estimation, $\ln(Y/N)$ and $\ln(Y/N)\bullet\text{Ed}$. Additionally, Model 2 includes N_{gr} and WA_{gr} to translate per-worker growth rates, $(Y/\text{WA})_{gr}$, into their more typical per capita variant, $(Y/N)_{gr}$. Thus, population is not explicitly modeled as having long-run productivity impacts. However, any of these coefficients

Table 2.1. Empirical results for five demographic specifications

Dependent variable		Simple Demography $(Y/N)_{gr}$ (1)	Translations Demography $(Y/N)_{gr}$ (2)	$(Y/WA)_{gr}$ (3)	Enriched Demography $(Y/WA)_{gr}$ (4)	$(Y/WA)_{gr}$ (5)
Productivity model						
Convergence						
$\ln(Y/N)$	(1–3)	-1.19^{***}	-1.18^{***}	-1.18^{***}	-1.31^{***}	-1.26^{***}
$\ln(Y/WA)$	(4–5)	(4.27)	(4.30)	(4.30)	(4.63)	(4.47)
$\ln(WA/N)$			11.56^{***}	11.56^{***}		
			(4.77)	(4.77)		
$\ln(Y/N)\bullet Ed$	(1–3)	-0.04	0.00	0.00	-0.08	$-.03$
$\ln(Y/WA)\bullet Ed$	(4–5)	(0.30)	(0.02)	(0.02)	(0.51)	(0.18)
$\ln WA/N\bullet Ed$			0.27	0.27		
			(0.14)	(0.14)		
Z_e: economic core						
TT %chg		0.16^{***}	0.15^{***}	0.15^{***}	0.14^{***}	0.15^{***}
		(5.13)	(5.16)	(5.16)	(4.92)	(5.20)
Gcons/Y		-0.11^{**}	-0.06	-0.06	-0.07^{*}	-0.07^{*}
		(2.01)	(1.17)	(1.17)	(1.35)	(1.40)
Inflation		-0.04^{***}	-0.04^{***}	-0.04^{***}	-0.04^{***}	-0.04^{***}
		(4.80)	(4.51)	(4.51)	(4.63)	(4.77)
$\ln(e_0)$		6.51^{***}	4.49^{***}	4.49^{***}	4.40^{***}	5.22^{***}
		(4.92)	(3.56)	(3.56)	(3.14)	(3.99)
MaleEduc		0.38	0.17	0.17	0.23	0.20
		(1.50)	(0.71)	(0.71)	(0.95)	(0.83)
Rule Law		2.42^{***}	1.93^{**}	1.94^{**}	2.04^{**}	2.03^{**}
		(2.50)	(2.15)	(2.15)	(2.18)	(2.13)
Democracy		7.99^{***}	5.15^{**}	5.16^{**}	5.68^{***}	6.28^{***}
		(3.33)	(2.31)	(2.31)	(2.49)	(2.69)
Democracy^2		-8.41^{***}	-6.11^{***}	-6.12^{***}	-6.57^{***}	-7.10^{***}
		(3.79)	(2.94)	(2.95)	(3.03)	(3.20)
Z_d: demographic core						
$\ln(D_1)$					-2.95^{***}	-2.17^{***}
					(3.45)	(2.99)
$\ln(D_2)$					0.01	-0.32
					(0.01)	(0.58)
Density					0.14	0.15
					(0.66)	(0.69)
$\ln(N)$					0.10	0.10
					(0.99)	(1.04)
Translations model						
N_{gr}		-0.29^{**}	-1.12^{***}	-0.12	0.13	
		(1.71)	(3.63)	(0.40)	(0.40)	
WA_{gr}			1.51^{***}	0.51^{*}	0.23	
			(4.96)	(1.68)	(0.75)	

(continued)

Table 2.1.   Continued

Dependent variable	Simple Demography	Translations Demography		Enriched Demography	
	$(Y/N)_{gr}$ (1)	$(Y/N)_{gr}$ (2)	$(Y/WA)_{gr}$ (3)	$(Y/WA)_{gr}$ (4)	$(Y/WA)_{gr}$ (5)
Exogenous influences					
Regional fixed effects					
N. and C. America	−0.01	0.26	0.26	0.34	0.22
	(0.01)	(0.62)	(0.62)	(0.78)	(0.51)
S. America	1.24**	1.24**	1.24**	1.29***	1.32***
	(2.37)	(2.57)	(2.57)	(2.61)	(2.61)
Europe	0.91	1.12**	1.12**	0.76	0.70
	(1.55)	(2.04)	(2.04)	(1.32)	(1.20)
Asia	1.47***	1.35***	1.35***	1.27***	1.21***
	(3.78)	(3.72)	(3.72)	(3.39)	(3.19)
Oceania	0.87	0.61	0.61	0.96	0.89
	(1.23)	(0.92)	(0.92)	(1.44)	(1.31)
Period fixed effects					
Pd:1970–80	−0.47	−0.91***	−0.91***	−0.98***	−0.91***
	(1.36)	(2.68)	(2.68)	(2.91)	(2.76)
Pd:1980–90	−1.83***	−2.37***	−2.37***	−2.47***	−2.37***
	(4.81)	(6.41)	(6.40)	(6.65)	(6.44)
Pd:1990–95	−2.27***	−2.84***	−2.84***	−2.87***	−2.83***
	(5.80)	(7.48)	(7.48)	(7.47)	(7.35)
Intercept					
Constant	−23.95***	−9.80	−9.79	−3.78	−9.03
	(4.59)	(1.83)	(1.83)	(0.54)	(1.41)
R Squared	0.55	0.61	0.60	0.59	0.58
Adj. *R*-Sq.	0.53	0.58	0.57	0.56	0.56
Std Error	1.88	1.74	1.74	1.76	1.78
# of Obs	344	344	344	344	344

Note: Descriptive Statistics, the country sample, and estimation details are provided in the appendix. The change of dependent variable between Models 2 and 3 eliminates the need for "translations." By definition, the coefficients for N_{gr} and WA_{gr} in model 3 are those of Model 2 minus the translations values of −1 and +1, respectively. Within the limits of estimation precision, all other coefficients and *t*-values are identical.
* denotes 10% significance,
** denotes 5% significance, and
*** denotes 1% significance for the appropriate 1- or 2-tailed test. *t*-values are in parentheses.

could deviate from its translations' prediction (e.g., WA_{gr} or N_{gr} could deviate from 1 or −1) either if it has direct long-term impacts, or if the model is specified incompletely (e.g., if the translations variables are correlated with omitted impacts of population).

By contrast, Model 3 specifies $(Y/WA)_{gr}$ as the dependent variable [Model 2 employs $(Y/N)_{gr}$]. Having removed their translations role, Model 3's inclusion of N_{gr} and WA_{gr} provides an explicit test for direct productivity impacts. A statistically significant coefficient for N_{gr} and/or WA_{gr} would indicate a role beyond translations, perhaps for one of the reasons discussed above in the section outlining the roles of population.

Models 4 and 5, termed *Enriched Demography*, append four demographic variables $[\mathbf{Z}_d = \ln(D_1), \ln(D_2), \text{Density}, \ln(N)]$ that have the potential for influencing long-run output per worker. Additionally, Model 4 constrains two translations parameters $[\ln(WA/N)$ and $\ln(WA/N){\bullet}Ed]$ to their theoretical expectations in a translations framework, whereas Model 5 constrains all four (also N_{gr} and WA_{gr}).

2.3.2.1. *Overall fit and economic core results*

The convergence framework appears to be a reasonable paradigm for assessing the roles of population. The models fit the data satisfactorily with R^2's ranging from 55 to 61%. All economic core variables are of the expected sign, and 9 of those 12 variables are significant at the 5% level in each of the five variants. Over half of the coefficients are significant at the 1% level. Two variables are never significant (the convergence term's interaction with education and the education variable itself), and one variable (government consumption's share in GDP) is significant at the 5% level in the simplest demographic variant and at the 10% level in the enriched demographic variants. For the most part, the $\mathbf{Z}_e$ variables are not particularly sensitive to the demographic specification either in coefficient magnitude or in statistical significance.

A qualification on the education impacts is in order. Our weak results are not uncommon in the convergence literature. Although those results have been found to be somewhat sensitive to the education measure used as well as to functional form, we have chosen not to experiment with the core model. Rather, we have adopted Barro's formulation given our methodological posture of building upon an arm's-length specification of the core economic and political variables. Having said this, we did rerun Model 5 without the $\ln(Y/WA){\bullet}Ed$ interaction as a sensitivity experiment. The MaleEduc coefficient fell slightly and remained insignificant. Coefficients and *t*-values of other variables changed very little.

2.3.2.2. *Population results: Translations*

Considering first Model 1, we observe that population growth (N_{gr}) has a negative impact on per capita output growth that almost quadruples (it declines from -0.29 to -1.12) when working-age growth (WA_{gr}) is taken into account (see Model 2). Presumably WA_{gr}'s positive impacts are incorporated into the estimated coefficient on N_{gr} in Model 1, muddying the measurement of population's impact (see also Bloom and Williamson 1997). Such a result plausibly accounts for the mixed results of N_{gr} in numerous empirical studies. Thus, while population growth may well have mattered in those studies, impacts were offsetting because the frameworks were excessively parsimonious. Kelley (1988, 1701) observes that such results "... provide little *prima facie* information about the size and nature of the net impact..." We further argue (Kelley and Schmidt 1995, 545) that the insignificant result "... does not mean that demographic processes are unimportant; ... [rather, it] may imply that strong intertemporal demographic effects are offsetting."

Turning to the Harvard translations model (Number 2 in Table 2.1) in which N_{gr} and WA_{gr} are included to translate per-worker into per capita growth, note that N_{gr} does not play a role beyond pure translation. That is, its coefficient is not statistically different from -1 at the 10% level (the *p-value* from that test, not included in the table, is 0.689). By contrast, WA_{gr}'s coefficient of 1.51 is notably larger than the pure translations coefficient of $+1$ and that discrepancy is significant at the 10% level (*p-value* of 0.094). Model 3 makes these points more directly since it eliminates the need for such translation by using Y/WA_{gr} rather than $(Y/N)_{gr}$ as the dependent variable. In this variant, the coefficient for N_{gr} does not differ significantly from zero whereas that for WA_{gr} is positive (0.51) and significant at the 10% level.

This last result is quite surprising in light of the above discussion of measuring demographic impacts indirectly, which provides three separate rationales for including WA_{gr} in the labor productivity model. While each of those arguments implied a negative impact on productivity growth, the estimated impact here is positive, quantitatively notable, and statistically significant at the 10% level. We believe this perverse outcome to be the result of omitted variable bias. We argued above that the savings influence attributed to WA_{gr} might be captured better by direct measures of the age structure. We have done that in Model 4, which enriches the Harvard model by adding youth and elderly dependency ratios, $\ln(D_1)$ and $\ln(D_2)$, as well as density, Density, and population size, $\ln(N)$. In that model, the perverse estimate disappears—the coefficient for WA_{gr} drops to 0.23 and it is insignificant at the 10% level (*t*-value of 0.75). Neither N_{gr} nor WA_{gr} plays any significant role beyond translations.

A surprising story emerges as well for the translations variable $\ln(WA/N)$, included in Models 2 and 3, to translate the convergence term from $\ln(Y/WA)$ to $\ln(Y/N)$. Its coefficient (11.56) differs statistically and substantively from its translations prediction of the negative of the convergence term (-1.18). Although this result is not new to the literature (see, for example, Bloom,

Canning, and Malaney 2000), the striking disparity between the coefficients has not been explained satisfactorily. As was the case with WA_{gr}, we would argue that this disparity is likely the result of omitted variable bias rather than an impact of WA/N on long-run, steady-state productivity.

We have suggested a theoretical reason, in our discussion of the roles of population, for including two correlates of $\ln(WA/N)$, the youth and elderly dependency ratios $[\ln(D_1)$ and $\ln(D_2)]$, in the productivity model. We believe that their omission from the model has resulted in a coefficient estimate for $\ln(WA/N)$ that is dramatically different from the convergence coefficient. Unfortunately, we cannot include all three variables in the model owing to the high correlations between $\ln(WA/N)$ and $\ln(D_1)$ (-0.96) as well as $\ln(D_2)$ (0.79). We have taken a different tack. Models 4 and 5 use $\ln(Y/WA)$ as the convergence term rather than $\ln(Y/N)$ in conjunction with $\ln(WA/N)$. Neither variant is preferable theoretically, and to our knowledge no empirical growth model has included $\ln(WA/N)$ among Z vector influences on the steady-state productivity level. Having eliminated the need for including $\ln(WA/N)$, Models 4 and 5 do include youth and elderly dependency ratios as well as additional demographic variables.

2.3.2.3. Demography results: Z_d variables

We turn finally to the productivity roles that population may play in the Barro convergence model. Models 4 and 5, denoted as enriched demography, append four demographic variables to the list of variables influencing an economy's long-term productivity level. This Z_d vector includes $\ln(D_1)$, $\ln(D_2)$, Density, and $\ln(N)$. While each carries its predicted sign, only $\ln(D_1)$ is significant (at the 1% level). Moreover, the coefficients on $\ln(D_1)$ appear to be large. Of course, the relative importance of the various variables cannot be determined solely by reference to their coefficients. As a result, the following section of this chapter assesses the magnitude of these impacts in the context of the world's experience.

Before turning to that, however, we consider again the key theoretical insight of our section on the roles of population and the empirical lesson of the current section on population and growth. Population plays multifaceted roles in the economy. Certain influences are negative whereas others are positive; and some are felt immediately whereas others are felt with lags of 10, 15, 20, or more years. But all are interrelated. Consequently, modeling demographic effects by any single variable such as N_{gr} is overly simplistic and potentially misleading. Moreover, these influences are separable into two distinct categories—a translations set (N_{gr} and WA_{gr}) and a productivity set [in our rendering, $\ln(D_1)$, $\ln(D_2)$, Density, and $\ln(N)$]. Furthermore, this dichotomy is pure in the sense that the results from Models 3 and 4 demonstrate no productivity influence of the translations variables. Indeed, the more demographic detail incorporated into the model, the more sharply separable are the two models.

Additionally, the finding of a strong and significant coefficient for (D_1) provides insight into the interpretation of the translations demography in convergence modeling. Specifically, in theoretical terms, the impacts of the age distribution on the saving rate (S/Y), and thus $(Y/N)_{gr}$, are typically specified in terms of the age-structure *levels*, such as dependency rates or similar summary measures. Thus, while dependency is correlated with the *growth rates* of population and the working-age population, the appropriate analytical connection is arguably better measured as dependency levels. This point is made most forcefully for WA_{gr}. Its productivity impact when $\ln(D_1)$ is excluded (col. 3 of Table 2.1) is estimated to be 0.51 and significant at the 10% level, two-tail. That impact falls to 0.23 and insignificance with the inclusion of the extended demography (col. 4). In short, adding $\ln(D_1)$ in the Barro core tends to provide more plausible estimates of the translations variables. For further elaboration of saving's role, see Mason (1988), Higgins and Williamson (1997), and Lee, Mason, and Miller (2001).

Finally, the insignificance of several demographic variables within this broad country sample does not necessarily diminish their importance within specific settings. For example, the influence of aging $[\ln(D_2)]$ is difficult, if not impossible, to identify given that aging was noteworthy in only a few countries by the mid-1990s. Furthermore, the impacts of density might be quite different in advanced economies such as Japan, South Korea, Taiwan, and much of Europe than in poorer countries such as India, Indonesia, Pakistan, and Bangladesh. Greater distinction between demographic effects in developed and developing countries merits additional consideration. Regional and geographic factors using the parameter estimates from this study are explored in Chapter 3 of this volume. Those findings offer considerable encouragement to these directions of research.

2.4. Population matters: But how, and by how much?

A common methodology for assessing impacts within a regression model is to apply estimated coefficients to period means of the corresponding variables. However, assessing the "importance" of demographic trends must account not only for the size of the coefficients and mean levels of the variables, but also for changes in the variables over time. Such a reckoning is compiled in Table 2.2, which applies the regression coefficients from Model 5 of Table 2.1 (our preferred rendering) to *changes* in

Table 2.2. Accounting for changes in $(Y/N)_{gr}$ over time: Impacts of interdecadal change

	World Sample				North and Central America				South America			
	1960s to 70s	1970s to 80s	1980s to 90s	Avg.	1960s to 70s	1970s to 80s	1980s to 90s	Avg.	1960s to 70s	1970s to 80s	1980s to 90s	Avg.
Change in $(Y/N)_{gr}$	**−0.84**	**−1.73**	**0.28**	**−0.77**	**−1.15**	**−2.44**	**1.02**	**−0.86**	**0.27**	**−3.58**	**3.31**	**0.00**
Productivity model												
Convergence	**−0.38**	**−0.26**	**−0.03**	**−0.22**	**−0.36**	**−0.18**	**0.14**	**−0.13**	**−0.28**	**−0.27**	**0.17**	**−0.13**
Z_c: economic core	**−0.05**	**−0.29**	**0.58**	**0.08**	**−0.38**	**−0.75**	**1.48**	**0.12**	**−0.26**	**−1.82**	**1.56**	**−0.17**
Financial	−0.34	−0.66	0.19	−0.27	−0.67	−1.03	0.83	−0.29	−0.71	−2.03	1.30	−0.48
Human K: $\ln(e_0)$	0.37	0.35	0.28	0.33	0.45	0.36	0.34	0.38	0.32	0.35	0.29	0.32
Human K: Male Educ	0.06	0.09	0.07	0.07	0.06	0.11	0.08	0.08	0.02	0.09	0.04	0.05
Political	−0.13	−0.07	0.04	−0.05	−0.22	−0.19	0.23	−0.06	0.12	−0.23	−0.07	−0.06
Z_0: demographic core	**0.09**	**0.26**	**0.18**	**0.18**	**0.16**	**0.34**	**0.22**	**0.24**	**0.15**	**0.26**	**0.19**	**0.20**
$\ln(D_1)$	0.08	0.24	0.17	0.17	0.14	0.32	0.21	0.22	0.13	0.24	0.18	0.18
$\ln(D_2)$	−0.02	−0.01	−0.01	−0.01	−0.01	−0.01	−0.01	−0.01	−0.01	0.00	−0.01	−0.01
Density	0.00	0.01	0.00	0.00	0.00	0.00	0.00	0.00	0.00	0.00	0.00	0.00
$\ln(N)$	0.02	0.02	0.02	0.02	0.03	0.02	0.02	0.02	0.02	0.02	0.02	0.02
Translations model												
Demographic translations	**0.40**	**0.02**	**0.01**	**0.14**	**0.62**	**−0.03**	**−0.02**	**0.19**	**0.46**	**−0.09**	**0.07**	**0.15**
N_{gr}	0.13	0.14	0.19	0.15	0.29	0.23	0.05	0.19	0.24	0.26	0.17	0.22
WA_{gr}	0.27	−0.12	−0.17	−0.01	0.33	−0.25	−0.06	0.00	0.22	−0.35	−0.10	−0.08
Exogenous influences												
Period fixed effects	**−0.91**	**−1.47**	**−0.46**	**−0.94**	**−0.91**	**−1.47**	**−0.46**	**−0.94**	**−0.91**	**−1.47**	**−0.46**	**−0.94**

(continued)

Table 2.2. *Continued*

	Europe				Africa				Asia			
	1960s to 70s	1970s to 80s	1980s to 90s	Avg.	1960s to 70s	1970s to 80s	1980s to 90s	Avg.	1960s to 70s	1970s to 80s	1980s to 90s	Avg.
Change in $(Y/N)_{gr}$	**-1.55**	**-0.48**	**-1.21**	**-1.08**	**-0.90**	**-2.30**	**-0.81**	**-1.34**	**-0.23**	**-0.84**	**0.74**	**-0.11**
Productivity model												
Convergence	**-0.53**	**-0.33**	**-0.24**	**-0.37**	**-0.28**	**-0.16**	**0.14**	**-0.10**	**-0.47**	**-0.41**	**-0.33**	**-0.40**
Z_e: Economic core	**-0.39**	**0.38**	**0.09**	**0.03**	**-0.15**	**-0.26**	**-0.07**	**-0.16**	**0.77**	**0.07**	**0.82**	**0.55**
Financial	-0.67	0.21	-0.13	-0.20	-0.20	-0.80	-0.47	-0.49	0.20	-0.43	0.32	0.03
Human K: $\ln(e_0)$	0.14	0.18	0.15	0.16	0.46	0.43	0.28	0.39	0.43	0.41	0.38	0.41
Human K: Male Educ	0.12	0.17	0.08	0.12	0.02	0.03	0.05	0.03	0.06	0.10	0.10	0.09
Political	0.01	-0.18	-0.01	-0.06	-0.43	0.08	0.06	-0.09	0.08	-0.02	0.01	0.03
Z_d: Demographic core	**0.06**	**0.43**	**0.23**	**0.24**	**-0.04**	**0.03**	**0.09**	**0.03**	**0.22**	**0.36**	**0.26**	**0.28**
$\ln(D_1)$	0.10	0.44	0.24	0.26	-0.06	0.01	0.06	0.00	0.20	0.33	0.25	0.26
$\ln(D_2)$	-0.05	-0.01	-0.02	-0.03	0.00	0.00	0.00	0.00	-0.02	-0.02	-0.03	-0.02
Density	0.00	0.00	0.00	0.00	0.00	0.00	0.00	0.00	0.02	0.02	0.02	0.02
$\ln(N)$	0.01	0.01	0.00	0.01	0.03	0.03	0.03	0.03	0.03	0.02	0.02	0.02
Translations model												
Demographic translations	**0.34**	**0.18**	**-0.26**	**0.08**	**0.24**	**0.10**	**0.21**	**0.18**	**0.53**	**-0.14**	**0.03**	**0.14**
N_{gr}	0.19	0.21	-0.13	0.09	-0.11	-0.11	0.50	0.09	0.18	0.31	0.18	0.23
WA_{gr}	0.14	-0.03	-0.13	-0.01	0.35	0.22	-0.29	0.09	0.34	-0.46	-0.15	-0.09
Exogenous influences												
Period fixed effects	**-0.91**	**-1.47**	**-0.46**	**-0.94**	**-0.91**	**-1.47**	**-0.46**	**-0.94**	**-0.91**	**-1.47**	**-0.46**	**-0.94**

Note: "Convergence" includes initial economic level and its interaction with education; "Financial" includes terms of trade, government consumption share, and inflation; separate "Human Capital" rows are included for the reader who prefers to treat life expectancy as a demographic variable; and "Political" includes rule of law and democracy. Exogenous impacts include only period fixed effects and are the same for all regions since the regional fixed effects and the intercept are constant across decades. By definition, regression impacts will add up (except for rounding) to "Change in $(Y/N)_{gr}$" for each World Sample column but not for the regional columns. The calculations are based on Table 2.1, col. 5, augmented by the theoretically specified coefficients for N_{gr} and WA_{gr}, -1 and $+1$, respectively. Although Oceania is not included as a separate region in this table, its three countries are included in the worldwide sample.

mean values across decades, thereby estimating impacts on interdecadal changes in $(Y/N)_{gr}$.

Table 2.2 groups impacts into broad categories denoted as "productivity model" (convergence, $\mathbf{Z}_e$: economic core, and $\mathbf{Z}_d$: demographic core), "translations model," or "exogenous influences" (period fixed effects). The table presents these results first for our "world" sample and for five regions (North and Central America, South America, Europe, Africa, and Asia) as described in the appendix. Given the extensive results in Table 2.2, we focus initially in this section on net impacts of the major components of the model. Next we provide additional detail by assessing contributions from the variables within those components. Finally, we summarize the major lessons and provide bottom-line estimates of the relative contributions of the various influences.

2.4.1. Population matters: Broad conclusions from the world and regional samples

Table 2.2 provides some interesting insights into trends during the last four decades of the twentieth century and in the process provides a warning against overaggregation. For example, were we to focus exclusively on the world's "average" column (the equivalent of estimating from a single 35-year cross-section) and the five variable groupings, we would conclude that both the core demographic trends (0.18) and the demographic translations (0.14) have dominated the impact of the economic trends (0.08) on $(Y/N)_{gr}$ changes. Furthermore, at -0.94, exogenous shocks have had several times the impact of the economic and demographic core variables. These conclusions hold across all regions except Asia, where economic impacts (0.55) dominated the demographic core (0.28) and translations (0.14). While interesting, these generalizations conceal considerable variability across the individual decades and regions.

Consider, first, time patterns in the global aggregates. Worldwide, positive economic impacts ($\mathbf{Z}_e$) between the 1980s and 1990s (0.30) reversed two decades of growth-inhibiting trends (-0.05 and -0.64). By contrast, demographic trends have been consistently growth enhancing. Thus, while $(Y/N)_{gr}$ declined notably between the 1960s and 1970s and again between the 1970s and 1980s, those declines would have been even larger without the ameliorating impacts of favorable demographic trends. Although the positive impacts of changes in the demographic core ($\mathbf{Z}_d$) displayed no obvious trend over time (0.09, 0.26, 0.18), a favorable net trend in the demographic translations variables was largely exhausted in the 1970s (0.40, 0.02, 0.03)—a fascinating finding.

How do these global conclusions fare across the regions of the world? The Americas follow the worldwide Z_e pattern, with South American countries experiencing the largest negative (-1.82) and positive (1.56) impacts. While Africa suffered negative Z_e impacts throughout, positive impacts were enjoyed in Europe in two periods and in Asia in all three periods. By contrast, the regions followed global demographic patterns quite well. Trends in the Z_d variables contributed positively and notably to growth throughout the period in four of the five regions. As is the case worldwide, favorable impacts from the translations variables were largely exhausted in the 1970s in the same four regions. Indeed, in each of those regions, translations impacts were negative in at least one of the last two periods. Africa displays demographic impacts different from those of the other regions because of stubbornly high fertility rates throughout most of the period. Correspondingly, translations impacts are smaller initially but remain positive and are nearly as large in the last period as in the first $(0.24, 0.10, 0.21)$. On the other hand, Z_d impacts are quite small in Africa, starting out negative but rising gradually $(-0.04, 0.03, 0.09)$.

Finally, we briefly consider the impacts of "convergence" and exogenous influences. Since the log level of per-worker income $[\ln(Y/WA)]$ is inversely related to $(Y/N)_{gr}$, the estimated convergence impact will be negative between any two decades of growth in $\ln(Y/WA)$ and positive after a decline. For the world as a whole and in three of the five regions, convergence had a negative impact during the first two periods because economic growth dictated higher $\ln(Y/WA)$ in 1970 than 1960 and in 1980 than 1970, but a positive impact due to the widespread decline over the 1980s, resulting in a lower Y/WA in 1990 than 1980. Europe and Asia bucked this trend, enjoying growth in every decade—implying negative convergence impacts in all three periods. Humbling to the growth literature is the role played by the largely unexplained exogenous factors. They exert the largest influences in Table 2.2, and they are consistently negative. (Note that exogenous impacts are the same across all regions because regional fixed effects are held constant across all periods and thus drop out when interdecadal changes are calculated.)

2.4.2. Population matters: Digging deeper into components of Z_e, Z_d, and translations

A review of the components of these broad categories enriches this analysis further, both temporally and spatially. Within the economic core, trends in human capital (life expectancy and education) have been strongly growth inducing globally $(0.42, 0.44, 0.35)$ as well as in every region. That consistency is not found in the financial (terms of trade, government consumption, and inflation) and political (rule of law and democracy) components, the combined negative impacts of which more than offset these gains in the first two periods before enhancing the gains with favorable impacts in the last period (−0.34, −0.66, 0.19). This worldwide trend was largely followed in North and Central America (−0.67, −1.03, 0.83) and in South America (−0.71, −2.03, 1.30), but not in Africa, which suffered throughout (−0.20, −0.80, −0.47), nor in Europe (−0.67, 0.21, 0.13) or Asia (0.20, −0.43, 0.32), which enjoyed positive impacts in one of the earlier periods. We find that the largest negative *and* positive financial impacts were experienced in South America, followed by North and Central America (acknowledging that this model is not designed to fully capture the Asian monetary crisis of the late 1980s). Although the political component is the least influential worldwide (−0.13, −0.07, 0.04), this is the net result of advances and retreats regionally. For example, whereas South America made strides in the political arena between the 1960s and the 1970s, the region fell back in the latter two periods (0.12, −0.23, −0.07). Africa demonstrated the opposite pattern (−0.43, 0.08, 0.06) after the colonial era ended on that continent.

Turning to population, we see several interesting results emerge. First, youth dependency [$\ln(D_1)$] strongly dominates other components of the demographic core [$\ln(D_2)$, $\ln(N)$, Density] in influence on $(Y/N)_{gr}$ trends, and its impact has been consistently positive. This is true in every region of the world with the exception of Africa, where, because of delayed fertility declines, youth dependency remained high throughout the latter half of the twentieth century. By contrast, aged dependency has had a negligible effect to date. The impacts of aging may well reveal themselves as the twenty-first century progresses. Large youth-dependency ratios have already been observed, and their impacts can therefore be estimated. By contrast, the largest elderly dependency ratios lie in the future, and those effects cannot be estimated well from this sample.

Second, the positive economic impacts of the demographic core could be enhanced considerably in all regions and in all periods depending upon how much of the gains from rising life expectancy one ascribes to demographic variables rather than to human capital. As we argued earlier, we believe that the demographic side of life-expectancy impacts is largely controlled for within this model by other demographic indicators. Nevertheless, were an analyst to disagree and impute all life-expectancy impacts to demographic variables, the effect on $\mathbf{Z}_d$ impacts would be substantial.

Third, within the Translations Model, declining population growth (N_{gr}) positively impacted trends in $(Y/N)_{gr}$ relative to $(Y/WA)_{gr}$ throughout the last four decades of the twentieth century worldwide and in three of the five regions of Table 2.2. The exceptions are Africa in the first two periods for reasons discussed above and Europe in the last period. Trends in the growth of the working-age population (WA_{gr}) enhanced $(Y/N)_{gr}$ change six times in the first two periods but not a single time since.

In short, the prevailing pattern throughout the world of a positive and strong net translations impact between the 1960s and the 1970s, followed by small and even negative net impacts in the latter two periods, has been driven to date largely by initially strong but eventually declining growth rates of the working-age population. Again, the notable exception is in Africa where, subject to the ravages of HIV-AIDS, such a period may lie ahead as the countries of that continent pass through the various phases of the demographic transition.

2.4.3. Population matters: Summary lessons and bottom-line calculations

What lessons can be learned from the rich regional detail of Table 2.2? First, population can and has exerted quantitatively large impacts on changes in $(Y/N)_{gr}$, especially if one combines the impacts of both core and translations demography (and even more if one includes life expectancy in the demographic core).

Second, the translations impacts trace out a fairly consistent pattern following a fertility boom and decline (for example, over the course of the demographic transition). That pattern consists of (a) strong positive impacts (as N_{gr} declines from lower fertility while WA_{gr} rises from earlier high fertility); and (b) small impacts, and possibly negative impacts (as N_{gr} stabilizes and WA_{gr} eventually slows due to earlier fertility declines). This result both qualifies and elaborates the renderings of the recent literature. The magnitude and timing of these impacts can vary dramatically across countries and regions. Africa (with a delayed transition and positive impacts throughout the period) and Asia (with a rapid transition in key countries and negative impacts by the second period) provide stark contrasts in this regard.

Third, the demographic core variables, especially youth dependency, change more slowly and therefore exert their influences over longer periods than do the translations variables. For this reason we argue the importance of a richer modeling of demographic change to an improved understanding of economic change.

Having said all of this, we remain curious about the relative contributions of the various influences to variability in $(Y/N)_{gr}$ changes around the world. Table 2.2 is inadequate for this task since $(Y/N)_{gr}$ changes derive from variables that have both positive and negative impacts. As a result, $(Y/N)_{gr}$ change can be quite small by comparison with its component influences. (See, for example, the 1980s–1990s in Table 2.2.) The *net* value masks considerable "economic activity," which can be negative as well as positive. As an alternative approach, we have computed component shares in total "movements"—the sum of the unsigned impacts of all variables (including the exogenous variables that result from period shifts in events such as OPEC decisions and debt overhang). These movements are shown in Table 2.3. For the world sample, core demography accounts for 8% of total movements across the interdecadal periods. Among the other factors, human capital (education, health) and financial and economic factors have the most important impacts (15% apiece), followed by demographic translations (13%), the convergence adjustments (9%), and politics (4%). As previously noted, exogenous factors dominate interdecadal changes (36%).

As can be seen in Table 2.3, these figures vary notably by region. They can also vary over time and by the degree of disaggregation, justifying caution in interpreting the results. However, the general conclusion that "population matters" is beyond dispute and holds everywhere: in the aggregate it ranges from 8% of "movements" in the demographic core to 21% if translations impacts are included, and to 34% if life expectancy is interpreted not as a proxy for health but rather as largely a demographic variable.

Table 2.3. *Accounting for changes in $(Y/N)_{gr}$ over time: Percentage shares in total movements*

	World Sample	N. & C. America	South America	Europe	Africa	Asia
Productivity model						
Convergence	9	7	6	13	7	12
Z_c: economic core	35	46	55	35	43	34
Financial	15	25	35	16	21	13
Human K: $\ln(e_0)$	13	11	8	5	13	12
Human K: Male Educ	3	2	1	4	1	3
Political	4	7	10	9	8	7
Z_d: demographic core	8	8	5	24	3	28
Translations model						
Demographic translations	13	12	11	10	17	16
Exogenous influences						
Period fixed efects	36	28	23	33	31	28

2.5. Conclusion

This chapter has examined various ways in which demography has been incorporated into "convergence modeling," as pioneered by Robert J. Barro and extended by Harvard scholars and others. Our interpretation of this literature distinguishes somewhat sharply between the impacts of Harvard translations additions and the more traditional demographic impacts on the economy. We have proposed, and found in our empirical analysis, that the impacts of translations demography are best viewed as largely "neutral" on economic production, although the translations framework nicely exposes effects on potential consumption (and welfare) and, importantly, significantly clarifies the roles of other demographic variables (e.g., dependency, size, and density).

These demographic impacts (deriving mainly from declining birth and death rates) combine to exert positive contributions to trends in per capita GDP growth. Worldwide, the combined impacts of demographic change have accounted for approximately 20% of per capita output growth impacts, with larger shares in Asia and Europe. And, in the not too distant future, demographic change (this time deriving from low and stable death and birth rates) will likely exert negative impacts on growth. To see how these results can materialize, we propose that future modeling build on the type of demographic disaggregation illustrated in this chapter, where greater distinction is made between demographic change that affects output growth per worker and that which translates such growth into per capita terms. A theoretical modeling perspective that synthesizes the Barro convergence framework, augmented to include several traditional demographic variables such as population age structure and size, and unified within the Harvard translations framework, provides a promising and relatively clear structure for revealing the roles of demographic change on the economy.

Appendix

Table 2.A1 presents descriptive statistics and data sources for the variables in this study. Following Barro (1991, 1997), we use a panel with 10-year growth periods. Our sample, grouped by region, includes the following 86 countries. **Africa (26)**: Algeria, Benin, Cameroon, Central Africa, Ivory Coast, Egypt, Ethiopia, Ghana, Kenya, Madagascar, Malawi, Morocco, Niger, Nigeria, Rwanda, Senegal, Sierra Leone, South Africa, Sudan, Tanzania, Togo, Tunisia, Uganda, Zaire, Zambia, Zimbabwe. **North and Central America (12)**: Canada, Costa Rica, Dominican Republic, El Salvador, Guatemala, Haiti, Honduras, Jamaica, Mexico, Nicaragua, Panama, United

Table 2.A1.   *Variable definitions, sources and descriptive statistics*

Variable	Description	Source	Mean	Std. Dev.	Min	Max
$(Y/N)_{gr}$	Per capita GDP (PPP) growth rate	Trans	1.65	2.69	−10.77	8.64
$(Y/WA)_{gr}$	Per working-age GDP (PPP) growth rate	Trans	1.46	2.66	−11.14	7.94
$\ln(Y/N)$	Per capita GDP (PPP, log)	SH	0.85	1.03	−1.35	2.89
$\ln(Y/WA)$	Per working-age GDP (PPP, log)	SH, UN	1.42	0.96	−0.72	3.31
$\ln(WA/N)$	Ratio of working-age to total pop. (log)	UN	−0.57	0.10	−0.76	−0.32
$\ln(Y/N) \bullet$ Ed	Interaction: $\ln(Y/N) \bullet$ MaleEduc	Trans	0.95	1.48	−0.84	10.98
$\ln(Y/WA) \bullet$ Ed	Interaction: $\ln(Y/WA) \bullet$ MaleEduc	Trans	0.86	1.36	−0.91	10.14
$\ln(WA/N) \bullet$ Ed	Interaction: $\ln(WA/N) \bullet$ MaleEduc	Trans	0.09	0.14	−0.14	0.83
TT %chg	Terms-of-Trade, percentage change	WB	−0.43	3.54	−13.73	19.25
Gcons/Y	Pct share of gov't consumption in GDP	WB, BL93	7.27	3.60	0.01	27.19
Inflation	Inflation rate	WB	15.71	28.71	0.74	317.10
$\ln(e_0)$	Life expectancy at birth (log)	WB	4.07	0.21	3.46	4.37
MaleEduc	Avg years post-primary educ, Males 25+	BL96	1.29	1.19	0.02	6.67
Rule Law	Index: Law & order tradition	ICRG	0.56	0.24	0.10	1.00
Democracy	Democracy (political rights index)	G	0.58	0.33	0.00	1.00
N_{gr}	Population Growth Rate	Trans	2.02	1.01	−2.18	4.06
WA_{gr}	Working-age population growth rate	Trans	2.21	1.05	−1.81	4.23
$\ln(D_1)$	100 $\bullet$ Ratio of ages 0–14 to 15–64 (log)	UN	4.14	0.41	3.14	4.67
$\ln(D_2)$	100 $\bullet$ Ratio of ages 65+ to 15–64 (log)	UN	2.14	0.51	1.21	3.31
Density	Density: 1,000 population per Sq. Km	WB	0.17	0.61	0.00	5.77
$\ln(N)$	Population size (log)	WB	9.37	1.26	7.06	13.65

Note: Additional definitional details are found in Kelley and Schmidt (2001). Data fills and extrapolations were made by imposing rates of change from an alternative data set with more complete series. For SH, WB was the primary filling source with UN and IMF as alternatives. WB was generally filled from earlier versions, UN sources, or SH. Fills for ICRG and G are too complicated to describe here; a description is available upon request. The "Source" column from the appendix table uses the following key for data sources:

BL93   Barro and Lee's data set used in Barro and Lee (1993).
BL96   Barro and Lee (1996) update of their education attainment series.
G   Gastil (1991).
ICRG   International Country Risk Guide.
SH   Summers and Heston (1994) Penn World Tables, version 5.6.
Trans   Transformation of variable described elsewhere in the table.
UN   United Nations (1996).
WB   World Bank's (1994, 1995, 1997, 1999, and 2000) *World Development Indicators* CD-ROM.

States. **South America (10)**: Argentina, Bolivia, Brazil, Chile, Colombia, Ecuador, Paraguay, Peru, Uruguay, Venezuela. **Asia (18)**: Bangladesh, Hong Kong, India, Indonesia, Iran, Israel, Japan, Malaysia, Myanmar, Nepal, Pakistan, Philippines, Singapore, South Korea, Sri Lanka, Syria, Taiwan, Thailand. **Europe (17)**: Austria, Belgium, Denmark, Finland, France, Greece, Germany, Ireland, Italy, Netherlands, Norway, Portugal, Spain, Sweden, Switzerland, Turkey, United Kingdom. **Oceania (3)**: Australia, New Zealand, Papua New Guinea.

Barro employs three-stage least-squares estimation, with the third stage correcting for possible serial correlation. Since he found little evidence of serial correlation, we opted for two-stage estimation instead for the variables identified by Barro to be endogenous: $\ln(Y/N)$, $\ln(Y/WA)$, $\ln(Y/N) \bullet Ed$, $\ln(Y/WA) \bullet Ed$, Gcons/Y, Democracy and its square, and Inflation. Following Barro, the first-stage equations include all exogenous or predetermined variables [$\ln(WA/N)$, TT% chg, $\ln(e_0)$, MaleEduc, Rule Law, N_{gr}, WA_{gr}, $\ln(D_1)$, $\ln(D_2)$, Density, and $\ln(N)$] together with 5-year lags of $\ln(Y/N)$ or $\ln(Y/WA)$, $\ln(Y/N)$'s or $\ln(Y/WA)$'s interaction with contemporaneous education, Gcons/Y, Democracy, and Democracy's squared term. Finally, binaries for former colonies of Spain and Portugal and former colonies of Great Britain and France are included as instruments for inflation. The first-stage equations are run separately for each period. The second-stage equation is pooled but includes period-specific binaries.

Table 2.A2 includes R^2s from the first-stage regressions for our preferred variant, Model 5 from Table 2.1. As might be expected, inflation is the hardest variable to predict with R^2s ranging from 0.279 to 0.507. Although these are low relative to the others, they are quite acceptable for an instrumental-variables approach, and predicted inflation is consistently significant in the second-stage regressions of Table 2.1. As might also be expected, regressions for $\ln(Y/WA)$ and $\ln(Y/WA) \bullet Ed$ are the strongest, partly due to the inclusion of their lagged values among the instruments.

Table 2.A2. **R^2s from first-stage regressions for Model 5 of Table 2.1**

Endogenous Variable	Regression Period			
	1960s	1970s	1980s	1990–95
$\ln(Y/WA)$	0.995	0.984	0.987	0.995
$\ln(Y/WA) \bullet Ed$	0.994	0.993	0.996	0.994
Gcons/Y	0.740	0.508	0.556	0.520
Inflation	0.385	0.507	0.417	0.279
Democracy	0.921	0.843	0.869	0.851
Democracy^2	0.946	0.863	0.884	0.912

With R^2s ranging from 0.987 to 0.996, the predicted values nearly replicate the actual values. The full set of results from these first-stage regressions is available upon request.

Problems of reverse causation may plague demographic variables as well, although here the case is less clear. On the one hand, fertility rates are likely to be more sensitive to the level than to the growth of income. On the other hand, the length of the observations used in empirical studies ranges from 5 to 25 years, resulting in periods sufficiently long that the levels can change notably through growth. Our estimation uses an intermediate period of 10 years. Consequently, we assessed the need to instrument key demographic variables [WA_{gr}, N_{gr}, $\ln(D_1)$] through the Durbin-Wu-Hausman test (appending lagged demographic variables to the above list of instruments). In no demographic variant was that test significant at the 5% level. This result is consistent with that of Brander and Dowrick (1994), who present one of the most econometrically intensive analyses in the literature using instrumental variables for birth rates in a production function setup. They conclude that, "there is no evidence that the demographic variables are endogenous with respect to income growth rates" (p. 18). As a result, we do not instrument any of the demographic variables in the estimation presented in this study. As a sensitivity experiment, we ran an additional set of 2SLS regressions that included first-stage regressions for WA_{gr}, N_{gr}, and $\ln(D_1)$, which are thought to be most sensitive to fertility changes. Coefficient estimates changed negligibly.

A more thorough explanation and rationale for our estimation procedures can be found in Barro (1997) and Kelley and Schmidt (2001).

References

Barro, Robert J. 1991. "Economic growth in a cross section of countries". *Quarterly Journal of Economics* 106(2): 407–44.

———. 1997. *Determinants of Economic Growth: A Cross-country Empirical Study.* Cambridge, MA: MIT Press.

Barro, Robert J., and Jong-Wha Lee. 1993. "Losers and winners in economic growth". Working Paper 4341. NBER, Cambridge, MA.

———. 1994. "Sources of economic growth". *Carnegie-Rochester Conference Series on Public Policy* 40: 1–46.

———. 1996. "International measures of schooling years and schooling quality". *American Economic Review* 86(2): 218–23.

Bloom, David E., and David Canning. 2001. "Cumulative causality, economic growth, and the demographic transition", in: Nancy Birdsall, Allen C. Kelley, and Steven Sinding, eds, *Population Matters: Demographic Change, Economic Growth, and Poverty in the Developing World*, pp. 165–97. New York: Oxford University Press.

———. 2003. "From demographic lift to economic liftoff: The case of Egypt". *Applied Population and Policy* 1: 15–24.

Bloom, David E., David Canning, and Bryan Graham. 2003. "Longevity and life cycle savings". *Scandinavian Journal of Economics* 105: 319–38.

Bloom, David E., David Canning, and Pia Malaney. 2000. "Population dynamics and economic growth in Asia", in: C. Y. Cyrus Chu and Ronald Lee, eds, *Population and Economic Change in East Asia. Population and Development Review*, Supplement to Vol. 26: 257–90.

Bloom, David E., and Jeffrey G. Williamson. 1997. "Demographic change and human resource development", in: *Emerging Asia: Changes and Challenges*, pp. 141–97. Manila: Asian Development Bank.

———.1998. "Demographic transitions and economic miracles in emerging Asia". *World Bank Economic Review* 12(3): 419–55.

Brander, J.A., and Steven Dowrick. 1994. "The role of fertility and population in economic growth: Empirical results from aggregate cross national data". *Journal of Population Economics* 7: 1–25.

Gastil, Raymond D. 1991. "The comparative survey of freedom: Experiences and suggestions", in: Alex Inkeles, ed., *On Measuring Democracy: Its Consequences and Concomitants*, pp. 21–46. New Brunswick, NJ: Transaction Publishers.

Higgins, Matthew, and Jeffrey G. Williamson. 1997. "Age structure dynamics in Asia and dependence on foreign capital". *Population and Development Review* 23(2): 261–93.

ICRG (International Country Risk Guide). 1982–95. "International country risk guide". Political Risk Services; obtained from IRIS Center, University of Maryland, College Park, MD.

Kelley, Allen C. 1988. "Economic consequences of population change in the Third World". *Journal of Economic Literature* 26(4): 1685–1728.

Kelley Allen C., and Robert M. Schmidt. 1994. "Population and income change: Recent evidence". World Bank Discussion Papers, No. 249. Washington, DC: World Bank.

———. 1995. "Aggregate population and economic growth correlations: The role of the components of demographic change". *Demography* 32(4): 543–55.

———. 1996. "Saving, dependency and development". *Journal of Population Economics* 9(4): 365–86.

———. 2001. "Economic and demographic change: A synthesis of models, findings, and perspectives", in: Nancy Birdsall, Allen C. Kelley, and Steven Sinding, eds, *Population Matters: Demographic Change, Economic Growth, and Poverty in the Developing World*, pp. 67–105. New York: Oxford University Press.

Kinugasa, Tomoko. *Life Expectancy, Labor Force, and Saving.* Ph.D. dissertation. University of Hawaii at Manoa.

Kinugasa, Tomoko, and Andrew Mason. 2005. "Why nations become wealthy: The effects of adult longevity on saving". Working Paper No. 200514. Department of Economics, University of Hawaii at Manoa.

Lee, Ronald D., Andrew Mason, and Tim Miller. 2001. "Saving, wealth, and population", in: Nancy Birdsall, Allen C. Kelley. And Steven Sinding, eds, *Population Matters: Demographic Change, Economic Growth, and Poverty in the Developing World*, pp. 137–64. New York: Oxford University Press.

Levine, Ross, and David Renelt. 1992. "A sensitivity analysis of cross-country growth regressions". *American Economic Review* 82(4): 942–63.

Mason, Andrew. 1988. "Saving, economic growth, and demographic change". *Population and Development Review* 14 (March): 113–44.

Radelet, Steven, Jeffrey Sachs, and Jong-Who Lee. 2001. "The determinants and prospects of economic growth in Asia". *International Economic Journal* 15(3): 1–29.

Summers, Robert, and Alan Heston, 1994. PWT 5.6. Data update based on *The Penn World Table (Mark 5): An Expanded Set of International Comparisons, 1950–1988*. These data can be downloaded from http://pwt.econ.upenn.edu/Downloads/index.htm.

UNPD (United Nations Population Division). 1996. Sex and age annual data: 1950–2050 (1996 revision). Data diskettes. New York.

World Bank. 1994, 1995, 1997, 1999, 2000. *World Development Indicators*. CD-ROM. Washington DC.

CHAPTER 3

A Century of Demographic Change and Economic Growth: The Asian Experience in Regional and Temporal Perspective

Allen C. Kelley and Robert M. Schmidt

Assessing the impacts of demographic change on economic growth has spurred an outpouring of research. The literature in the period since World War II has vacillated between pessimism and optimism, with broad eclecticism representing the median judgment. Very few empirical studies have uncovered robust and strong macroeconomic effects of demographic change, one way or the other—a surprise to pessimists in the Malthusian tradition.[1]

The 1990s witnessed a modest shift in judgment about population consequences based on the use of convergence (or technology-gap) modeling pioneered by Robert J. Barro (1991). His early empirical studies uncovered negative consequences of high birth rates on economic growth. In 1994 Kelley and Schmidt expanded this demography to include density and population size, and in the late 1990s several Harvard economists (e.g., David Bloom, David Canning, Jeffrey Sachs, and Jeffrey Williamson) argued convincingly that whereas theorists conceptualize the economic growth process in labor-productivity terms, empirical growth models are generally specified in per capita terms. Without an accounting structure to translate labor-productivity impacts into per capita terms, demographic coefficient estimates (mainly population growth) will be biased. In that case the population-growth coefficient would capture net demographic impacts that could be positive, negative, or neutral, depending upon time and place. Correspondingly, the Harvard rendering specified what we have labeled a "translations model" to accommodate these accounting considerations. The resulting model is elegant in its simplicity, incorporating only two demographic variables that have unambiguous

---

[1] A history of various assessments is provided in Kelley (2001).

POPULATION CHANGE, LABOR MARKETS, AND SUSTAINABLE GROWTH
VOLUME 281   ISSN 0573-8555/DOI 10.1016/S0573-8555(07)81003-0

predicted coefficient values of -1 (for N_{gr}, population rate of growth) and $+1$ (for WA_{gr}, working-age population rate of growth) when used to expose population's impact on Y/N_{gr} relative to Y/WA_{gr}.

In Chapter 2 of this volume we examine the theoretical underpinnings of the Harvard translations model and argue that, properly formulated, its demographic terms would not be expected to have any economic-growth impacts beyond translations accounting. Various estimates have corroborated this interpretation. This outcome encouraged us to "enrich" the demographic specification. Specifically, we added a set of four variables—youth and aged dependency (D_1 and D_2), density (Density), and population size (N)—for an expanded demographic structure. This "enriched demography" is then combined with the "translations demography" (WA_{gr} and N_{gr}) into what we term a "synthesis" formulation. We fitted that model with Barro's core economic and political variables using a cross-section of 86 developed and developing countries over the period 1960–95. The results revealed the usefulness of the synthesis framework by exposing the impacts of observed demographic change on changes in per capita GDP growth rates over the period. We found that several aspects of demographic change influenced economic growth, that the impacts of dependency (mainly youth) exceeded those of the "translations" specifications, and that the relative and absolute magnitudes of these separate influences varied notably over time.

The present chapter is divided into two sections. In Section 3.1, "Modeling population in development," we further assess and compare the impacts of the "translations" and "enriched" demographic structures on growth. We begin by summarizing the theoretical structure. We next extend the empirical period of evaluation beyond the past (1950–2000) to include the future (2000–50). In addition, we examine regional effects. This detail nicely exposes the dynamics of economic–demographic interactions over the demographic transition. Our central finding is that the impacts of population over the full century do not result primarily from "translations effects" (N_{gr} and WA_{gr}), but rather from the "enriched" demographic structure variables—mainly from youth-dependency rates. Section 3.2, A return to basics: Saving, investment, and capital flows, builds upon this finding by asking the question, what are the linkages between youth and aged dependency that would lead to sizable impacts on economic growth in the convergence-modeling framework? These two variables played prominent roles in the early population debates (*a la* Coale and Hoover 1958), which emphasized the impacts of dependency on saving and investment but have been "behind the scenes," as it were, in recent convergence studies of population's impact on economic growth. Accordingly, using our data set, we undertake an exploratory empirical analysis of demographic impacts on saving and investment.[2] Some intriguing results emerge. First, both youth- and aged-dependency impacts are not only statistically significant, but are also exceptionally large in size. Moreover, and most surprisingly, aged-dependency impacts dominate youth-dependency impacts in the recent past—even for developing countries—and this relationship is predicted to continue and increase in importance at least until 2050. These patterns are strongest for East Asia, but they are increasingly prevalent in other regions as well.

3.1. Modeling population in development

This section of the chapter applies the methodology developed in Chapter 2 to assess the impacts of a century of demographic change on economic growth. We first summarize the theory of the economic growth model; then review the empirics from our estimation; and finally estimate the impacts of demographic change on changes in per capita GDP growth.

3.1.1. Population in development: The methodology

An initial taxonomy for organizing an assessment of demographic change is presented in equation (3.1),

$$(Y/N)_{gr} \equiv \underbrace{Y/L_{gr}}_{Productivity\ Component} + \underbrace{(L_{gr} - N_{gr}),}_{Translations\ Component} \quad (3.1)$$

which decomposes per capita output growth (Y/N_{gr}) into two components: an economic component (per-hour labor productivity growth, Y/L_{gr}), and an accounting or translations component ($L_{gr} - N_{gr}$), which converts output growth per labor hour into output growth per person (a possible welfare measure).

This definition explicitly acknowledges the fact that per capita GDP growth rates will deviate from per-worker growth rates whenever the number of workers grows at a rate different from that of the population as a whole. Many growth models focus exclusively on the economic component, implicitly or explicitly assuming the equivalence of the rates (L_{gr} vs. N_{gr} and, therefore, Y/L_{gr} vs. Y/N_{gr}). In some cases, these

---

[2] Although there have been several studies of these relationships (Higgins 1998; Taylor and Williamson 1994; Taylor 1995), we wish to evaluate such relationships with a country data set, where they have been shown to be relevant.

assumptions hold, at least approximately. In times of rapid demographic change (e.g., during the demographic transition), however, the available pool of workers (the working-age population, traditionally ages 15–64) grows faster or slower than the population as a whole. Accordingly, per worker GDP grows faster or slower than per capita GDP. Indeed, in certain countries over certain periods, the disparity can be quite large.[3]

3.1.1.1. An empirical model of per capita GDP growth

To estimate the magnitude of this and other demographic impacts over a full century (1950s through 2040s) and for several country classifications requires an empirical model corresponding to the definitional taxonomy represented by equation (3.1). Here we consider three types of variables in such an empirical model—demographic variables in the translations (accounting) component, economic and political variables in the economics component, and demographic variables in the economics component.

For the translations component we have made two key choices. First, we follow the practice of the Harvard studies and proxy L with WA (working-aged population), based on the absence of employment rates and the problematic quality of labor force estimates. Second, we have elected to include WA_{gr} and N_{gr} separately rather than in net form as the equation appears to suggest. The implied coefficients for these variables are $+1$ and -1, respectively, if neither plays an additional role in influencing Y/WA_{gr} (our proxy for Y/L_{gr}). We have tested for that possibility and found that neither differs from its hypothesized value at the 10% significance level. (Similar results are found in other studies as well; see Bloom and Williamson 1997, 1998; Bloom and Canning 2001.) Accordingly, we restrict the coefficients for WA_{gr} and N_{gr} to $+1$ and -1, respectively.[4]

While the economic-growth literature provides numerous ways to model productivity growth, we have elected to employ the "convergence" or "technology-gap" framework to model the economics component. Rooted in neoclassical growth theory, this paradigm explores the relationships between economic growth and the level of economic development. It focuses on the pace at which countries move from their current economic

---

[3] Bloom and Williamson (1997, 1998) highlighted this phenomenon with special reference to the "Asian Tigers" over the period 1965–90. They found that a notable portion of the Tigers' per capita GDP growth over that period was caused by the translations component.

[4] Experimenting with the unrestricted variant of the model, we found in Chapter 2 that the conclusions are little affected by these restrictions.

level to their long-run, or potential, or steady-state equilibrium level of per-worker output. The steady-state level is modeled to be both country- and time-specific, and variables thought to influence that level are included explicitly in the empirical model. We denote such variables as Z_e variables. The economic component, then, consists of the Z_e variables and the level of per-worker GDP (Y/WA) at the beginning of the growth period.[5]

An extensive literature has evolved on how to model the Z_e vector. Since its specification is not our focus, we have adopted without notable modification the economic–political core and methodology of Barro (1997), a pioneer in this area. While one can easily imagine alternative variables, suffice it to say that Barro's empirical inquiries have been expansive. Briefly, Barro's core Z_e variables posit economic growth to be enhanced by health (e.g., life expectancy), education (male secondary and tertiary), strong terms of trade, a low government consumption share in GDP, strong rule of law, slow inflation, and robust democratic institutions whose impact is at first positive and then negative beyond a certain point.

Given that population's impact on economic growth is our primary focus, it merits greater attention. For modeling demographic influences within the economic component, therefore, we have appended a demographic vector of four variables, denoted Z_d, to the economic component of equation (3.1). These include youth (D_1, 0–15/WA) and aged (D_2, 65+/WA) dependency ratios to capture possible age-structure impacts on investment. To the extent that a population's age structure influences the rate of domestic saving (e.g., life-cycle influences; see Mason 1988), it can affect investment and the pace of productivity growth, especially where international capital flows are limited.

Additionally, population size (N) is included as a proxy for the scale of production, while higher population density (Density) can decrease per-unit costs and increase the efficiency of transportation, irrigation, extension services, markets, and communications. Earlier development studies have highlighted scale effects, particularly with reference to specialization and diversification between firms. Recent endogenous growth models of technical change posit positive scale effects where an R&D industry produces a nonrival stock of knowledge. Overall, evidence on scale and density effects is mixed and sparse, especially with respect to the experience of Third World countries.

In Chapter 2 we provide an extensive discussion of the theoretical model, the variables and their justifications, the functional form, the data

---

[5] Barro (1991) adds a term "interacting education" with Y/N based on the hypothesis that technology transfer is faster in countries with higher levels of education.

Table 3.1. **Empirical results for a model of per capita GDP growth**

	Coefficient	(t-value)
Barro convergence terms		
Convergence: Initial Y/WA (log)	−1.38**	(4.99)
Interaction with education	−0.17	(1.15)
Barro economic/political core (Z_e)		
Terms of trade, percentage change	0.16**	(5.67)
Gov. consumption share in GDP	−0.09*	(1.68)
Inflation (log)	−0.03**	(4.06)
Life expectancy at birth (log)	5.72**	(4.67)
Education, males aged 25+	0.42*	(1.87)
Rule-of-Law index	2.16**	(2.34)
Democracy index	7.59**	(3.20)
Squared	−8.14**	(3.61)
Kelley/Schmidt enriched demography (Z_d)		
Youth dependency ratio ($\ln D_1$)	−2.50**	(3.69)
Elderly dependency ratio ($\ln D_2$)	−0.46	(0.88)
Population density (Density)	0.24	(1.16)
Population size ($\ln N$)	0.16*	(1.79)
Harvard translations accounting from Y/WA$_{gr}$ to Y/N$_{gr}$		
Working age growth rate (WA$_{gr}$)	1.00	*Restricted*
Population growth rate (N_{gr})	−1.00	*Restricted*
Exogenous growth determinants		
Period binary: 1970–80	−0.96**	(2.89)
Period binary: 1980–90	−2.60**	(7.11)
Period binary: 1990–95	−3.16**	(8.30)
Constant	−9.62	(1.55)

Note: The sample consists of a panel of 86 countries and four time periods, 344 observations in all. Details of estimation are provided in Kelley and Schmidt (2001).
* indicates significance at the 5% level.
** indicates the 1% level, 1- or 2-tail tests as appropriate. The R^2 is 0.57 while the adjusted R^2 is 0.54.

set, and the estimation methodology.[6] Table 3.1 presents the empirical results from that study for our preferred modeling variant. These demographic coefficients are used for the remainder of this chapter to estimate

---

[6] Briefly, the data comprise 86 countries and four growth periods spanning 1960–95, resulting in a panel with 344 observations. Included countries have market economies, GDPs not dominated by raw material exports, populations of at least 1 million in 1970, and reasonably reliable data. We followed Barro (1997) in employing two-stage least squares estimation, running period-specific first-stage regressions for the convergence terms, inflation, government consumption, and democracy. Since Durbin-Wu-Hausman tests were insignificant, we have not run first-stage equations for any demographic variables. We include period binaries (i.e., period fixed effects) to allow for exogenous shocks.

the impacts of demographic change on changes in per capita economic growth.

The convergence framework appears to provide a reasonable paradigm for assessing the roles of population. The model fits the data satisfactorily with an R^2 of 57%. Although the convergence term's interaction with education is insignificant, all Z_e variables are of the expected sign and are significant at the 5% level and most are significant at the 1% level. Furthermore, the addition of demographic variables to the economic component of the model appears to be useful. Each of the Z_d variables carries its predicted sign and two are statistically significant: ln D_1 at the 1% level and ln N at 5%. Moreover, the coefficient on ln D_1 is large.

3.1.1.2. Estimating the impacts of demographic change on Y/N_{gr} change

As we have noted, a major objective of this chapter is to gain insight into the impacts of demographic change on economic growth by level of development and region, both historically and as projected over the next 50 years. The effects of variables are determined not only by the size of the regression coefficients, but also by the size of changes in the variables over time. For example, our results in the next section show the impacts of variables such as N_{gr} and WA_{gr} to be quantitatively important as much because of notable swings in their values as because of the magnitude of their coefficients. Our focus on change is a little unusual. Many studies apply regression coefficients to sample means in order to "explain" past and predict future growth rates for the desired subsamples. We have opted for a "changes" approach because policymakers work at the margin in attempting to effect change in the variables they can influence. The "levels" approach provides no insight into real-world experience of plausible magnitudes of demographic change and the economic changes that policymakers can effect.[7]

The approach we will follow is to apply the regression coefficients of Table 3.1 to interdecadal changes in mean levels of the demographic variables. The estimated impact, then, is on the change in Y/N_{gr} from one decade to the next. Interestingly, while the net demographic influence on Y/N_{gr} is nearly always negative, global changes in these demographic variables are generally growth enhancing. The net influence of global demographic change on Y/N_{gr} change has been positive in each interdecadal period from the 1960s through the 1990s (see Table 2.2.).

---

[7] An alternative way to confront this issue would be to construct counterfactual experiments. For example, in assessing Kenya's experience, one might ask, "What if Kenya's demography mirrored that of South Korea?" While methodologically useful, this approach is sensitive to the selection of comparisons, and these must be convincing and robust.

Given the detailed demographic data available by country for the 1950s through the 1990s and projections through the 2040s, we have a century of data upon which to apply this methodology. This provides nine periods of interdecadal change: the 1960s vs. 1950s through the 2040s vs. 2030s. (Clearly, many of the projections to 2050 are substantially "out of sample" within our empirical modeling. At a minimum, we must not overinterpret the results. They assume parameter stability over an extended period of time, a qualification of note.)

We have grouped our sample into eight country categories. At the broadest level, we compare 23 developed countries with 63 less-developed countries (LDCs). We further summarize the LDCs by region—Africa, Latin America, and Asia. Finally, given the focus in this chapter on Asia, we subcategorize that region (using ILO categorizations) into East, South Central, Southeast, and Other (the last not shown in our estimates). Our sample, grouped by region, includes 86 countries.[8]

3.1.2. Population in development: A century of demographic change, 1950–2050

The beginning of a new millennium seems a propitious time to evaluate the impacts of population change on the economy. Widely varying trends in mortality and fertility reduction across regions from around 1950 have resulted in major changes in numerous demographic indicators. These will continue to vary for decades to come, including the ones we have chosen to explore in our synthesis paradigm [N_{gr}, WA_{gr}, D_1, D_2, Density, N]. To date, a rich historical base of experience has provided considerable scope for analysis of the past; specifically, it provides both sufficient variation and a reasonable empirical foundation to support some exploratory projections into the future. This effort is facilitated by the availability of age-specific

---

[8] The 23 developed countries are Austria, Australia, Belgium, Canada, Denmark, Finland, France, Greece, Germany, Ireland, Israel, Italy, Japan, Netherlands, New Zealand, Norway, Portugal, South Africa, Spain, Sweden, Switzerland, Great Britain, and the United States. The 25 African countries are Algeria, Benin, Cameroon, Central Africa, Ivory Coast, Egypt, Ethiopia, Ghana, Kenya, Madagascar, Malawi, Morocco, Niger, Nigeria, Rwanda, Senegal, Sierra Leone, Sudan, Tanzania, Togo, Tunisia, Uganda, Zaire, Zambia, and Zimbabwe. The 20 Latin American countries are Argentina, Bolivia, Brazil, Chile, Colombia, Costa Rica, Dominican Republic, Ecuador, El Salvador, Guatemala, Haiti, Honduras, Jamaica, Mexico, Nicaragua, Panama, Paraguay, Peru, Uruguay, and Venezuela. Asia, containing 18 countries, is further categorized into East Asia, with 3 countries—Hong Kong, South Korea, and Taiwan; South Central Asia, with (6 countries: Bangladesh, India, Iran, Nepal, Pakistan, and Sri Lanka; Southeast Asia, with 7 countries—Indonesia, Malaysia, Myanmar, Papua New Guinea, Philippines, Singapore, and Thailand; and Western Asia, with 2 countries— Syria and Turkey.

population projections by country compiled by the United Nations. These projections enable us to take stock and assess the impacts of population change on per capita GDP growth over a considerable period of time.

Here we examine the economic impacts of such regional variety in demographic change over the century covering the 1950s through the 2040s. We proceed in two stages. The section that follows examines mean impacts over three broad periods to arrive at several general conclusions. The subsequent section illustrates the patterns and timing behind these conclusions by graphing the demographic impacts for eight country groupings and the nine interdecadal periods.

3.1.2.1. Impacts of historical and projected demographic changes

Table 3.2 presents the mean changes in annualized, per capita GDP growth rates resulting from changes in three demographic measures: (1) the "synthesis" of translations (WA_{gr}, N_{gr}) plus Z_d impacts (D_1, D_2, N, Density); (2) the Z_d impacts; and (3) the net translations impacts. These mean impacts are presented for eight country groupings and three broad periods:

Table 3.2. *Mean impacts on annual Y/N_{gr} of demographic change over two epochs: The past and the future*

				Synthesis: Translations $+ Z_d$				
Row	Period	DCs	LDCs	Africa	L. America	Asia	East	S. Cntr.	SE
1	1950s–90s	0.29	0.34	0.18	0.40	0.52	0.83	0.40	0.48
2	2000s–40s	−0.10	0.17	0.31	0.13	0.02	−0.20	0.12	0.04
3	Total	0.07	0.25	0.25	0.25	0.24	0.26	0.24	0.23

$$Z_d = \ln D_1 + \ln D_2 + \ln N + \text{Density}$$

Row	Period	DCs	LDCs	Africa	L. America	Asia	East	S. Cntr.	SE
4	1950s–90s	0.21	0.12	0.02	0.16	0.23	0.51	0.09	0.27
5	2000s–40s	−0.06	0.30	0.38	0.27	0.21	−0.02	0.33	0.18
6	Total	0.07	0.22	0.22	0.22	0.22	0.22	0.22	0.22

$$\text{Translations} = WA_{gr} + N_{gr}$$

Row	Period	DCs	LDCs	Africa	L. America	Asia	East	S. Cntr.	SE
7	1950s–90s	0.09	0.22	0.16	0.25	0.28	0.32	0.32	0.21
8	2000s–40s	−0.05	−0.13	−0.07	−0.14	−0.19	−0.18	−0.21	−0.14
9	Total	0.01	0.03	0.03	0.03	0.02	0.04	0.02	0.01

Note: The "1950s–90s" represents the means of four interdecadal impacts (the 1960s vs. 1950s through the 1990s vs. 1980s), whereas the "2000s–40s" averages five interdecadal impacts (the 2000s vs. 1900s through the 2040s vs. 2030s). $\ln D_1$ comprises the bulk of the impact within the Z_d vector.

the past (1950s–1990s), the future (2000s–2040s), and the full period (1950s–2040s).

Consider first the combined influences of all demographic impacts as represented in the Synthesis panel (rows 1–3).

Trends of declines in birth and death rates, translating into various measures of demographic change (D_1, D_2, N, Density, N_{gr}, WA_{gr}), have exerted in the past, and will continue into the foreseeable future to exert, sizable net positive impacts on economic growth per capita both world-wide and by region. The only exceptions are in East Asia and the DCs, where negative impacts of demographic changes are slated to characterize the upcoming decades.

Surprisingly, the net impacts for the entire century are quite similar at around 0.25% per annum across all LDC regions. The basis of this constancy is explored below.

With the exception of Africa, the bulk of the positive demographic impacts have already occurred (see rows 1 and 2). The net average impact for Latin America and South Central Asia for the first half of the twenty-first century is predicted to be about one-third that of the last half of the twentieth century, whereas positive impacts have nearly ended for South-east Asia. The extreme cases are represented in East Asia and the DCs, where the net impacts turn negative in the future. By contrast, Africa, a late starter in the fertility transition, can look forward to favorable impacts almost twice as large in the future as in the past.

How do the translations and Z_d components contribute to these combined effects? Consider the full century's experience, shown in rows 6 and 9.

Importantly, for the full century of experience, the driving force is not "translations demography" (i.e., net impacts of WA_{gr} and N_{gr}). Unsurprisingly, the mean translations impact over the 100-year period is close to zero in all regions (see row 9). Recall that this impact results from an accounting translation from per-worker into per capita GDP growth rates. It is positive early in the fertility transition as the relatively large pretransition birth cohorts work their way into working age. As the transition matures, changes in working-age growth rates slow and eventually turn negative. The effect is transitory and never affects productivity growth. Over the course of 100 years, the translations impact tends to balance out in these country groupings.

Nearly all of the net positive impacts derive from growth-enhancing trends in the Z_d variables, primarily from declines in the youth dependency ratio (see row 6). Over the century, the average contribution of Z_d changes in explaining Y/N_{gr} change dominates strongly. It is around ten times the size of the impact of "translations" accounting (i.e., 0.22 in row 6 versus roughly 0.025 in row 9).

The combined impacts of Z_d changes over the century are surprisingly consistent across LDC regions at 0.22, rounded to two decimal places (row 6). This appears to be a remarkable coincidence of the groupings. We have calculated these impacts at the country level and find that they range from 0.06 to 0.30. Moving selected countries across regions would eliminate the near constancy. Furthermore, Z_d impacts result from the influences of four separate variables. Since trends in youth dependency dominate in all regions, they are the focus of much of our discussion of Z_d impacts. Nevertheless, other components make proportionately different contributions across LDC regions. Youth dependency plays the smallest proportionate role in East Asia, with aged dependency and population density playing the largest roles. Conversely, youth dependency plays the largest relative role in Africa, as does population size.[9]

Finally, the story changes when one moves from an entire century's experience to the half-century epochs of the past (rows 1, 4, and 7) versus the future (rows 2, 5, and 8).

With the exception of East Asia, translations impacts accounted for the majority of favorable impacts of demographic change in the last half of the twentieth century (row 7). For the LDCs, the translations' share in the total averaged 65%, ranging from 38% in East Asia to 89% in Africa (compare rows 1 and 7). It will be seen below that this dominance is mainly for the early period (the first two decades). Thereafter it largely disappears.

The positive twentieth-century translations impacts turn negative in the twenty-first century (row 8). These negative impacts nearly offset past gains. The century's average is positive but close to zero in all regions (row 9).

The transition from high to low fertility rates has been said to provide a demographic "gift" to LDCs through the translations model. On net, that has been true over the past half-century, and especially in the period 1950–80. But it is not a gift that countries are allowed to keep. Rather, given the dynamics of demographic change, it more resembles a gift that must be returned in the long run.

3.1.2.2. Visualizing the impacts on Y/N_{gr} of interdecadal demographic changes

Our synopsis of a century of demographic change, summarizing the economic impacts of demographic change over two 50-year periods, has shown surprising uniformity across LDC regions for the mean 100-year

---

[9] Youth dependency comprises from 56% (East Asia) to 78% (Africa) of the total unsigned (absolute value) impacts of these four Z_d components. Aged dependency ranges from 7% (Africa) to 26% (East Asia) of the total while density ranges from 1% (Africa) to 14% (East Asia) and population size ranges from 5% (East Asia) to 14% (Africa).

50 Allen C. Kelley and Robert M. Schmidt

impacts on changes in per capita GDP growth rates of the $\mathbf{Z}_d$ variables, the translations model, and the synthesis of the two. The results also reveal, however, that those similarities mask differences when the longer period is divided into the past and the future. That there are differences in the timing of demographic impacts is not surprising. The transition from high to low fertility rates was long completed among most DCs before the period began and was completed very quickly and early in East Asia. Southeast Asia and Latin America followed, but at a more moderate pace. The countries of South Central Asia began later in the period with some African nations beginning their transition only recently.[10]

We find it useful, therefore, to depict the full set of interdecadal impacts. We do that in this section through a set of eight graphs. Given the extensive detail covered in the graphs, we highlight our major conclusions in italics.

Before we turn to that analysis, however, we make one observation. The results in Table 3.2 indicate that East Asia is in many respects an "outlier" in world experience. The graphs discussed in this section will make that even more apparent. Generalization from this region's experience must be undertaken with care. At the same time, in some respects East Asia will be the leader in a path-breaking experiment on how countries may respond to the future demographic effects of exceptionally rapid demographic change in the past. The policies that are designed in East Asia to cope with these conditions will be on the cutting edge of world experience. Interestingly, the "developed countries" that are entering the last phase of the demographic transition at a much more modest rate may be able to benefit from the unfolding experience of the East Asian paradigm. Is there an "ideal" pace at which the demographic transition might have proceeded? The way East Asia responds to the "payback time" may well furnish the world with some insights into this intriguing question.

Figure 3.1 illustrates the impacts on Y/N_{gr} change of the two highlighted components of demographic change (translations and Z_d), both separately and in combination. We discuss the individual graphs shown in Figure 3.1 in conjunction with the summary means of Table 3.2.

Considering first the broadest country groupings, the DCs versus the LDCs, we see that demographic change has enhanced per capita GDP growth rates over the past half century by 0.29 percentage points annually among the DCs and by 0.34 for the LDCs. Their paths diverge in the future. Economic growth will be lowered by up to 0.5 percentage point in the 2010s, 2020s, and 2030s in the DCs. This is ameliorated somewhat by positive

---

[10] We recognize that these generalizations do not hold for all countries in a region. There may be as much, or more, variability across countries within a region as across regions.

Figure 3.1.   Demographic impacts on Y/N_{gr} change: 1960s vs. 1950s through 2040s vs. 2030s

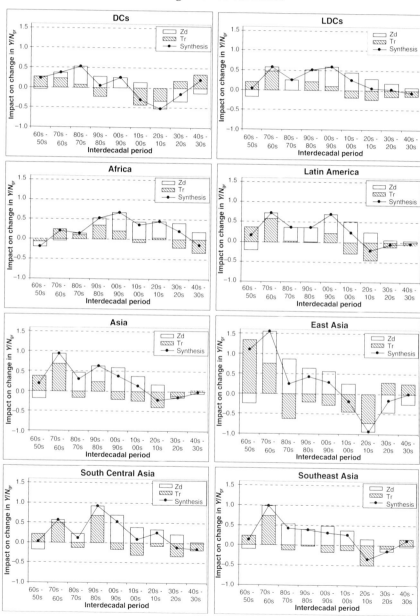

impacts in the current decade and the 2040s for an average annual impact of -0.10 percentage points. By contrast, demographic change will continue to raise economic growth for the average LDC during the next 50 years. At 0.17 percentage points annually, the projected rate is about half that of the past 50 years. Furthermore, all of the gains for LDCs will be achieved during the first two decades of this century. Thereafter, the net influence of demographic change on economic growth rate changes will be negligible.

Time trends in the split of these net impacts between the translations model and the Z_d variables are particularly interesting. The fertility transition set off a fairly consistent chain of events, albeit at different times and with different magnitudes of impacts. With the exception of Africa, all LDC regions enjoyed notable positive translations impacts in the first two decades of the period. Those boosts were short-lived, however. The majority of the remaining seven decades experienced negligible or negative translations impacts. Africa follows this general pattern, but somewhat later, translations gains from fertility declines occurred during the fourth and fifth decades of the period.[11] South Central Asia also deviates from the general timing as a result of a transition that preceded Africa's but lagged behind that of other regions.

Briefly stated, the translations impact was positive in the past (especially in the first two decades), is projected to be negative in the future, and is close to zero for the full period. This is true for each of our eight country groupings. In marked contrast to the transitory and offsetting nature of the translations impact among the LDCs, growth-enhancing Z_d impacts (dominated by the economic impacts of declining youth dependency) are enjoyed for five to seven decades. Changes in the Z_d variables have generally positive economic impacts whether looking to the past, the future, or overall.

This important result is quite plausible upon further consideration. As the fertility transition begins, declining N_{gr} enhances economic growth. WA_{gr} rises as well due to entry from earlier large birth cohorts and declining childhood mortality. These two influences typically reinforce each other in enhancing economic growth. Within 15–20 years, however, smaller birth cohorts begin to enter working ages, often producing declining WA_{gr}, which offsets the growth-enhancing influence of falling N_{gr}. In Latin America they offset each other completely by the 1980s and into the 1990s. In East Asia the negative influence of declining WA_{gr} swamped the positive influences of declining N_{gr} by the 1980s, a trend that continues for five decades. To the

---

[11] Actually, Africa did enjoy moderate positive impacts in the 1970s and 1980s. These were not due to fertility declines, however. Rather, falling childhood mortality rates resulted in working-age growth rates rising slightly faster than the population at large. This partially explains South Central Asia's early experience as well.

contrary, youth-dependency ratios (D_1), which dominate the economic influences in the Z_d vector, can decline for decades after the beginning of the fertility transition. For this to occur, the denominator (population age group 15–64) must grow faster than the numerator (population age group 0–14). This begins to occur soon after fertility begins to decline and continues throughout the transition. Beyond that, it can continue while mortality improvements proceed among the adult population. Such improvements are projected among LDCs well into the twenty-first century.

Turning to the individual LDC regions, on the one hand, we see that the mean positive demographic impact over the full period is remarkably consistent across the regions at around 0.25 percentage points annually. On the other hand, the disparity between historical impacts (averaging 0.47) and projected impacts (averaging 0.07) is notable, exposing the variety in the patterns of demographic influence on economic growth. East Asia once again proves to be an outlier with respect to both the magnitudes of the demographic influences (positive and negative) and the speed of its transition. Demographic forces added an astounding 1.4 and 1.5 percentage points, respectively, to changes in its annual per capita GDP growth rate for the 1960s vs. 1950s and the 1970s vs. 1960s. Even though the translations impacts turned negative by the 1980s, the combined demographic impact remains positive through the current decade in East Asia. For the 2020s vs. 2010s, demographic factors are projected to lower economic growth by almost 1.0 percentage point. On net, East Asia enjoyed the largest demographic boost historically (0.83 annual average) and is the only LDC region projected to suffer from demographic change over the next 50 years (−0.20 annual average).

Africa again illustrates the other extreme among the LDC regions. Africa enjoyed the smallest positive demographic impact historically (0.18 annual average) but will likely experience the largest in the future (0.31 annual average). Although the world has long been concerned by continued high fertility among African nations, demographic trends have been moderately growth-enhancing and will continue to be so for the next four decades. Latin America and Southeast Asia will continue to gain economically from demographic trends for the first two decades of this century, but their impacts will turn negative by the 2020s. Finally, South Central Asia enjoyed its largest boost between the 1980s and 1990s (close to 1.0 percentage point annually) and smaller growth enhancements during the first three decades of this period before turning modestly negative.

3.1.3. Population in development: Conclusions

Our analysis in Section 3.1 has exposed the ebb-and-flow dynamics of two major demographic forces on trends in per capita output growth rates:

"translations accounting," highlighted in the Harvard studies (the impacts of population and working-age growth rates), and "enriched demography," highlighted by us and others (the impacts of dependency, population size, and density). On the one hand, trends in enriched demography are found to exert a steady and strong positive impact on growth over most of the period. On the other hand, trends in translations demography are assessed to be positive over the past 50 years, negative in projections for the next 50 years, and small overall. While future negative translations impacts are noteworthy, they must be viewed within context. If these variables continue to play the same role they did in the past, then they will exert no causal influence on labor productivity growth. Simply stated, over the past half-century, changes in per capita output growth rates were higher than per-worker rates owing to the translations accounting. Over the next half-century, they are projected to be lower. Over the full century, they are about the same. And at no time is labor productivity notably and demonstrably affected. We thus view the translations accounting of the past not to represent a "no-strings gift," but rather as a gift that will be returned in the future as working-age growth rates decline relative to those of other age cohorts.

Our estimates imply quite different conclusions for enriched demography. In the developing countries the impacts of demographic trends were strongly positive in the past and promise to remain so in the future. Indeed, in three of six developing regions, these impacts are projected to be higher in the future than in the past. Furthermore, with the sole exception of East Asia, the positive impacts of the enriched demography are projected to more than offset the negative translations impacts in these regions. The net demographic impacts are projected to be positive in five of six developing regions. Those regions that began their transition early (most notably East Asia and to a lesser extent Southeast Asia) have largely exhausted their net demographic benefits. Africa, which began its transition only recently, can expect to reap the bulk of these benefits in the future. Latin America and South Central Asia have enjoyed the majority of these benefits already and will continue to experience notable gains in the future.

There are two major qualifications to these conclusions. The first lies in the uncertain impact of HIV-AIDS. Age-specific population projections must be tempered appropriately. The second qualification concerns the impact of aged dependency given the limited empirical evidence with this variable. All we know is that the impacts of aging will be felt most heavily by East Asia and the developed countries. The size and nature of the impacts is uncertain.

In summary, the repercussions of demographic change over the past 50 years will continue to be felt economically over the foreseeable future.

Favorable advances in infant and childhood health, rather remarkable fertility transitions in developing regions, aging, and advances in fighting chronic diseases will continue to modify population growth rates and age structure. Whatever the origin of demographic changes, our analysis illustrates that the impacts can be nicely divided between translations impacts, which occur whenever the working-age population grows faster or slower than the general population, and age-structure and population-size impacts, which affect labor-productivity growth rates. Predictably, the translations impacts resulting from a fertility decline are positive early, negative later, and approximately zero over a long period. In contrast, age-structure impacts resulting, say, from the fertility transition are generally favorable and extend over a long time period. What is clear is that distinguishing between per capita versus per-worker productivity impacts, and the quite varied impacts of demographic variables, is useful to making overall demographic assessments. The impacts of aging on labor-productivity growth must be at center stage in formulating assessments of population impacts and policies in the future.

3.2. A Return to basics: Saving, investment, and capital flows

We have argued in Section 3.1 and in greater detail in Chapter 2 for the inclusion of dependency among the Z_e variables in growth models primarily because of its potential influence on savings and investment. Levine and Renelt (1992) surveyed numerous empirical growth studies to identify a common set of influential variables. They found investment rates to constitute the most robust variable. Nevertheless, the investment share in GDP is conspicuous by its absence from the list of variables in a convergence model. Why is that?

Simply stated, from a neoclassical perspective, physical and human investments flow fluidly within and across countries toward highest returns (e.g., to regions and countries with large gaps between potential and current labor productivity). However, not all countries finance investment with equal ease. Thus, a second category of variables is added to the **Z** vector to "condition" the convergence rate. These variables include country- and time-specific factors that enhance or deter international capital flows, domestic saving, domestic investment, or migration. Commonly included among these factors are, for example, restrictive licensing, the risk of expropriation, political conditions, the rule of law, and migration regulations.

We believe that dependency belongs in that list as well. Using here the basic methodology of country samples that we used in Section 3.1, we provide a preliminary assessment of the impacts of youth and aged dependency on savings and investment.[12] We draw heavily on a sizable literature, including our own work (Kelley and Schmidt 1996), in modeling the influence of dependency on savings shares in GDP. Why examine domestic savings in this study? After all, it is investment that plays the driving role in growth, and domestic savings is but one source for financing investment. One important reason is the extensive literature, dating back to Coale and Hoover (1958), arguing the significant role that high rates of youth dependency play in inhibiting savings and, in turn, development among poor countries. The argument from those days applies as well today, although perhaps to a lesser extent in an age of globalization. Specifically, in an economy closed entirely to capital flows, domestic savings impose an effective constraint to investment. While globalization has to some extent opened the world to rising financial capital flows, restrictions remain in many countries through laws and institutions, domestic instability, or perceived lack of credit worthiness. Domestic savings remain an important and often dominant source of finance.

Studies that examine linkages between age structure and investment are not all that plentiful. They are most prevalent in the historical literature and appear with a theme of "population-sensitive" investments. Some studies have examined demographic impacts on school spending, although in recent years attention has shifted to the impacts of medical spending and financing pensions for the aged. Recently, several studies, such as those by Taylor and Williamson (1994) and Higgins (1998), have begun redressing this issue by formulating empirical models to estimate the impact of age structure on GDP shares of both savings and investment, as well as international capital flows (the current account balance).

Here we build on both of these literatures to examine the impact of youth and aged dependency on GDP shares of saving, investment, and capital flows. There are no new theoretical innovations. Rather, we wish to evaluate the impacts of population using a data set and methodology that

---

[12] Thus, we model dependency to indirectly influence growth through its impacts on savings and investment. Using the chain rule of calculus, we find that the estimated coefficient for either dependency term in the growth model we used in part one is the product of the partial derivative of dependency's impact on investment (or savings) times that of investment's (or savings') impact on growth. For D_1 and I, for example, $\hat{\beta}_{D_1} \equiv \left(\frac{\partial(Y/WA_{gr})}{\partial D_1} \right) \equiv \left(\frac{\partial(Y/WA_{gr})}{\partial I} \right) \left(\frac{\partial I}{\partial D_1} \right)$. In Section 3.2 we estimate $\left(\frac{\partial I}{\partial D_1} \right)$ as well as $\left(\frac{\partial S}{\partial D_1} \right)$. The questions to be answered are, Do youth and elderly dependency influence savings and investment? And, if so, how large are their impacts?

conform to those used in Section 3.1 and that extend the time from around 1990 (the end point in most published studies) through 2000. Hopefully this highly exploratory excursion will expose some of the sources of demographic impacts in the convergence framework. Our guiding questions are, what are the demographic impacts of aging on saving, investment, and the current account balance over the period 1960–2000? And what are the plausible impacts in the future (2000–2050)?

Some of our results are provocative. For example, we find a much more substantive role for aged dependency in savings and investment than we have seen in previous studies. Indeed, while we do find important positive impacts historically of declining youth dependency on savings and investment, we find even larger negative impacts of rising aged dependency in many regions. And, as might be expected, the impacts of rising aged dependency over the next 50 years are projected to swamp any positive impacts of declining youth dependency in most regions of the world.

3.2.1. Return to basics: The methodology

Following Taylor and Williamson (1994) and Higgins (1998), the model is parsimonious and the same for each of our three dependent variables— GDP shares of S, gross national saving; I, gross domestic investment; and CAB, current account balance.[13] The independent variables include the level of per capita GDP (Y/N), the growth rate of GDP (Y_{gr}), youth and elderly dependency rates (D_1 = ages 0–14/N and D_2 = ages 65+/N),[14] three decadal binaries (1970s, 1980s, and 1990s with the 1960s in the intercept), and five regional binaries (Asia, Europe, North and Central America, South America, and Oceania with Africa in the intercept). The regions correspond to UN designations and conform to those used in our modeling of population in development.

---

[13] These series, downloaded from the World Bank's online version of the World Development Indicators in April 2005, represents period averages and are expressed as percentages. S includes gross domestic saving and net income from abroad but excludes net current transfers from abroad because of data gaps, especially for the 1960s. This approach follows Higgins (1998). The series used for I is "gross capital formation (percentage of GDP)." CAB was calculated as the difference between S and I.

[14] Per capita GDP is the chained-index variant in 1996 dollars from version 6.1 of the Penn World Tables (Heston, Summers, and Aten 2002; downloaded from http://pwt. econ.upenn.edu/php_site/pwt_index.php). D_1 and D_2 represent mid-period values and were downloaded from the United Nations site (*http://esa.un.org/unpp/*) in September 2005. Population by age and sex are available for quinquennial years 1950–2000 with the medium projections used for impacts analysis from 2005 to 2050. Y_{gr}, D_1, and D_2 are expressed in percentages.

The savings model is in the tradition of Leff (1969), Taylor and Williamson (1994), and Higgins (1998). Mason (1987), followed by Kelley and Schmidt (1996), adds an interaction term between youth dependency and the rate of growth in GDP. Higgins (1998) considers this term but argues that one of the underlying assumptions for its inclusion is demographic steady state, an assumption that he questions for the period under study. Like Higgins, we do not include this term in our basic model but did run an experimental regression that included D_1 and D_2 both individually and as interaction terms with GDP_{gr}. Neither of those terms was significant at the 5% level in either the savings or the investment equation.

The investment model is in the tradition of Taylor and Williamson (1994) and Higgins (1998), who employ the same framework for investment as they do for savings. The linkages between dependency and investment are more complicated than they are for savings. Recall that dependency can impact investment both by influencing the "supply" (financing) of investment in the form of domestic savings as well as the "demand" for investment through age-sensitive investment. Recall further that domestic savings present an effective supply constraint in an economy closed to international capital flows, and there is no impact in a global environment of perfect capital mobility. The world lies somewhere in between, with countries more or less open to capital flows and countries more or less attractive to foreign capital. As noted previously, the economic-demography and historical literatures examine both the level and the form that investment might take for different age structures (schools and housing when D_1 is high and medical infrastructure when D_2 is high). Higgins (1998, 346) argues that investment demand should be "most closely related to the youth share (through its connection with labor force growth)" as well as through additional demands for schools and housing. By contrast, a relatively high elderly share would boost the demand for medical infrastructure but lower the demand for productive investment through its correlation with labor force exit. The investment demand boost for D_1 will at least partially offset its negative savings impact in a country open (but not perfectly so) to foreign capital. The prediction for D_1 is ambiguous. In contrast, both the investment-demand and the savings-supply effects of D_2 are negative and the predicted impact on I is negative.

Coefficients in the CAB equation are, by definition, the simple difference between the coefficients in the S and I equations, given that each employs the same model and the definition that $CAB \equiv S - I$. Nevertheless, we present them and the coefficient significance tests for the reader's interest.

As was the case in our modeling of population in development, estimation is through ordinary least squares[15] within a fixed-effects model. Period binaries include those for the 1970s, 1980s, and 1990s with the 1960s serving as the reference point as in Section 3.1. Here, however, we follow Higgins (1998) and employ 5-year periods. Regional binaries include those for Asia, Europe, North and Central America, and South America with Africa serving as the numeraire. Higgins (1998) tested for fixed versus random effects and found the fixed-effects model to be preferred.[16]

The data set includes 87 of the 89 countries listed in footnote 9. Myanmar and the Sudan were excluded from version 6.1 of the Penn World Tables and were thus dropped from the sample. Missing data precluded 37 observations (1960s: 28, 1970s: 6, 1980s: 2, and 1990s: 1), resulting in the use of 659 of 696 possible quinquennial observations covering the period 1960–2000.

3.2.2. Return to basics: The regression results

Regression results from this model are presented for savings (*S*), investment (*I*), and current account balance (CAB) shares in Table 3.3. Although we present the CAB results, for expositional brevity we concentrate our discussion on savings and investment. The model's explanatory power is solid with an R^2 of 60% for savings, 47% for investment, and 31% for CAB. All four of the core variables—the log of per capita GDP [$\ln(Y/N)$], GDP growth rate [Y_{gr}], youth's dependency share [D_1], and elderly's dependency share [D_2]—are of the anticipated signs and are significant at the 1% level in the *S* and *I* regressions. Furthermore, with these influences held constant, the mean rate of both savings and investment varies by decade and region at the 1% level when a test for joint significance (not shown) is used.

---

[15] Standard errors and *t*-values are White-corrected for the possible presence of heteroscedasticity. We would have preferred to use the Newey-West technique to estimate standard errors that are both heteroscedasticity and autocorrelation consistent, but the packages available to us at this time (Stata, Limdep, and SAS) do not allow missing observations for their techniques. We will remedy this in future work. For now, we note that our analysis is based on the coefficient estimates that remain unbiased in the presence of autocorrelation.

[16] We do not follow Higgins precisely, because he used country fixed effects but not period fixed effects. Indeed, we do not employ the FEM as it is conventionally applied. That is, we specify broader aggregations than our data (regions instead of countries and decades instead of quinquennial periods) to retain some of the cross-sectional (within regions) and temporal (within decades) variation.

Table 3.3. *Empirical results for a model of savings, investment, and current account balance*

	Savings		Investment		CAB	
	Coeff. (*t*-value)	Std. Coeff.	Coeff. (*t*-value)	Std. Coeff.	Coeff. (*t*-value)	Std. Coeff.
$\ln(Y/N)$	8.394** (13.87)	0.85	4.909** (10.71)	0.77	3.474** (6.41)	0.50
Y_{gr}	0.479** (4.57)	0.14	0.516** (6.57)	0.23	−0.037 (0.38)	−0.02
D_1	−0.402** (4.26)	−0.38	−0.224** (3.18)	−0.33	−0.178* (2.08)	−0.24
D_2	−1.591** (7.56)	−0.63	−1.181** (7.22)	−0.72	−0.407* (2.19)	−0.23
Pd 1970s	0.571) (0.69)	0.02	2.974** (4.84)	0.19	−2.395** (3.50)	−0.14
Pd 1980s	−3.472** (4.26)	−0.15	1.419* (2.43)	0.09	−4.882** (7.28)	−0.29
Pd 1990s	−3.938** (4.84)	−0.17	0.918 (1.53)	0.06	−4.846** (6.55)	−0.29
N.&C. America	−5.860** (5.43)	−0.20	−2.063* (2.45)	−0.10	−3.782** (3.46)	−0.18
S. America	−2.367* (2.57)	−0.07	−2.336** (3.14)	−0.11	−0.014 (0.02)	−0.00
Europe	1.865 (1.35)	0.07	2.149 (1.92)	0.13	−0.277 (0.22)	−0.02
Asia	1.719 (1.72)	0.07	0.893 (1.35)	0.05	0.848 (0.90)	0.05
Oceania	−5.996** (3.68)	−0.10	−0.438 (0.44)	−0.01	−5.559** (3.25)	−0.14
Constant	−28.027** (3.44)		−7.282 (1.25)		−20.697** (2.83)	
R Squared	0.602		0.469		0.306	
Adj *R*-Sq.	0.595		0.459		0.293	
Mean	15.743		20.888		−5.145	
Std Dev.	10.44		6.784		7.327	
Std Error	6.648		4.99		6.159	

Note: The sample consists of a panel of 87 countries, eight 5-year time periods, and 659 observations.
* indicates significance at the 5% level.
** indicates the 1% level, 1- or 2-tail tests as appropriate; *t*-values are White-corrected.
Note that *t*-values and significance levels apply to the standardized coefficients as well.

Table 3.3 presents two variants of regression coefficients—traditional coefficients and standardized coefficients.[17] We focus our discussion on the standardized coefficients since they are unaffected by scaling differences. Consequently, they provide an indication of the relative importance of the various independent variables in their effects on savings and investment.

The qualitative lessons are similar across savings and investment. Per capita GDP is the most important influence on either savings or investment. With the other variables held constant, a one standard deviation increase in $\ln(Y/N)$ is estimated to raise savings by 0.85 standard deviations and investment by 0.77 standard deviations. Of the four core variables, the GDP growth rate appears to be the least influential, with standardized coefficients of 0.14 for savings and 0.23 for investment.

Dependency falls between per capita GDP and GDP growth in its influence on both savings and investment. Contrary to much of the discussion in this literature, elderly dependency appears to have a greater impact than youth dependency. A one standard deviation increase in D_2 is estimated to lower savings by 0.63 standard deviations and investment by 0.72 standard deviations (rivaling per capita GDP). By contrast, youth dependency's standardized coefficients are −0.38 for savings and −0.33 for investment. The stronger influence of elderly dependency for savings is surprising but not unprecedented in the literature. Higgins (1998, 350) illustrates regression coefficients over the full age spectrum, and for savings and investment those coefficients for ages 65+ (our D_2) are more negative than are those for ages 0–14 (our D_1). In fact, contrary to our expectations and results, Higgins depicts coefficients for youth dependency that are positive relative to working ages for investment.

With respect to period and regional effects, when the other model influences are held constant savings was significantly lower in the 1980s and 1990s than in the 1960s. By region, both of the Americas and Oceania saved significantly less than Africa after we controlled for per capita GDP, GDP growth, dependency, and time period. By contrast, investment was significantly higher in the 1970s and 1980s than in the 1960s. Again, only the Americas fared significantly worse than Africa, with the other regions statistically the same.

---

[17] Standardized coefficients result from a regression in which all variables are standardized to a zero mean and unitary standard deviation. Thus, everything in the regression is interpreted in terms of standard deviation changes and the regression's intercept is zero by definition.

3.2.3. Return to basics: A century of dependency change, 1950–2050

Dependency appears to exert statistically and quantitatively important influences on savings and investment both by conventional and standardized regression coefficients. Furthermore, these results reveal a finding that is new to the literature and quite surprising: the influence of elderly dependency appears to have been stronger for both savings and investment than that of youth dependency. Of course, the impact of any variable is determined by its coefficient as well as by its magnitude. As a result, we assess here the extent to which changes in dependency rates have affected changes in savings and investment rates over the last 40 years. We estimate these impacts using the same methodology we employed when modeling population in development. Specifically, we apply the estimated coefficient from Table 3.3 to the interdecadal change in mean levels of youth and elderly dependency. Since these coefficients are negative, a rising dependency level implies a decline in savings and investment across the two decades, whereas a declining dependency level implies rising savings and investment.

We proceed in two stages. The section that follows examines mean impacts over three broad periods to arrive at several general conclusions. The subsequent section illustrates the patterns and timing behind these conclusions by graphing the demographic impacts for eight country groupings and the nine interdecadal periods.

3.2.3.1. Impacts of historical and projected dependency changes

Table 3.4 summarizes these impacts retrospectively for the 1950s through the 1990s, prospectively for the 2000s through the 2040s, and also for all nine interdecadal periods. The table presents impact estimates for the

Table 3.4. *Mean impacts on savings and investment of dependency change over two epochs: The past and the future*

		Savings			Investment		
		D_1	D_2	D_1+D_2	D_1	D_2	D_1+D_2
DCs	1950s–90s	0.78	−1.99	−1.20	0.44	−1.48	−1.04
	2000s–40s	0.33	−3.82	−3.49	0.19	−2.84	−2.65
	Total	0.53	−3.01	−2.47	0.30	−2.23	−1.94
LDCs	1950s–90s	0.27	−0.24	0.04	0.15	−0.18	−0.02
	2000s–40s	1.25	−2.43	−1.19	0.70	−1.81	−1.11
	Total	0.81	−1.46	−0.64	0.45	−1.08	−0.63

Note: The "1950s–90s" represents the means of four interdecadal impacts (the 1960s vs. 1950s through the 1990s vs. 1980s) whereas the "2000s–40s" averages five interdecadal impacts (the 2000s vs. 1900s through the 2040s vs. 2030s).

23 DCs and the 64 LDCs in the sample. Before proceeding, it is instructive to interpret results from Table 2.2 for D_1 and savings. Interdecadal declines in youth dependency raised the annual savings rate by an average of 0.78 percentage points from the 1950s through the 1990s. This savings boost is projected to decline to 0.33 percentage points from the 2000s through the 2040s. The average for the full period is somewhere in between, 0.53 percentage points.

There are similarities across the past and the future of savings and investment changes as well as across the DCs and LDCs. For all of these aggregates, youth-dependency changes are estimated to raise both savings and investment shares while elderly dependency changes are estimated to lower them. There are other notable differences as well.

Within the DCs, the boost to saving and investment from falling youth-dependency shares was larger in the past than is projected for the future (0.78 vs. 0.33 for S and 0.44 vs. 0.19 for I), but relatively small in both cases. The impact of rising elderly dependency shares presents a stark contrast. Its impact is not only negative, but also much larger than the youth impact and will be about twice as large in the future as it was in the past (−1.99 vs. −3.82 for S and −1.48 vs. −2.84 for I). As a result, the combined impact of dependency changes in the past has been to lower both savings and investment by about 1 percentage point per decade (−1.20 for S and −1.04 for I). This negative impact is projected to grow to 3.49 percentage points for savings and 2.65 percentage points for investment for the first half of the twenty-first century.

A different story emerges for the LDCs. Over the last half of the twentieth century, the positive impacts of declining youth dependency were small (0.27 for S and 0.15 for I) and approximately offset by the negative impacts of rising elderly dependency (−0.24 for S and −0.18 for I). This was true for both savings (combined impact of 0.04) and for investment (−0.02). These effects are predicted to grow in magnitude in the first half of the twenty-first century and will no longer offset each other. While declines in youth dependency will continue at a faster pace (with average impacts of 1.25 for savings and 0.70 for investment), rises in elderly dependency will grow even faster (with impacts of −2.43 and −1.81, respectively). As a result, the combined negative impact is projected to grow to over 1 percentage point per decade for both savings and investment for the first half of the twenty-first century.

Overall, these preliminary findings are surprising. They challenge the assessments in the literature, which has focused on youth dependency. However, when the impacts of D_2 are reckoned, the D_1 impacts of the past are seen to be fairly small and largely netted out by elderly effects. Indeed, D_2 effects appear to be taking center stage, especially with respect to the future. The most amazing aspect of these results is that they are found for both the DCs and the LDCs. It appears that the "population pressures" of the past that have focused on schooling demands and skewed investment in favor of children may have missed the strong, yet important, elderly-dependency effects of the past. Clearly, our findings are less novel for the DCs, although the magnitudes of the D_2 impacts are quite exceptional in both sets of countries.

3.2.3.2. *Visualizing the impacts on savings and investment of interdecadal dependency changes*

Our summary of dependency impacts over the two broad aggregations of countries (DCs and LDCs) and our broad aggregations of decades (the last half of the twentieth century and the first half of the twenty-first century) have provided an interesting overview, but such a high level of aggregation tends to mask disparities across regions. Therefore, we find it useful to follow the approach we used when visualizing the economic impacts of demographic change, and therefore depict the full set of interdecadal changes. We do this in Figure 3.2 for savings, Figure 3.3 for investment, and Figure 3.4 for the current account balance (included for the interested reader but not discussed below). Each figure includes eight stacked-bar graphs, depicting the impacts of interdecadal changes in D_1, D_2, and $D_1 + D_2$ for the DCs, LDCs, three regions (Africa, Latin America, and Asia), and three Asian subregions (East, South Central, and Southeast).

Notice first the qualitative similarity between savings (Figure 3.2) and investment (Figure 3.3). Although there are differences in the magnitudes of the impacts and the relative size of the D_1 and D_2 impacts, these differences are small compared with the overall stories told by these graphs. As noted in the previous section, those stories are qualitatively the same for both series. Consequently, we focus our attention on the savings impacts, which can best be understood by viewing Figure 3.2 in conjunction with Table 3.5, which summarizes the mean savings impacts by region for the past, future, and overall.

Before proceeding, it is instructive to learn the mechanics by interpreting the Figure 3.3 graph for East Asia. Both youth and elderly dependency rose between the 1950s and 1960s, resulting in reinforced negative impacts on savings. The graph depicts this by stacking the D_2 bar below the D_1 bar and positioning both below zero. Since they reinforce each other, the dot in the line graph representing their combined impact is at the bottom of the stacked bars (about -1.3). By contrast, in every subsequent period, D_1 and D_2 impacts partially offset each other: the D_1 bar rises above zero and the D_2 bar falls below zero. Through the 1990s, positive D_1 impacts dominate and the dot for the aggregate line graph lies within the

Figure 3.2. Impacts of dependency on savings change: 1960s vs. 1950s through 2040s vs. 2030s

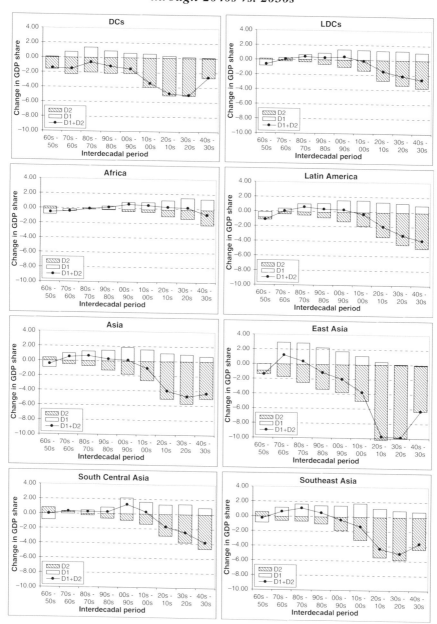

**Figure 3.3.   *Impacts of dependency on investment change:*
*1960s vs. 1950s through 2040s vs. 2030s***

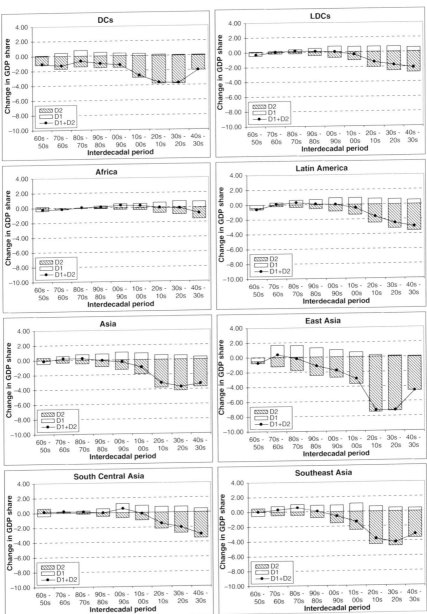

Figure 3.4. Impacts of dependency on current-account balance change: 1960s vs. 1950s through 2040s vs. 2030s

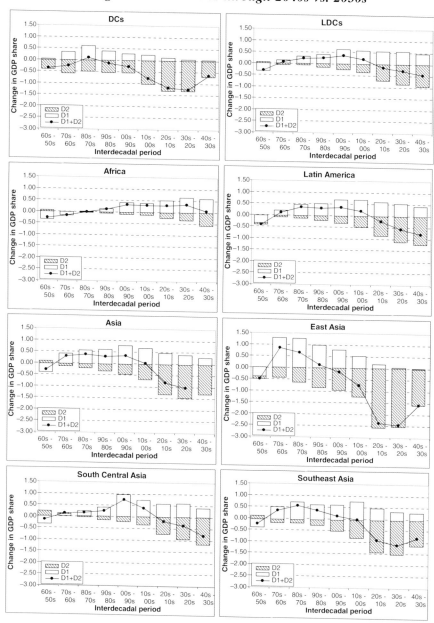

Table 3.5.   Mean impacts on savings of demographic change over two epochs: The past and the future

D_1: Youth Dependency

Row	Period	DCs	LDCs	Africa	L. America	Asia	East	S. Cntr.	SE
1	1950s–90s	0.78	0.24	−0.17	0.48	0.73	1.78	0.18	0.88
2	2000s–40s	0.33	1.10	1.20	1.33	1.23	0.69	1.43	1.19
3	Total	0.53	0.72	0.59	0.96	1.01	1.17	0.87	1.06

D_2: Elderly Dependency

Row	Period	DCs	LDCs	Africa	L. America	Asia	East	S. Cntr.	SE
4	1950s–90s	−1.99	−0.24	0.06	−0.44	−0.47	−1.95	0.01	−0.36
5	2000s–40s	−3.82	−2.43	−0.99	−3.08	−3.96	−6.87	−2.71	−4.04
6	Total	−3.01	−1.46	−0.53	−1.91	−2.41	−4.68	−1.50	−2.40

$D_1 + D_2$: Youth and Elderly Dependency

Row	Period	DCs	LDCs	Africa	L. America	Asia	East	S. Cntr.	SE
7	1950–90s	−1.20	0.04	−0.11	0.04	0.26	−0.17	0.19	0.52
8	2000s–40s	−3.49	−1.19	0.20	−1.75	−2.73	−6.18	−1.28	−2.84
9	Total	−2.47	−0.64	0.06	−0.95	−1.40	−3.51	−0.63	−1.35

Note: The "1950s–90s" represents the means of four interdecadal impacts (the 1960s vs. 1950s through the 1990s vs. 1980s) whereas the "2000s–40s" averages five interdecadal impacts (the 2000s vs. 1900s through the 2040s vs. 2030s).

D_1 bar and above zero. Beginning with the 2000s, negative D_2 impacts dominate and the dot for the aggregate line graph lies within the D_2 bar and below zero.

One is struck in Figure 3.2 by the large areas of darkly shaded bars relative to clear bars—i.e., by the comparatively large negative impacts of rising elderly dependency relative to the positive impacts of declining youth dependency. Two interesting points are included in this observation. First, subsequent to the first period (1950s to the 1960s), the impacts of changes in youth dependency are uniformly positive while the impacts of changing elderly dependency are uniformly negative. Although relatively small in magnitude, the impacts are generally of opposite signs in the first period. Second, the magnitude of impacts for rising elderly dependency approached and sometimes exceeded that of impacts for declining youth dependency over the last half of the twentieth century. To our knowledge, both of these results are new to the literature. Part of the explanation for this might be our focus on demographic change. Given the negative regression coefficients, both youth and elderly dependency will always exert a negative influence on savings and investment levels, even when a trend facilitates rising savings and investment. Another part of the explanation, however, is the magnitude of our estimated regression coefficient for elderly dependency. It appears to be larger than in some other studies. We addressed this issue above when assessing the regression results.

Even more interesting, rising aged dependency clearly will be the dominant demographic influence on savings and investment over the first half of the twenty-first century. Indeed the phenomenon builds as the century progresses. Over the first period or two, youth and elderly dependency approximately offset each other in all regions other than the DCs and East Asia, where elderly dependency dominates from the very first period. From the third period (2010s to 2020s) forward, the disparity in influence of rising elderly dependency over declining youth dependency is dramatic in all regions other than Africa. Again, East Asia, where these impacts are largest by far, is a clear outlier. Surprisingly, Africa is least influenced by changing dependency throughout the full century.

3.2.4. Return to basics: Conclusions

These results leave us with new insights and some new questions as well. If these results are to be believed, elderly dependency played a larger role in determining savings and investment over the last half of the twentieth century than earlier studies have indicated. This is true both with respect to the regression coefficients themselves and, more importantly, in the role that rising aged dependency appeared to play in lowering savings and investment shares. Projecting the analysis into the future, we estimate that rising population shares of the elderly will swamp declining youth shares in all regions other than Africa. Their negative impact will be large (much larger in East Asia than elsewhere), and that impact will grow in magnitude typically through the 2030s.

How do these results conform to our findings in Section 3.1? Compare the Y/N_{gr} impacts depicted in Figure 3.1 with the savings impacts of Figure 3.2. A general consistency appears to hold across all regions. Positive savings (and investment) impacts from dependency change tend to correspond to periods of positive demographic impacts on Y/N_{gr} as well. Conversely, negative dependency impacts on savings tend to correspond to periods of negative demographic impacts on Y/N_{gr}. This pattern is most obvious for East Asia, which stands out as an outlier in each set of graphs. Demographic change provided by far the largest positive boost in East Asia for both Y/N_{gr} and savings over the last 50 years, and it is projected to have notably larger negative impacts over the next 50 years. The magnitude and consistency of these impacts tend to corroborate our argument from Section 3.1 for the inclusion of dependency in an economic growth model: it plays a substantive role in savings and investment. There is, however, a discordant note. Although multiple demographic variables are combined in the Z_d influences on Y/N_{gr} in Figure 3.1, youth dependency is the driving force. By contrast, whereas youth dependency evinces notable savings and investment impacts in Figures 3.2 and 3.3, it is elderly dependency that is the dominant force. Clearly, population is influential in both arenas. Equally clearly, work remains to be done to understand the linkages in modeling savings, investment, and economic growth.

Appendix: Robustness experiments and future directions for modeling the impact of dependency on savings and investment

The results from five "robustness" experiments are summarized in Table 3.A1. To conserve space, the table includes only the D_1 and D_2 coefficients for the savings and investment equations. The full results are available upon request. Results from both the base and the experimental regressions are presented for each experiment to simplify comparisons. In some instances (experiments 2, 3, and 5), the base regression is the same as that in Table 3.3. In other instances (experiments 1 and 4), the base results differ because a new base regression was run on the sample subset dictated by the experiment. We consider each in turn, identifying directions for future research where appropriate.

"Lagged Y_{gr}" assesses the use of lagged Y_{gr} as an instrument for contemporaneous Y_{gr}. The dependency coefficients are little changed and we use OLS in Section 3.2 as a consequence. Even though this approach to instrumentation does not affect our results, the potential endogeneity of the GDP growth rate remains a serious concern in the investment as well as savings equations. Higgins (1998) noted that he could not identify a set of instruments to resolve satisfactorily the endogeneity issues raised by the Wu-Hausman test. Consequently, he used OLS regression. Nevertheless, we hope to address it in a rigorous manner in our model. Section 3.1 provides a candidate list of instrumental variables through a well-explicated model of economic growth. That data set must be extended through the end of the 1990s, however, before we can satisfactorily address the endogeneity issue.

"Include RPI" appends a variable, the relative price of capital, argued by Taylor (1995) and Higgins (1998) to be potentially important in the investment equation. In our model, RPI is never significant and scarcely changes dependency coefficient estimates.

Experimentation with additional variables by Taylor and Higgins highlights the Spartan nature of the empirical models in this literature. Higgins

Table 3.A1. Estimated dependency coefficients from a series of robustness experiments

| | | Savings | | | | Investment | | | |
| | | Base Model | | Experimental | | Base Model | | Experimental | |
	n	D_1	D_2	D_1	D_2	D_1	D_2	D_1	D_2
(1) Lagged Y_{gr}	640	−0.39**	−1.62**	−0.44**	−1.58**	−0.24**	−1.19**	−0.28**	−1.21**
(2) Include RPI	659	−0.40**	−1.59**	−0.40**	−1.62**	−0.22**	−1.18**	−0.23**	−1.17**
(3) JPE Data	474	−0.29**	−1.31**	−0.04	−0.48	−0.13	−0.98**	−0.23*	−0.86**
(4) Drop 1990s	659	−0.40**	−1.59**	−0.32**	−1.39**	−0.22**	−1.18**	−0.13	−0.96**
(5) Period Spec.	659	−0.40**	−1.59**			−0.22**	−1.18**		
1960s				0.09	0.03			−0.22	−1.70
1970s				−0.07	−0.89**			−0.02	−0.45
1980s				−0.67**	−2.19**			−0.22	−1.19**
1990s				−0.67**	−2.10**			−0.21*	−1.31**
(6) Dep. Denom.	659	−0.40**	−1.59**	−0.38**	−1.57**	−0.22**	−1.18**	−0.13	−1.07**

Note: The sample consists of a panel of 87 countries, eight 5-year time periods, and 659 observations.
* indicates significance at the 5% level.
** indicates significance at the 1% level using 1-tail tests; *t*-values are White-corrected.

also experimented with proxy measures for openness to capital flows since dependency should play a less important role in investment for an economy open to foreign capital, than for one closed to it. He had more success with an openness-to-trade proxy than with an openness-to-capital measure that he created. Further experimentation with this and other institutional measures may prove to be productive, especially for investment. Additionally, within a life-cycle framework, the availability of old-age pension programs, both government and employer, should also influence household savings decisions. Moreover, domestic savings may well be affected by current levels of wealth as well as income. Recent speculation concerning a worldwide savings glut is predicated partially upon the necessity of countries such as Japan to raise savings, given declines in wealth due to a falling stock market and falling real-estate values. By contrast, the very low savings rates in the United States are argued to be rational because of the rapid run-up of the stock market in the 1990s and housing values through the present time. Such conjectures could be put to the test in the present savings model.

"PWT Data" compares results we obtained when using the current data set versus the data set used in Kelley and Schmidt (1996), since our new results differ qualitatively from those in our earlier study. This experiment employs the 474 observations that overlap between the two data sets. The more important difference between these two studies, however, is the use in the current study of GDP shares based on nominal, local currency units. By contrast, our 1996 study's GDP shares were based on real, purchase-price parity prices from the Penn World Tables, version 5.6. We found dramatic differences in coefficient estimates between the two series, in both magnitude and statistical significance. We switched from PPP GDP shares to those more commonly used in the literature when we discovered that the simple correlation between GNS/GDP in versions 5.6 and 6.1 of the PWT was only 0.73 for our country set (versus 0.99 for per capita GDP). We subsequently learned that GDP shares in PPP tend to be unstable from vintage to vintage.

"Drop 1990s" addresses the question of how much our results are influenced by extending the data set beyond that of most published work in this literature, i.e., through the 1990s. Dependency exhibits weaker impacts when the 1990s are dropped from the sample. D_1 coefficients decline by about 0.08 for both the savings and investment equations, whereas while D_2 coefficients decline by about 0.10 in both instances. Furthermore, the D_1 coefficient drops from significance in the investment equation.

"Period Spec." further examines the apparently stronger dependency coefficients of the 1990s than in earlier decades by estimating decade-specific dependency coefficients. The results are striking. The number of statistically significant dependency coefficients rose consistently over the four decades: there were none in the 1960s, one in the 1970s, three in the 1980s, and all four in the 1990s. Furthermore, the dependency coefficients became increasingly negative through the 1980s and appeared to stabilize in the 1990s. These results raise more questions than they answer, and they also suggest that some important variables may be missing from these models.

"Dep. Denom." assesses the influence of alternative denominators that could be used for D_1 and D_2. Following the savings literature, we use population size in the denominator in Section 3.2 and use D_1 and D_2 to represent population shares. Consistent with the convergence model's focus on the working-age population, in Section 3.1 we use the working-age population in the denominators for the growth model. How much are the results from Section 3.2 influenced by this choice? Coefficients change very little for savings but are somewhat weaker for investment. The D_1 coefficient drops from significance in the investment equation, and the coefficients decline by about 0.09 for D_1 and 0.11 for D_2, when dependency is expressed as a ratio to the working-age population. Neither of these changes affects our qualitative conclusions.

References

Barro, Robert J. 1991. "Economic growth in a cross section of countries". *Quarterly Journal of Economics* 106(2): 407–44.
———. 1997. *Determinants of Economic Growth: A Cross-country Empirical Study.* Cambridge, MA: MIT Press.
Bloom, David, and David Canning 2001. "Cumulative causality, economic growth, and the demographic transition", in: Nancy Birdsall, Allen C. Kelley, and Steven Sinding, eds, *Population Matters: Demographic Change, Economic Growth, and Poverty in the Developing World,* pp. 165–197 New York: Oxford University Press.
Bloom, David E., and Jeffrey G. Williamson. 1997. "Demographic change and human resource development". In *Emerging Asia: Changes and Challenges,* pp. 141–197. Manila: Asian Development Bank.
———. 1998. "Demographic transitions and economic miracles in emerging Asia". *World Bank Economic Review* 12(3): 419–55.
Coale, Ansley J., and Edgar M. Hoover. 1958. *Population Growth and Economic Development in Low-income Countries: A Case Study of India's Prospects.* Princeton, NJ: Princeton University Press.
Heston, Alan, Robert Summers, and Bettina Aten. 2002. *Penn world tables Version 6.1.* Philadelphia: Center for International Comparisons at the University of Pennsylvania (CICUP).
Higgins, Matthew. 1998. "Demography, national savings, and international capital flows". *International Economic Review* 39(2): 343–69.

Kelley, Allen C. 2001. "The population debate in historical perspective: Revisionism revisited", in: Nancy Birdsall, Allen C. Kelley, and Steven Sinding, eds, *Population Matters: Demographic Change, Economic Growth, and Poverty in the Developing World*, pp. 24–54. New York: Oxford University Press.

Kelley, Allen C., and Robert M. Schmidt. 1994. "Population and income change: Recent evidence". World Bank Discussion Papers, No. 249. Washington, DC: World Bank.

————. 1995. "Aggregate population and economic growth correlations: The role of the components of demographic change". *Demography* 32(4): 543–55.

Leff, Nathaniel H. 1969. "Dependency rates and savings rates". *American Economic Review* 59(5): 886–96.

Levine, Ross, and David Renelt. 1992. "A sensitivity analysis of cross-country growth regressions". *American Economic Review* 82(4): 942–63.

Mason, Andrew. 1987. "National saving rates and population growth: A new model and new evidence", in: D. Gale Johnson and Ronald D. Lee, eds*Population Growth and Economic Development: Issues and Evidence*, pp. 523–560 Madison, WI: University of Wisconsin Press.

————. 1988. "Saving, economic growth, and demographic change". *Population and Development Review* 14 (March): 113–44.

Taylor, Alan M. 1995. "Debt, dependence and the demographic transition: Latin America into the next century". *World Development*. 23(5): 869–79.

Taylor, Alan M., and Jeffrey G. Williamson. 1994. "Capital flows to the New World as an intergenerational transfer". *Journal of Political Economy* 102(2): 348–71.

CHAPTER 4

Demographic Dividends: The Past, the Present, and the Future

Andrew Mason

All countries in the world have experienced and will continue to experience substantial changes in their age structures. These can be traced, first, to fertility decline that reduced the numbers of children in populations and later the number of workers, and, second, to improvements in life expectancy that will eventually produce populations with many more people concentrated at the older ages. The macroeconomic implications of these changes have been the subject of considerable interest in the last few years.

Analysis of the effects of age structure comes in three forms. First, a series of empirical studies based on aggregate-level panel data conclude that demographic factors have a strong, statistically significant effect on aggregate saving rates (Bloom, Canning, and Graham 2003; Deaton and Paxson 2000; Kelly and Schmidt 1996; Kinugasa 2004; Kinugasa and Mason 2007 forthcoming; Williamson and Higgins, 2001) and on economic growth (Bloom and Canning 2001; Bloom and Williamson 1998; Kelley and Schmidt 1995). In contrast, earlier studies based on shorter time series found little statistical support for strong demographic effects (e.g., Kelley 1988). Second, detailed case studies of the East Asian "miracle" provide compelling and consistent evidence that the demographic dividend was an important contributor to that region's economic success (Bloom and Williamson 1998; Mason 2001b; Mason, Merrick, and Shaw 1999). Bloom and Williamson (1998) use econometric analysis to conclude that about one-third of East Asia's increase in per capita income was due to the demographic dividend. In a previous study (Mason 2001a), I use growth-accounting methods to estimate that the dividend accounted for about one-fourth of the region's economic growth.

This research was supported by NIA, R01-AG025488-01. My thanks to Ronald Lee for making US age profiles of consumption and production available; to Tomoko Kinugasa, Rikiya Matsukura, and Naohiro Ogawa for help with identifying historical age data for Japan; and to Comfort Sumida and Turro Wongkaren for their able research assistance.

POPULATION CHANGE, LABOR MARKETS, AND SUSTAINABLE GROWTH
VOLUME 281   ISSN 0573-8555/DOI 10.1016/S0573-8555(07)81004-2

The third approach, the one employed here, relies on macroeconomic simulations to explore the effects of changing age structure (Cutler et al. 1990; Lee, Mason, and Miller 2001, 2003; Mason 2005). This chapter extends two earlier studies. The first formally establishes the potential for two demographic dividends (Mason and Lee 2006). The first dividend arises because over the demographic transition, countries experience an increase in the share of their populations concentrated in the working ages. On its face, this has a direct, favorable effect on per capita income. Whether or not the first dividend is realized, however, will depend on how wages, labor-force-participation rates, and unemployment are affected by the rapid growth in the working-age population that typically leads to the first dividend. The second dividend arises as a response to the prospect of population aging. A key economic challenge for aging populations is to provide for old-age consumption in the face of substantially reduced labor income. Some societies are trying to meet this challenge by relying on transfer systems—either public programs or familial-support systems. Other societies are responding by increasing their saving rates and accumulating greater physical wealth or capital. It is in this latter response that prospects for capital accumulation and more rapid economic growth are enhanced.[1]

The second study employs the two-dividend framework to construct measures of the demographic dividends for the countries of the world for the period from 1950 to 2000 (Mason 2005). The analysis supports several conclusions. First, the demographic dividends are potentially quite important—contributing as much as 1 to 2 percentage points of growth of per capita income between 1970 and 2000 in the industrial countries, East and Southeast Asia, Latin America, the Middle East and North Africa, and the Pacific Islands. Second, the greatest gains were in the developing world, although this reflects their relatively unfavorable demographic situation in 1970. Third, in some parts of the world, favorable changes in demographic conditions have not yet begun; sub-Saharan Africa is a notable example. Fourth, the record of translating favorable demographic conditions into more rapid economic growth is quite mixed. It appears that East and Southeast Asia were very successful in this effort, whereas Latin America was not.

The purpose of the analysis presented in this chapter is to examine the effects of demographic change over a longer time horizon. The analysis focuses on the experience of three countries: India, Japan, and the United States. They have been selected, in part, because of their distinctive

---

[1] Changes in age structure may have additional important effects (Bloom, Canning, and Sevilla 2002). Recent studies suggest that demographic change may have favorable effects on human capital (Jensen and Ahlburg 2001; Montgomery and Lloyd 1996), although the effects on education are uncertain (Ahlburg and Jensen 2001; Kelley 1996).

demographic experiences. The demographic transition began earliest in the United States, later in Japan, and later still in India. The United States experienced a substantial baby boom from 1946 to 1964. Japan experienced high fertility for a short period following the end of World War II, but nothing on the order of the US baby boom.

A second reason for selecting those three countries is that data availability allows us to explore the economic affects of changes in age structure over an extended period of time. Those changes began in 1850 in the United States, in 1880 in India, and in 1900 in Japan.

A third reason is that the future of these countries is of considerable interest both because of their size in the world economy and also because of their demographics. India will soon have the largest population in the world. Japan now has the oldest population in the world, and the United States has a relatively young population for an industrial country. Using long-term population projections, it is possible to explore the potential effects of demographic change well into the future.

The fourth and most important reason for selecting these countries is that their diverse demographic experiences make it possible to judge whether or not changes in age structure have played an important role in their development experiences.

4.1. Two demographic dividends

The first demographic dividend arises and dissipates as changes in age structure interact with the life cycle of production and consumption. Children and the elderly produce much less than they consume, whereas working-age adults, on average, produce much more than they consume. Populations with heavy concentrations at the working ages are advantaged at producing high levels of per capita income. Child- and old-age dependency ratios are often used to capture the key features of the economic life cycle, but more detailed and precise estimates are becoming available. Estimated age profiles of production and consumption are broadly consistent with general characterizations of the economic life cycle, but two features of country profiles are striking. The first is that the ages of dependency are often not very close to those used to delineate the dependent ages (under 15, and 65 and older). In 2000, US residents under the age of 26 and over the age of 57 were dependents in the sense that they consumed more than they produced through their labor. Estimates for Taiwan are similar: in 1998, residents under the age of 25 and over the age of 56 consumed more than they produced. In Indonesia, the crossing points for consumption and production are ages 20 and 60 (Lee, Lee, and Mason 2005, 16). The second striking feature of the individual country profiles is that the estimates of production and consumption imply a gradation of dependency. Persons who are 25 and those who are 60 are dependents, but to a much smaller degree than those who are 18 and those who are 75.

The manner in which the economic life cycle interacts with the age distribution to influence per capita income is apparent from the production and consumption weights in the upper panel of Figure 4.1 and the three extreme age distributions in the lower panel of Figure 4.1. The production and consumption weights are based on US estimates of labor income and total consumption in 2000. The production weights have been scaled so that the average value of production is 1.0 for ages 30–59. The consumption weights have been scaled so that the 1950 population of the world has a support ratio of 1.0 if constructed using the US-based weights. A value of 0.9 for the support ratio, for example, indicates that the effective number of producers per consumer is 90% of the worldwide value for 1950 (Mason 2005).

The youngest population age distribution in Figure 4.1 is for the United States in 1850. Over half of its population was under the age of 20 and only 43% was of "working age" (20–59). In contrast, the Indian distribution projected for 2040 has an unusually high concentration of the population in the working ages: 56% is between the ages of 20 and 60. The projection for Japan in 2070 represents a third extreme. In this population only 40% is in the 20–59 age group, while over 40% is 60 and older. The Japanese age structure appears to be even more unfavorable for current production than the US age distribution, because such a low percentage of its population falls in the working ages. A central issue in this chapter, however, is whether an old dependent population and a young dependent population are equivalent. As will be shown, they are not.

Taking these three cases together illustrates the changes in age structure over the demographic transition, perhaps in extreme form, and the implication for the first demographic dividend. The transition from the US to the Indian distribution is marked by a substantial relative increase in the working-age population and, assuming that workers can be fully employed, an increase in per capita income. The transition from the Indian to the Japanese age distribution would undo the gains from the first part of the age transition. During this part of the age transition, changes in age structure represent a drag on growth in per capita income.

The second dividend arises to the extent that consumers and policy-makers are forward-looking and respond effectively to the demographic changes that are coming. With a rise of the elderly dependent population on the horizon, consumption in the future can be maintained only through the accumulation of wealth in some form. One possibility is that individuals or firms and governments, acting on the behalf of consumers, accumulate

Figure 4.1. *Consumption and production weights by age: United States, 2000*

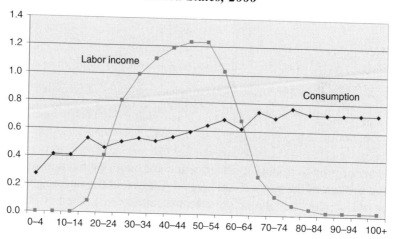

Age distributions: Three extremes

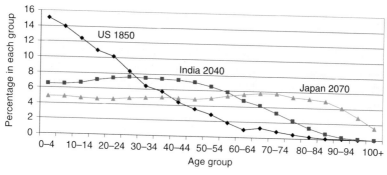

capital. If invested in the domestic economy, the result will be capital deepening and more rapid growth in output per worker. If invested abroad, the result will be an increase in the current account and national income. In either case, per capita income will grow more rapidly.

The first and second dividends are formalized in Mason and Lee (2006), which draws on earlier work by Cutler et al. (1990).The effective number of consumers (*N*) and the effective number of producers (*L*) are defined as

$$N(t) = \sum_a \alpha(a)P(a,t)$$

$$L(t) = \sum_a \gamma(a)P(a,t) \qquad (4.1)$$

where $\alpha(a)$ is a vector of consumption weights, $\gamma(a)$ is a vector of production weights, and $P(a,t)$ is the population. Output per effective consumer (Y/N), is given by:

$$\frac{Y(t)}{N(t)} = \frac{L(t)}{N(t)} \times \frac{Y(t)}{L(t)} \qquad (4.2)$$

Equation (4.2) is readily converted from levels to rates of growth by taking the natural log of both sides and the derivative with respect to time:

$$\dot{y}(t) = \dot{L}(t) - \dot{N}(t) + \dot{y}^{l}(t) \qquad (4.3)$$

The rate of growth in output per effective consumer ($\dot{y}$) is the sum of the rate of growth of the support ratio ($\dot{L}(t) - \dot{N}(t)$) and the rate of growth of labor productivity, i.e., output per effective worker ($\dot{y}^{l}$). The first dividend is defined as the rate of growth of the support ratio. The second dividend operates through productivity growth by inducing the accumulation of wealth and capital-deepening as discussed more extensively below.

4.1.1. Methods and sources

Estimates of the first demographic dividend require an age profile of consumption and labor income and population age distributions. The results are based on estimates of consumption and labor income by age for the United States in 2000. Consumption includes both private and public consumption. Private consumption is estimated primarily by using consumer-expenditure surveys. Public-consumption estimates are based on administrative records, estimates of utilization, and other information that can be used to allocate public spending on education, health, and other public programs for the intended beneficiaries of those programs. Labor-income estimates are based on wage and income surveys and include earnings of employees, estimates of the return to labor in family businesses, and other forms of labor income. Detailed estimation procedures are described in Mason et al. (2006) or at www.ntaccounts.org.

Historical population data are taken from a variety of sources available upon request. Data from 1950 to 2050 are based on the most recent population projections of the UN Population Division (UNPD 2005). Data for 2050 to 2150 are based on UN long-range population projections (UNPD 2004). Results for individual countries are not published, but were provided to me by the UN Population Division. The historical pre-1950 estimates for the United States and Japan are consistent with UN estimates for 1950. In the case of India, however, there is a sharp discontinuity between the historical data and the UN estimates.

Figure 4.2. Support ratios for India, Japan, and the United States

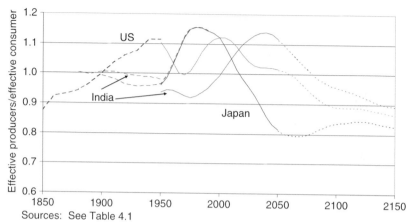

Sources: See Table 4.1

4.1.2. The first dividend: Long-term effects

The support ratios are very different for Japan, the United States, and India (Figure 4.2). The United States had a very young age structure and an unfavorable support ratio in 1850. Over the next 90 years, however, it experienced a steady and pronounced rise in the support ratio—again exceeding 20%. The effects of the post–World War II baby boom are pronounced and quite apparent. Between 1950 and 1970, the support ratio declined sharply, only to return to pre-baby boom levels in 2000. During the first half of the twenty-first century the support ratio is projected to decline steadily in the United States, dropping back to very nearly the 1850 value.

The Japanese experience is tracked from 1900. Japan's population was quite young at that time, with 44% under the age of 20. In this respect, Japan's population was very similar to the US population and its support ratio was nearly identical to the US support ratio. The percentage under the age of 20 was rising gradually and the support ratio was declining. Fertility decline began in the 1930s, but it was accompanied by a decline in infant and child mortality. Japan experienced a mini-baby boom in the early 1950s and a dramatic fall thereafter, with replacement fertility reached in 1959. The effect of fertility decline on the support ratio began to be felt in the early 1950s, and the ratio rose very rapidly, reaching a peak in 1980. During the last two decades of the twentieth century, the support ratio declined gradually in Japan. A much more precipitous decline has begun that is expected to push the support ratio strongly lower to a value of only 0.8 by 2050. The long-range projections of the UN

Andrew Mason

Figure 4.3. The first demographic dividend: India, Japan, and the United States

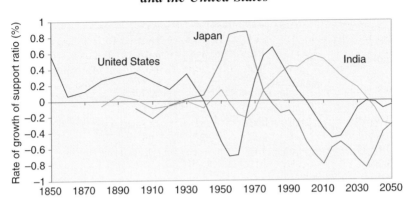

Population Division imply a relatively stable support ratio after 2050, but this will be so only if fertility recovers and life expectancy improves more slowly than it has in recent decades.

The trend in the Indian support ratio bears some similarity to Japan's. Both are single-peaked and their amplitudes are similar. Fertility decline began later in India and has proceeded more slowly than in Japan. As a consequence, the rise in the support ratio began later in India by several decades and the rate at which it increased has been slower. Based on the most recent UN population projections, India's support ratio will not peak until 2040. Another feature that India and Japan share is that both countries apparently experienced a pretransition period of relative stability during the first half of the twentieth century.

The first demographic dividend, i.e., the rate of growth of the support ratio, for the United States, Japan, and India are shown in Figure 4.3. The United States had two distinct dividend periods, the first lasting from 1850 to 1940 and the second lasting from 1970 to 2000. The dividend was strongly negative between 1950 and 1970. It has turned negative again and will continue to be a drag on economic growth for the foreseeable future.

Japan's first dividend was concentrated primarily in a 30-year period, from 1950 to 1980.[2] Before 1850, age structure played a moderately negative role. The first dividend turned negative again in 1980, and it will be an even greater drag on economic growth during the coming decades.

The support ratio deteriorated in India between 1955 and 1975 as declining rates of infant and child mortality produced an age structure

---

[2] See Ogawa and Matsukura (2005) for alternative estimates of the first dividend.

Table 4.1. Growth rates of the support ratio and GDP per effective consumer: India, Japan, and the United States during key demographic phases

Country and Years	Support Ratio	GDP Per Capita	Effective Consumers Per Capita	GDP Per Effective Consumer	Growth Rate of Support Ratio/Growth Rate of GDP Per Effective Consumer (%)
India					
1880–1955	−0.01	0.18	−0.01	0.18	−6.2
1955–75	−0.14	1.51	0.02	1.49	−9.1
1975–2005	0.34	3.12	0.13	2.98	11.5
2005–50	0.20				
Japan					
1900–40	−0.06	2.23	−0.02	2.24	−2.5
1950–80	0.61	5.19	0.26	4.93	12.3
1980–2005	−0.23	2.04	0.32	1.72	−13.2
2005–50	−0.65				
United States					
1850–1940	0.27	1.66	0.11	1.55	17.3
1950–70	−0.51	2.20	0.05	2.15	−23.7
1970–2000	0.40	2.15	0.11	2.04	19.5
2000–50	−0.20				

Note and sources: Growth rate of per capita GDP for 1970 and later based on World Development Indictors (World Bank 2005). Most recent growth rates for India and Japan are based on GDP per capita for 2003. Rates are calculated using real values in local currency. Growth rates of per capita GDP prior to 1970 calculated from Maddison (1995, table D). GDP per capita for India in 1880 is a simple average of values reported for 1870 and 1890.

with a large share of children. From 1975 to 2005, India experienced a demographic dividend that is anticipated to continue until 2040.

These key demographic phases are summarized in Table 4.1, which reports the average annual rate of growth of the support ratio. Japan experienced the strongest boost of the three countries during its dividend period. As reported in the column labeled "Support Ratio," changes in the support ratio led to an increase in GDP per effective consumer of 0.6% per year for a period of 30 years. The US baby boom–induced dividend was 0.4% per year, and its prewar dividend contributed a little less than 0.3% per year to economic growth. India's dividend contributed about one-third of 1% of economic growth per year between 1975 and 2005. To this point the largest negative dividend occurred in the United States. As a result of the baby boom, income growth slowed by 0.5% per year between 1950 and 1970. Japan is expected to experience an even larger negative effect (−0.65% per year) in the coming decades, and it is important to note that this will be experienced for a period of 45 years as compared with two decades for the US downturn.

To assess the magnitude of these effects it is useful to compare the first dividend to the rates of economic growth achieved during the same periods. The first step in carrying out this comparison is to construct an estimate of the rate of growth of output per effective consumer—our measure of economic growth. This is done by subtracting the rate of growth of effective consumers per capita from the rate of growth of GDP per capita. With the exception of pre-1955 India and pre-1950 Japan, the effective number of consumers grew more rapidly than the population because the share of high-consuming adults was increasing in the population. Thus, the rate of economic growth, incorporating changes in age-related "needs," is somewhat less than the rate of per capita GDP growth. The adjustments are relatively modest, typically resulting in a reduction of 5–10% or less. The only exception is in Japan during 1980–2005, where the adjustment reduced per capita GDP growth by 15%.

The first dividend has contributed the most to economic growth, in percentage terms, in the United States. It accounted for almost 20% of US growth in output per effective consumer between 1970 and 2000 and 17% between 1850 and 1940. In India and Japan, it contributed a little more than 10% of economic growth during the positive dividend periods. The largest negative effect was also felt in the United States, where the adverse effect of the baby boom was nearly equal to one-quarter of the growth achieved during that period. Also of note is the 13% reduction in economic growth in Japan between 1980 and 2005, attributable to the first dividend.

4.2. The second demographic dividend

The accumulation of wealth is implicit in the age profiles of consumption and production that lead to the first demographic dividend and its demise. Individuals in their late 50s and older will at every age over the remainder of their lives consume more than they produce—at many ages substantially more—if the current profiles persist. This is only possible if those individuals hold substantial wealth.

This wealth can take different forms, however (Lee 1994a, b). One possibility is that the old will rely on transfers from public pensions and welfare programs or from adult children and other family members. In this case, individuals accumulate transfer wealth as a means of financing consumption during their retirement years. A second possibility is that individuals accumulate capital during their working years and this serves as the source of support during retirement years. Both of these forms of wealth can be used to deal with the life-cycle deficit at older ages, but capital also influences economic growth—i.e., the productivity term in the economic growth model presented in equation (4.3). The pro-growth effect of capital accumulation is the source of the second demographic dividend.

Demographic factors lead to an increase in the demand for life-cycle wealth and a second demographic dividend in two ways. First, there is a compositional effect. A growing share of the population consists of individuals who are nearing or who have completed their productive years. Second, there is a behavioral effect. The rise in life expectancy and the accompanying increase in the duration of retirement lead to an upward shift in the age profile of wealth.

The second dividend is more complex to estimate than the first, in part because the accumulation of wealth is intrinsically forward-looking. Individuals accumulate wealth in anticipation of future needs to support consumption, to finance bequests, and to respond to other uncertain events. The analysis presented here emphasizes the life-cycle motive—i.e., the accumulation of wealth over the lifetime necessary to finance future consumption in excess of future labor income. The relevant demography is captured by the projections of the equivalent numbers of consumer and producers for each cohort. Each cohort's life-cycle wealth increases as the future person-years of consumption rises relative to the future person-years of production, both appropriately discounted.

Wealth is accumulated during the working years from the surplus—the excess of labor income over consumption—shown in Figure 4.1 top panel. The accumulation of wealth for retirement competes, however, with the support of children. Thus, some portion of the surplus is saved and some portion is transferred to children. To simplify calculations, I assume that surpluses at younger ages are transferred to children whereas surpluses at older ages are accumulated as wealth. Total life-cycle wealth, then, is the wealth held by all those older than the age at which the accumulation process begins. To be specific, I use the wealth held by those who are 50 and older to measure the effect of population aging on life-cycle wealth and the second demographic dividend. My interest is more in the rate at which wealth grows than in its absolute level. As long as the approximation is proportional to a more precise measure, this simplifying assumption will have no effect on the results.

Following the method introduced in Mason (2005), let $N(\leq b, t+x)$ be the number of effective consumers born in year b or less who are alive in year $t+x$. Letting $b = t - a$, then $N(\leq b, t+x)$ is the effective number of consumers a years or older in year t who are still alive in year $t+x$. If the

relative per capita cross-sectional age profile of consumption is fixed
and shifting upward at rate g_c, then the total consumption of the cohort
born before age b in year $t+x$ is equal to $\bar{c}(t)e^{g_c x}N(\leq b, t+x)$, where $\bar{c}(t)$
is consumption per effective consumer in year t.[3] The present value of
the future lifetime consumption of the cohort born in year $b = t - a$ or
earlier is

$$\bar{c}(t)PV[N(<b,t)] = \bar{c}(t)\sum_{x=0}^{\omega-a} e^{(g_c-r)x}N(\leq b, t+x) \tag{4.4}$$

where PV[] is the present-value operator. In similar fashion, if the shape
of the per capita cross-sectional age profile of production is fixed
and shifting upward at rate g_y, then the total production of the cohort born
before age b in year $t+x$ is equal to $\bar{y}^l(t)e^{g_y x}L(\leq b, t+x)$ where $\bar{y}^l(t)$ is
production or labor income per effective producer. The present value of the
future lifetime production of the cohort born in year $b = t - a$ or earlier is

$$\bar{y}^l(t)PV[L(<b,t)] = \bar{y}(t)^l\sum_{x=0}^{\omega-a} e^{(g_y-r)x}L(\leq b, t+x) \tag{4.5}$$

In the absence of bequests, the lifetime budget constraint insures that the
wealth in year t of those born in year b or earlier equals the difference
between the present value of future lifetime consumption and future lifetime production; i.e.,

$$W(\leq b, t) = \bar{c}(t)PV[C(\leq b, t)] - \bar{y}^l(t)PV[L(\leq b, t)] \tag{4.6}$$

Algebraic manipulation yields an expression for the ratio of wealth to total
labor income, $w(<b,t) = W(<b,t)/Y^l(t)$:

$$w(\leq b, t) = [C(t)/Y^l(t)]PV[C(\leq b, t)]/N(t) - PV[L(\leq b, t)]/L(t) \tag{4.7}$$

or alternatively:

$$w(\leq b, t) = [\bar{c}(t)/\bar{y}^l(t)]PV[C(\leq b, t)]/L(t) - PV[L(\leq b, t)]/L(t) \tag{4.8}$$

$PV[C(\leq b, t)]/L(t)$ is the present value of future lifetime consumption of
all persons born in year b of earlier per effective producer in year t.

---

[3] For the sake of simplicity, I assume that the rate of growth of per capita consumption and
the interest rate are constant. Although this is a standard steady-state assumption, there is
no reason to expect it to be the case during periods of transition. To treat g and r as
endogenous is not a tractable alternative without employing a detailed, country-specific
simulation model (Lee, Mason, and Miller 2000, 2003). A more general formulation that
allows for changing growth rates is provided by Mason and Lee (2006).

PV[$L(\leq b, t)$]/$L(t)$ is the present value of future lifetime production of all persons born in year b or earlier per effective producer in year t.

Under golden-rule, steady-state growth, equation (4.7) can be readily evaluated: the ratio of consumption to labor income is equal to 1 and drops out; the rate of productivity growth and the rate of growth of equivalent consumption, g_y and g_c, are constant and equal to each other.

The situation is more complex under the dynamic conditions that characterize the current world. If the ratio of wealth to income is rising over time because, for example, it is below its steady-state level, the ratio of consumption to labor income will be less than 1 and g_c will exceed g_y. In addition, the rate of growth of labor income will be varying in response to changes in the capital-intensity of the economy. Interest rates may be declining as the ratio of wealth to labor income rises. And whether and to what extent these variables change will depend on whether the economy is open or closed to capital flows and whether or not it is large enough to influence world capital markets. To fully incorporate all of these complexities would require a detailed, country-specific simulation model. The calculations here abstract from these many complexities and emphasize only the demographics.

To calculate the second dividend, g_y and g_c are assumed to equal 0.015, the rate of interest to equal 0.03, and the ratio of consumption to labor income to equal 1.0. The ratio of wealth of those aged 50 and older to total labor income is used to approximate the ratio of total wealth to total labor income. Analyses of the effects on productivity and economic growth are based on the assumption that the ratio of capital to life-cycle wealth is constant. In other words, the relative importance of capital and transfers in supporting consumption at older ages does not change.

4.2.1. Simulations of life-cycle wealth and the second dividend

The simulations of life-cycle wealth and the second demographic dividend are summarized in Figure 4.4, which charts the simulated ratio of wealth to income, and Figure 4.5, which charts the simulated ratio of output per worker, assuming that (1) the ratio of capital to income grows at the same rate as the ratio of life-cycle wealth to income; and (2) the elasticity of output with respect to capital is one-third.[4]

Simulated life-cycle wealth in the United States begins to increase around 1850. By 1900, simulated life-cycle wealth is twice that of India and about 10% greater than in Japan. During the next 40 years, life-cycle wealth grows rapidly

---

[4] This is the case with, for example, a Cobb-Douglas production function with labor augmenting technological change and an elasticity of one-third for capital and two-thirds for effective labor.

Andrew Mason

Figure 4.4. Wealth/income simulations: India, Japan, and the United States, 1850–2050

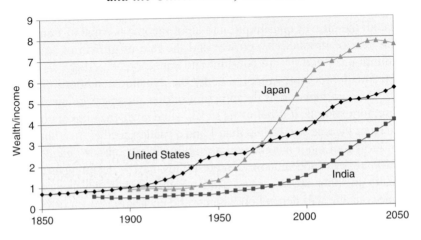

Figure 4.5. The second dividend: Rates of growth of output per worker

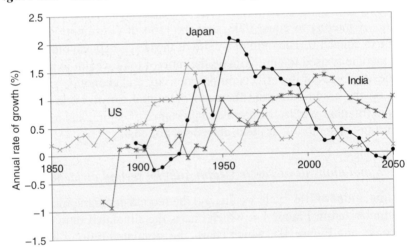

in the United States, but not in Japan or India. By 1950, US life-cycle wealth relative to income is four times that in India and about twice that in Japan. The year 1950 marks an important turning point for Japan, as simulated life-cycle wealth begins to grow very rapidly. By 1975 Japan passes the United States— establishing a lead that continues until 2000, when the ratio of life-cycle wealth to output is 6.0 in Japan and 3.6 in the United States.

In contrast, simulated life-cycle wealth in India increases quite slowly until recently. The ratio of life-cycle wealth to income does not reach

1.0 until 1985. Japan reaches this milestone in 1940 and the United
States in 1905. More rapid growth has begun, however, as India's age
structure has begun to change and as its life expectancy has continued to
improve.

Over the next 50 years, if UN population projections prove to be
accurate, life-cycle wealth will continue to grow more rapidly than income
in all three countries. Japan will maintain its lead, although the United
States will gain in relation to Japan, and India will gain substantially in
relation to both of the advanced industrial economies. Projected wealth in
Japan reaches a plateau around 2030 and declines slightly, thereafter.
Long-range projections to 2150 show this to be a temporary phenomenon,
however. For all three countries, wealth is projected to grow more rapidly
than income. The projected growth is slowest in Japan and most rapid
in India from 2050 to 2150, but the wealth-to-income ratio remains highest
in Japan, followed by the United States and then by India.

The implications for productivity growth are important if the increase
in life-cycle wealth translates into an increase in capital. There are interesting details in Figure 4.5, but here I will focus on the broad trends.
Before 1940, capital deepening induced by demographic change would
have increased output per worker by 0.6% per year in the United States, by
0.2% per year in Japan, and by about 0.1% per year in India. Between
1950 and 2000, the effect of life-cycle wealth on productivity would have
declined in the United States to 0.4% per year and increased substantially
in India to 0.8% per year and in Japan to 1.6% per year. The effects in
India and Japan are quite substantial. For the next 50 years (2000–50), the
productivity effect for the United States does not change, remaining at
0.4%. For India, the effect on productivity is 1.1% per year, while for
Japan the productivity effect drops to only 0.2% per year.

4.3. Combining the first and second dividends

The combined effects of the first and second dividends on economic
growth are readily calculated. Equation (4.3) can be used in conjunction
with the results presented above to calculate either the rate of growth of
per capita income or the rate of growth of total income attributable to the
first and second dividends. We compare the actual to the simulated trend
in GDP using the growth rates to calculate simulated values of GDP using
actual 1950 GDP as a base. The predicted values are set equal to the actual
GDP for 1950. The actual GDP deviates from the simulated GDP to the
extent that the actual growth rates of GDP deviate from the simulated
growth rates.

Growth in the effective labor force and growth in life-cycle wealth explain a remarkably high portion of economic growth in all three countries prior to 1950. The graphs are drawn using a log scale to facilitate comparisons and, of course, the slopes are equal to the rates of growth. In India, the "predicted" and the actual GDP are essentially indistinguishable (Figure 4.6). In Japan the rate of growth between 1900 and 1940 is significantly higher than that due solely to the first and second dividends (Figure 4.7). In the United States, the predicted growth in GDP induced by demographics was only slightly lower than the actual growth (Figure 4.8).

After 1950, rates of economic growth are consistently higher than predicted by population changes. In each country the gap between the predicted and the actual GDP grows steadily over time. The gap is

Figure 4.6.   Simulated GDP growth: India, 1890–1995 (US$1990 prices)

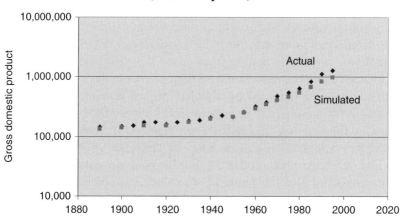

Figure 4.7.   Simulated GDP growth: Japan, 1920–95 (US$1990 prices)

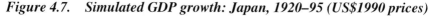
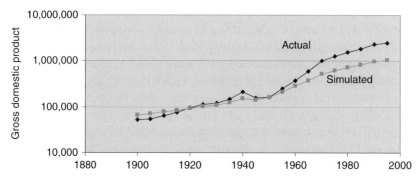

**Figure 4.8.   Simulated GDP growth: United States, 1850–1990
(US$1990 prices)**

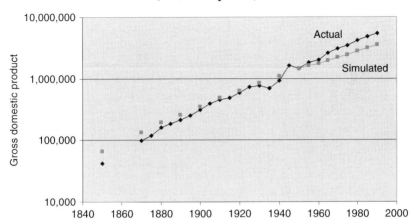

relatively modest for India, largest for Japan, and intermediate for the
United States.

The differences between actual and the predicted growth are summarized in Table 4.2. In India, actual real GDP growth was 0.7% per annum as
compared with a predicted growth of 0.8%. After 1950, actual growth
averaged 4.0% per year whereas the predicted was 3.4% per year. The
post-1950 demographic regime would have induced an increase in GDP
growth of 2.6% per year under the assumptions imposed. GDP growth
actually increased by 3.3% per year. The percentage of economic growth
"explained" by demographic factors was 115% before 1950 and 85% after
1950.

In Japan, actual GDP growth was 3.5% per year between 1900 and
1940 as compared with a predicted rate of increase of 2.0%. After 1950 the
actual rate increased to 6.1% and the predicted rate to 4.1%. Demographics accounted for almost 60% of the increase before 1940 and for
two-thirds of the increase after 1950. It is striking that in both Japan and
India the acceleration in economic growth after 1950 is closely tied to
substantial changes in the demographic regime.

The situation was quite different in the United States. Demographic
factors before 1950 were predicted to produce GDP growth of 3.1% per
year. Actual growth was 3.5% per annum. Demographics were less pro-
growth after 1950, when the combined effect of the demographic factors
was to produce GDP growth of 2.2% per year. Actual US GDP growth
declined very marginally, however—from 3.5 to 3.3% per annum. The
percentage of GDP growth explained by demographic factors dropped

Table 4.2. Actual and predicted GDP growth: India, Japan, and the United States

Country	GDP Growth			Predicted Growth Rates		Contribution to Growth		% Explained
	Actual	Predicted	Residual	Effective Labor Force	Wealth	Effective Labor Force	Wealth	
India								
<1950	0.7	0.8	−0.1	0.6	1.1	0.4	0.4	115.4
1950+	4.0	3.4	0.6	2.3	5.6	1.5	1.9	85.2
Change	3.3	2.6	0.7	1.7	4.4	1.1	1.5	
Japan								
<1940	3.5	2.0	1.4	1.1	3.9	0.7	1.3	58.6
1950+	6.1	4.1	2.0	1.6	9.3	1.0	3.1	67.9
Change	2.6	2.1	0.5	0.5	5.4	0.3	1.8	
United States								
<1950	3.5	3.1	0.4	2.2	4.8	1.5	1.6	87.4
1950+	3.3	2.2	1.1	1.3	4.1	0.9	1.4	67.0
Change	−0.2	−0.9	0.6	−1.0	−0.7	−0.6	−0.2	

from 87 to 67%. The demographics changed much less in the US than in Japan or India, as did the actual rates of economic growth.

Table 4.2 also reports the importance of growth in the effective labor force, and growth in wealth, to GDP growth. In India, predicted GDP growth increased after 1950 both because of an increase in the rate of growth of the effective labor force and because of an increase in the predicted rate of growth of wealth. In Japan the post-1950 effects of wealth are very large and substantially greater than before 1950. In the United States the rates of the growth of the effective labor force and the rates of growth of wealth both dropped, although the change was much greater in the rate of growth of the labor force than in the rate of growth of wealth.

As a final exercise, let us consider the contributions of the first and second dividend to growth in GDP per effective consumer. Recall from equation (4.3) that growth in output per effective consumer is equal to two additive factors: the rate of growth of the support ratio and the rate of growth of output per worker. Estimates of these two "dividends" are presented above and summarized and combined in Table 4.3 using the time periods distinguished in the analysis of the first dividend.

The second dividend is in all cases greater than the first dividend, and in most instances the differences are large. Of particular note are three periods during which the second dividend contributed or is projected to contribute at least 1 percentage point to growth in output per effective consumer: 1975–2005 India, 1950–80 Japan, and 1980–2025 Japan. The first dividend has varied in its effect in each country. It was negative in India before 1975, in Japan after 1980, and in the United States during the baby boom. With the exception of the US baby boom, the combined effects of the first and second dividend have been to increase the rate of growth of output per effective consumer. During these periods the share of growth attributable to these two factors has been very substantial. If we exclude India's slow growth period, the first and second dividend explained between 30 and 57% of the total growth in output per effective consumer. During the US baby boom, the second dividend dropped in magnitude, and it was not sufficient to offset the strong negative effect of the first dividend.

Demographic change appears to be favorable in India for some time to come. For 2005 to 2050, the combined effects of the first and second dividend are to raise per capita GDP growth by 1.24% per year. The picture is very different in the United States and particularly in Japan. In the United States the projected growth in GDP per effective consumer is expected to rise by 0.23% per year, while in Japan the projected growth effect of demographics is −0.45% per year.

Table 4.3. *First and second dividend as compared with actual GDP growth per effective consumer: India, Japan, and the United States*

Country and Years	Actual GDP Growth Per Effective Consumer	First Dividend: Growth of the Support Ratio	Second Dividend: Effect of Growth of Life-cycle Wealth	First + Second Dividend	First and Second Dividend as a % of Actual
India					
1880–1955	0.18	-0.01	0.13	0.12	63.7
1955–75	1.49	-0.14	0.60	0.47	31.2
1975–2005	2.98	0.34	1.02	1.37	45.8
2005–50		0.20	1.04	1.24	
Japan					
1900–40	2.23	-0.06	0.20	0.15	6.6
1950–80	6.23	0.61	1.72	2.32	37.3
1980–2005	1.72	-0.23	1.21	0.98	57.1
2005–50		-0.65	0.19	-0.45	
United States					
1850–1940	1.55	0.27	0.62	0.89	57.6
1950–70	2.15	-0.51	0.24	-0.27	-12.6
1970–2000	2.04	0.40	0.50	0.90	44.0
2000–50		-0.20	0.43	0.23	

Note: See text and Table 4.1.

4.4. Final remarks and qualifications

The analysis presented here supports the view that changes in age structure have been an important part of the development process for some time and may well be important for years to come. The US case is striking in this regard. Except for the interruption of the baby-boom period, changes in age structure have had an important effect on growth in GDP and growth in income per effective consumer for 150 years. Japan offers an interesting contrast, with demographics playing a much less important role prior to 1950 but a much more important role after 1950. India provides still another scenario. The positive growth effects were delayed in India, but during the last 50 years they have been important and potentially will continue to be important for decades to come.

For the United States it appears that changes in age structure will play a somewhat diminished role in the future, at least in their effect on economic growth. Although the share of the working-age population will decline over the next 50 years, the demand for life-cycle wealth may raise productivity more than enough to offset the negative first dividend. This is not the case in Japan, however, where the first dividend is negative, large, and swamps the second dividend.

No formal statistical analysis has been undertaken to formally test the validity of the theoretical model on which simulations are based. It is not entirely clear that formal analysis is warranted. Comparison of the simulations with the actual experience in these three countries is intriguing, however. In particular, rapid economic growth in both India and Japan occurred as demographic conditions shifted in a highly favorable way. Clearly, changes in age structure are only part of the story, but they are plausibly an important part. This contrasts with the United States, where demographic shifts have been relatively modest and generally consistent with the long-run trends in economic growth.

The results presented here are suggestive, then, but they are far from conclusive. Many issues need to be explored further. First, all of the calculations have been based on age profiles of consumption and labor income for the United States. These profiles vary over time and across countries. Over the long time span considered here perhaps they have changed substantially (see Lee, Lee, and Mason 2005). Second, all calculations of the second dividend are based on the assumption that capital is growing at the same rate as life-cycle wealth. Although this is a plausible starting point, it may be entirely wrong. Both Japan and the United States began and expanded major public pension programs during the periods under consideration. Thus, part of the increase in life-cycle wealth would have been met by transfers rather than by the accumulation of assets.

But in Japan and the United States, familial support for the elderly has declined substantially—in the late eighteenth and early nineteenth centuries in the United States and more recently in Japan. Hence, this would serve to increase capital as a share of life-cycle wealth.[5] Third, the implications of international capital flows have been neglected entirely. In recent years the United States has experienced substantial net capital inflows and Japan has invested heavily abroad—in other Asian countries and in the United States. A more complete analysis would surely take these developments into consideration.

References

Ahlburg, Dennis A., and Eric R. Jensen 2001. "Education and the East Asian miracle", in: Andrew Mason, ed., *Population Change and Economic Development in East Asia: Challenges Met, Opportunities Seized*, pp. 231–255. Stanford: Stanford University Press.

Bloom, David E., and Canning, David 2001. "Cumulative causality, economic growth, and the Demographic Transition", in: Nancy Birdsall, Allen C. Kelley, and Steven W. Sinding, eds, *Population Matters: Demographic Change, Economic Growth, and Poverty in the Developing World*, pp. 165–200. New York: Oxford University Press.

Bloom, David E., David Canning, Bryan Graham. 2003. "Longevity and life-cycle savings". *Scandinavian Journal of Economics* 105(3): 319–38.

Bloom, David E., David Canning, Jaypee Sevilla. 2002. *The Demographic Dividend: A New Perspective on the Economic Consequences of Population Change*. Santa Monica, CA: Rand.

Bloom, David E., and Jeffrey G. Williamson. 1998. "Demographic transitions and economic miracles in emerging Asia". *World Bank Economic Review* 12(3): 419–56.

Cutler, David M., James M. Poterba, Louise M. Sheiner, and Lawrence H. Summers. 1990. "An aging society: Opportunity or challenge?". *Brookings Papers on Economic Activity* 1990(1): 1–56.

Deaton, Angus, and Christina H. Paxson. 2000. "Growth, demographic structure, and national saving in Taiwan", in: C. Y. Cyrus Chu and Ronald Lee, eds, *Population and Economic Change in East Asia, A Supplement to Population and Development Review*, pp. 141–173. New York: Population Council.

Jensen, Eric R., and Dennis A. Ahlburg. 2001. "Child health and health care in Indonesia and the Philippines", in: Andrew Mason, ed., *Population Change and Economic Development in East Asia: Challenges Met, Opportunities Seized*, pp. 255–279. Stanford, CA: Stanford University Press.

Kelley, Allen C. 1988. "Economic consequences of population change in the Third World". *Journal of Economic Literature* 26(4): 1685–1728.

———. 1996. "The consequences of rapid population growth on human resource development: The case of education", in: Dennis A. Ahlburg, Allen C. Kelley, and

---

[5] A more detailed discussion and analysis of the implications for capital accumulation of changing transfer system can be found in Lee, Mason, and Miller (2003).

Karen O. Mason, eds, *The Impact of Population Growth on Well-Being in Developing Countries*, pp. 67–138. Heidelberg: Springer-Verlag.

Kelley, Allen C., and Robert M. Schmidt. 1995. "Aggregate population and economic growth correlations: The role of the components of demographic change". *Demography* 32(4): 543–55.

———. 1996. Saving, dependency and development. *Journal of Population Economics* 9(4): 365–86.

Kinugasa, Tomoko. 2004. *Life Expectancy, Labor Force, and Saving*. Ph.D. dissertation. University of Hawaii at Manoa.

Kinugasa, Tomoko, and Andrew Mason (2007 forthcoming). "Why Nations Become Wealthy: The Effects of Adult Longevity on Saving". *World Development* 35(1): 1–23.

Lee, Ronald D. 1994a. "The formal demography of population aging, transfers, and the economic life cycle", in: Linda G. Martin and Samuel H. Preston, eds, *Demography of Aging*, pp. 8–49. Washington, D.C.: National Academy Press.

———. 1994b. "Population age structure, intergenerational transfer, and wealth: A new approach, with applications to the US" in: Paul Gertler ed., *The Family and Intergenerational Relations. Journal of Human Resources* 19(4): 1027–63.

Lee, Ronald D., Sang-Hyop Lee, and Andrew Mason. 2005. "Charting the economic lifecycle". NTA Working Paper 05–08, November. National Transfer Accounts Data Base. www.ntaccounts.org.

Lee, Ronald D., Andrew Mason, and Tim Miller. 2000. "Life cycle saving and the Demographic Transition: The Case of Taiwan", in: C.Y. Cyrus Chu and Ronald Lee, eds, *Population and Economic Change in East Asia, A Supplement. Population and Development Review* 26:194–219.

———. 2001. "Saving, wealth, and population", in: Nancy Birdsall, Allen C. Kelley, and Steven W. Sinding, eds, *Population Matters: Demographic Change, Economic Growth, and Poverty in the Developing World*, pp. 137–164. New York: Oxford University Press.

———. 2003. "From transfers to individual responsibility: Implications for savings and capital accumulation in Taiwan and the United States". *Scandinavian Journal of Economics* 105(3): 339–57.

Maddison, Angus 1995. *Monitoring the world economy, 1820–1992*. Paris: Development Centre of the Organisation for Economic Co-operation and Development.

Mason, Andrew 2001a. "Population and economic growth in East Asia", in: Andrew Mason, ed., *Population Change and Economic Development in East Asia: Challenges Met, Opportunities Seized*, pp. 1–30. Stanford, CA: Stanford University Press.

———, ed. 2001b. *Population Change and Economic Development in East Asia: Challenges Met, Opportunities Seized*. Stanford, CA: Stanford University Press.

———. 2005. "Demographic transition and demographic dividends in developed and developing countries". Paper presented at United Nations Expert Group Meeting on Social and Economic Implications of Changing Population Age Structures, August 31– September 2, Mexico City.

Mason, Andrew, and Ronald Lee. 2006. "Reform and Support systems for the elderly in developing countries: Capturing the second demographic dividend". *GENUS* 62(2): 11–35.

Mason, Andrew, Ronald, Lee, An-Chi Tung, Mun Sim Lai, and Tim Miller. 2007. "Population aging and intergenerational transfers: Introducing age into national accounts", in: David Wise, ed., *Economics of Aging Series*, Chicago: NBER and University of Chicago Press (forthcoming).

Mason, Andrew, Thomas Merrick, and R. Paul Shaw. 1999. *Population Economics, Demographic Transition, and Development: Research and Policy Implications.* Washington, D.C.: World Bank Institute.

Montgomery, Mark R., and Cynthia B. Lloyd. 1996. "Fertility and maternal and child health", in: Dennis A. Ahlburg, Allen C. Kelley, and Karen O. Mason, eds, *The Impact of Population Growth on Well-being in Developing Countries*, pp. 37–66. Heidelberg: Springer-Verlag.

Ogawa, Naohiro, and Rikiya Matsukura. 2005. "The role of older persons' changing health and wealth in an aging society: The case of Japan". Paper presented at UN Expert Group Meeting on Social and Economic Implications of Changing Population Age Structure, Mexico City, 31 August to 2 September.

UNPD (United Nations Population Division). 2004. *World Population to 2300.* New York: United Nations.

———. 2005. *World Population Prospects: The 2004 Revision.* New York: United Nations.

Williamson, Jeffrey G., and Matthew Higgins. 2001. "The accumulation and demography connection in East Asia", in: Andrew Mason, ed., *Population Change and Economic Development in East Asia: Challenges Met, Opportunities Seized*, pp. 123–154. Stanford, CA: Stanford University Press.

World Bank. 2005. *World Development Indicators 2005.* Washington, DC.

CHAPTER 5

Demographic Change and Regional Economic Growth: A Comparative Analysis of Japan and China

Tomoko Kinugasa, Wei Huang, and Mitoshi Yamaguchi

How demographic characteristics affect economic growth has long been a controversial issue. Because many countries have experienced a demographic transition, the effects of demographic change are of great interest. In the early stage of economic development, both fertility and mortality are high and stagnant. As a country develops economically, mortality, especially infant mortality, declines rapidly, causing the population to increase dramatically for a period. After a while fertility also declines. When the demographic transition is completed, both fertility and mortality are low and population growth levels off.

The demographic transition causes significant changes in the age distribution of a population. At the beginning of the transition, the share of the working-age population decreases as infant and child mortality declines, causing the proportion of young dependents to grow. As fertility declines and babies born in the past enter the labor market, the share of the working-age population increases. The changes in age distribution have important implications for the labor force and hence the economy.

Today, low fertility is a serious problem in Japan and China. Japan's fertility declined rapidly in the 1960s after a post–World War II baby boom, and currently its fertility rate is less than the replacement level. China, which used to suffer from high fertility and rapid population growth, adopted policies to reduce its fertility, the most famous of which was the one-child policy. As a consequence, Chinese fertility dropped very rapidly and today is below the replacement level.

In this chapter, we analyze the effects of demographic characteristics on differences in economic growth among the regions of Japan and China.

We thank Kiyoshi Fujikawa, Allen Kelley, Andrew Mason, Robert Schmidt, and Sri Gowri Sanker for their helpful comments.

POPULATION CHANGE, LABOR MARKETS, AND SUSTAINABLE GROWTH
VOLUME 281   ISSN 0573-8555/DOI 10.1016/S0573-8555(07)81005-4

Many studies have analyzed the effects of demographic characteristics on growth using cross-country data. Kelley and Schmidt (1995) estimated the effect of population growth on GDP growth and found that the results were not significant. Using panel data from Japanese prefectures and Kelley and Schmidt's (1995) model, Kinugasa (2002) estimated the effects to be negative. Huang (2004) estimated the effects of population growth, using the same kind of model and data from Chinese provinces, and found population growth to have a negative effect on economic growth.

Convergence-patterns studies are based on neoclassical growth theory. Convergence means that a developing economy grows more rapidly than a developed economy, catching up with the developed economy in the long run.[1] Barro and Sala-i-Martin (1995) found that convergence could not be observed when they used data aggregated at the global level, but that the convergence hypothesis held if they controlled for regional effects. They observed convergence among Japanese prefectures. In contrast, the convergence hypothesis does not hold among the Chinese provinces. A large disparity of income exists there between coastal and inland areas. Several studies, however, have found evidence of conditional convergence. After controlling for such variables as education, marketization, and the degree of openness, Chen and Fleisher (1996), Yao and Zhang (2001), and Cai, Wang, and Du (2002) reported the support for the convergence hypothesis. Kelley and Schmidt (2001) also considered population size and density as demographic variables when testing the hypothesis and found population size and density to have a positive effect on economic growth.

In this chapter, we examine the effects of demographic variables on economic growth at the regional level in Japan and China. Demographic characteristics are germane to regional economic growth within a country. Empirical analyses of their effects based on worldwide panel data are problematic because social conditions, such as years spent in education, the cost of children, and intergenerational transfers, vary widely among countries. Analyses using regional data from a single country have an advantage in that such social conditions tend not to vary so much from region to region. Moreover, data from a single country are more useful for analyzing economic growth in that country.

5.1. Model and Data

We used convergence-pattern analysis to estimate the effects of demographic characteristics on economic growth. According to Kelley and

---

[1] This is the idea of β-convergence. Another concept of convergence, σ-convergence, suggests that income variance becomes smaller over time.

Schmidt (1994, 2001), two alternative methods of economic-demographic modeling are the simple correlation method and the production-function method. The simple correlation method, which regresses population growth and output per capita growth, has a disadvantage in that it fails to analyze many variables. Alternatively, the production-function method estimates production functions such as $Y = g(K,L,H,T)$, where Y is output, K is physical capital, L is labor, H is human capital, and T is technology. This method too has a disadvantage because physical or human capital stock is difficult to calculate. Kelley and Schmidt therefore employed the analytic method used in convergence-pattern studies. Such studies are based on neoclassical growth theory. In this method, productivity—that is, output (Y) per labor (L)—is described as

$$Y/L_{gr} = c[\ln(Y/L)^* - \ln(Y/L)] \tag{5.1}$$

where $(Y/L)^*$ is the steady-state value of productivity. This specification predicts "unconditional convergence," which means that all economies reach the same level of productivity, $(Y/L)^*$. "Conditional convergence" is expressed as

$$\ln(Y/L)^* = a + bZ \tag{5.2}$$

Conditional convergence insists that the level of steady-state productivity depends on characteristics (Z) that are specific to each economy. Combining equations (5.1) and (5.2), we derive the following equation:

$$Y/L_{gr} = a' + b'Z - c\ln(Y/L) \tag{5.3}$$

where $a' = bc$ and $b' = bc$. According to Barro and Sala-i-Martin (1994), convergence holds among Japanese prefectures when economy-specific characteristics are not controlled.

Demographic variables are included in Z and condition the transition to steady state. Kelley and Schmidt (2001) examined three types of studies that deal with demographic effects on economic growth. The first (Barro 1997; Kelley and Schmidt 1994) highlights long-run effects of population but includes a role for transitions. The second (Kelley and Schmidt 1995) deals with both long-run and transition effects. The third (Bloom and Williamson 1998) captures only transition effects.

Barro (1997) used a single demographic variable, the total fertility rate (TFR). A high total fertility rate prevents capital accumulation and increases the cost of raising children. Kelley and Schmidt (1994) focused on the effects of three demographic variables—population growth, size, and density—on output per capita. A large population size creates economies of scale. If the fruits of research and development are available without cost, a large population size directly and positively affects technological change. High population density can promote economic growth by stimulating technological growth and by reducing transport and communication costs. If resource scarcity or congestion has a large negative effect, high population density can retard growth.

The growth rate of a population can be decomposed into the effects of its birth rate and death rate if we ignore migration. During the early stage of a country's demographic transition, the population growth rate is remarkably high, but when the transition is completed, population growth is zero or negative. Because the timing of the declines in death rates and birth rates vary, it is important to analyze the effects of birth rates and death rates separately (Kelley and Schmidt 1995).

Examining the dynamic effects of demographic change on economic growth, Bloom and Williamson (1998) expressed productivity (Y/L) as

$$Y/L = (Y/N)(N/L) \qquad (5.4)$$

where N is population. Using this relationship, equation (5.3) can be transformed into per capita terms as

$$Y/N_{gr} = a' + b'Z - c'' \ln(Y/N) + d\ln(L/N) + L_{gr} - N_{gr} \qquad (5.5)$$

The effects of working-hour growth (L_{gr}) and population growth (N_{gr}) offset each other if they change at the same rate. In the calculation $d = c''$ Bloom and Williamson assumed that $d = 0$; that is, the workforce share has no impact on growth. They replaced L_{gr} with the growth rate of the working-age population. In this model, population does not affect Z's in equation (5.5). In this sense, the specification has a limitation, but estimating this equation is useful to see the transitional effect of population. Bloom, Canning, and Malaney (1999) augmented Bloom and Williamson's model by including the demographic variables $\ln(L/N)$ and density.

The variables used in the convergence-pattern studies are listed in Table 5.1. Kelley and Schmidt (2001) included demographic variables in their equation and found that those variables had important effects on economic growth. Specifically, the studies found that demographic transition plays an important role in the growth rate of GDP per capita. As the crude birth rate and the rate of population growth decline, the young-dependency burden decreases and the proportion of the working-age population increases, causing a great gain in GDP growth per capita.

Model 1 includes only one demographic variable, the total fertility rate. Model 2 includes the population growth rate. Model 3 adds population density and the size of population to Model 2. Models 4 and 5 consider the

Table 5.1.   Models and demographic specifications

Model	Variables
(1) Barro	ln(TFR)
(2) Early KS (1994)	N_{gr}
(3) Augmented KS	N_{gr}, Dns, ln(N)
(4) KS (1994, 1995) components, 15 years	CBR, CBR15, CDR, Dns, ln(N)
(5) KS components, 20 years	CBR, CBR20, CDR, Dns, ln(N)
(6) BW Trns	N_{gr}, L_{gr}
(7) BCM Trns	N_{gr}, L_{gr}, ln(L/N), Dns
(8) BCM TrnsExp	N_{gr}, L_{gr}, ln(L/N), Dns, ln(N)

Note: KS—Kelley and Schmidt; BW—Bloom and Williamson (1998); BCM—Bloom, Canning and Malaney (1999).

effects of the current crude birth rate, the current crude death rate, and the past crude birth rate. In Model 4 the current crude birth rate is included in order to see the effect of the youth dependency. It is expected that a high birth rate will have a negative effect on economic growth over the short run. After children become part of the labor force, however, the past high birth rate is expected have a positive effect on growth. Kelley and Schmidt (1994, 1995) include the crude birth rate lagged by 15 years, considering labor force entry to occur around age 15. In Model 5 the crude birth rate is lagged by 20 years, on the assumption that longer years of schooling delay labor force entry. Model 6 includes population growth and labor force growth in order to estimate the effect of the demographic transition. In Model 7, Bloom, Canning, and Malaney (1999) append the share of labor force in the population, and population density, to their basic framework. In Model 8, Kelley and Schmidt (2001) reformulate the BCM transformation and append population size [ln(N)]. In addition to the variables listed in Table 5.1, we include dummy variables for the 1970s, 1980s, and 1990s in each equation. In previous studies, data on the working-age population were used for the labor force variable. In our study, we use data on the employed population for the labor force. For comparison, we also estimate Models 6 through 8 using the working-age population instead of the employed population in the case of Japan.[2]

---

[2] For Japan, all data except for the working-age population are from the *Japan Statistical Yearbook*. Japanese data on working-age population are from the website of the National Institute of Population and Social Security Research. For China, data on the total fertility rate are from the China Population Information Centre. All other Chinese demographic data are from the *Almanac of China's Population*. Data on gross provincial product are from the *Statistical Yearbook of China*.

Table 5.2 presents the means and standard deviations of each variable used in our analysis.[3] The mean and standard deviation of the GDP growth rate are higher in China than in Japan during the period 1970–95. The mean population growth rate is higher in China, but the standard deviation of population growth is lower in Japan. Migration among prefectures is an important factor in the population growth of each Japanese prefecture. The means and standard deviations of the crude birth rate and the total fertility rate are lower in Japan than in China. Regional disparity of fertility is not very large in Japan, but it is great in China. Fertility is low in China's coastal areas but high in inland rural areas. Migration from rural to urban areas within a Chinese province appears to be common, but migration between provinces is less frequent than in Japan. The means of crude birth rates lagged by 15 years and by 20 years in China reveal a rapid fertility transition in that country.

We estimated the equations of the eight models listed in Table 5.1 using data from 47 prefectures of Japan for the period 1960–95 and from 29 provinces of China for the period 1970–95. The data set has panel (time-series and cross-sectional) characteristics. It may reveal characteristics specific to each prefecture and province that would be unobservable from time-series or cross-sectional data alone. If that were the case, the estimates by ordinary least squares (OLS) would be biased. The fixed-effect model (FEM) assumes that individual characteristics have a constant term.[4] FEM has a disadvantage in that it does not provide coefficients for unvarying variables. It is possible that wide geographical areas have special characteristics. For example, economic growth in the urban coastal areas of China is greater than that of the rural inland areas. In FEM, regional dummies cannot be included because they do not change over time. FEM also exacerbates measurement error. We estimated the equations by FEM and compared the results with OLS estimates using regional dummies. We discuss the results by contrasting them with the estimates made by Kelley and Schmidt using world panel data.

5.2. Results

The results estimated by Kelley and Schmidt (2001) from 86 countries for the period 1960–95 are presented in Table 5.A2. They indicate that the

---

[3] Appendix Table 5.A1 defines the variables used in the analysis.

[4] It is important to consider the interactive relationship between demographic change and economic growth because the economic situation in a country or region can influence demographic characteristics there. For simplicity, we ignored this issue in the current study. In future research, we will make simultaneous equation models to deal with it.

Table 5.2.   Summary of the variables: Japan and China

Country, Period, and Variable	Number of Observations	Mean	Standard Deviation
Japan, 1960–95			
Y/N_{gr}	188	4.859	3.248
ln(Y/N)	188	7.751	1.067
ln(TFR)	187	0.629	0.139
N_{gr}	188	0.508	0.921
L_{gr}	187	0.779	0.993
ln(L/N)	187	−0.724	0.065
CBR	187	1.361	0.311
CBR15	186	1.828	0.456
CBR20	93	1.636	0.148
CDR	187	0.731	0.117
Dns	188	0.569	1.006
ln(N)	188	7.514	0.692
Japan, 1970–95			
Y/N_{gr}	141	3.226	1.748
ln(Y/N)	141	8.108	0.902
ln(TFR)	141	0.588	0.131
N_{gr}	141	0.550	0.686
L_{gr}	141	0.609	0.684
ln(L/N)	141	−0.717	0.065
CBR	141	1.273	0.300
CBR15	140	1.601	0.209
CBR20	93	1.636	0.148
CDR	141	0.723	0.121
Dns	141	0.598	1.052
ln(N)	141	7.546	0.709
China, 1970–95			
Y/N_{gr}	86	7.891	2.160
ln(Y/N)	86	6.534	0.856
ln(TFR)	86	1.012	0.367
N_{gr}	86	1.486	0.608
L_{gr}	86	2.220	1.293
ln(L/N)	86	−1.728	0.967
CBR	86	2.002	0.598
CBR15	86	2.742	0.754
CBR20	86	2.981	0.669
CDR	86	0.660	0.095
Dns	86	0.301	0.362
ln(N)	86	10.161	0.954

effects of demographic characteristics on economic growth are significant. In Model 1 the total fertility rate exerts a negative effect on growth. In Models 2, 5, and 6, population growth has a negative effect on economic growth. In Model 4 the current crude birth rate depresses economic growth and the effect is significant. The coefficient of the birth rate lagged by 15 years is positive but not significant. The effect of population density on economic growth is positive and significant at the 1% level for one out of four models. The authors find that an increase in the working-age population during the demographic transition is a great source of economic growth. Four of the models show that the size of a population has a positive and significant effect on economic growth.

Table 5.3 presents our results using panel data from Japanese prefectures. In all specifications, the coefficient of output per capita is negative and significant, so that the convergence-pattern hypothesis is satisfied. In Model 1, the total fertility rate is negatively correlated with growth in output per capita, but it is not statistically significant. The population growth rate has a significantly negative effect on growth in Model 2. In Models 3, 5, and 7 the effect of population density is not statistically significant. In Models 4 and 8, the effect of population density is negative and significant. The effect of population density on economic growth seems to be sensitive to empirical specification. Kelley and Schmidt's positive result for this demographic variable (shown in Table 5.A2) suggests that the effect depends on how aggregated the data are. In Models 3, 4, and 8, the effect of population size on economic growth is positive and significant. Thus, population size appears to be a great source of economic growth.[5]

---

[5] Using general equilibrium growth accounting, Yamaguchi and Binswanger (1975) calculated the contribution of population variables to Japanese economic development and showed that population has a detrimental effect on per capita income. Yamaguchi (1982) showed that population has a negative effect on per capita income but that labor force has a positive effect. In sum, the negative contribution of population is larger than the positive contribution of labor force. Therefore, population and labor force together (called the "direct effect of population") negatively affect Japanese economic development. Yamaguchi and Kennedy (1984a) calculated the effect of population and labor force on technical change in both agriculture and nonagriculture sectors (calling this the indirect effect of population) by using three methods—the Verdoorn method, the residual method, and the factor-augmenting method. The authors found that the total effect of population, which is the sum of direct and indirect effects, were negative for the period from 1880 to 1930 but positive since 1930. This means that Japan's large population contributed substantially to the country's economic development after 1930. The finding is consistent with the result of ln$N$ for Japan; it contributes a strong t-value to the growth of per capita income. In other words, Japan's high-quality (educated) labor produced technical change. Major technical changes in agriculture pushed agricultural labor into nonagricultural occupations. Moreover, major technical changes in the nonagricultural sector pulled agricultural labor into that sector (i.e., technical change has an asymmetrical effect on labor). (See Yamaguchi and Kennedy 1984b for details.) Labor pushed or pulled into nonagricultural occupations has had greater productivity and contributed to rising per capita income. (See Appendix 5.1 for details.)

Table 5.3. Estimated results from FEM: Japanese prefectures

	Barro	Early KS	Augmented KS	KS Comp. 15 years	KS Comp. 20 years	BW Trns	BCM Trns	BCM TrnsEx
	(1)	(2)	(3)	(4)	(5)	(6)	(7)	(8)
ln(Y/N)	-3.213*** (-5.485)	-3.489*** (-5.158)	-6.026*** (-5.053)	-8.276*** (-7.268)	-8.989*** (-3.182)	-2.689*** (-3.862)	-2.734*** (-3.951)	-5.539*** (-4.526)
ln(TFR)	-6.378*** (-4.263)							
N_{gr}		-0.336** (-2.449)	-0.109 (-0.458)			-0.834*** (-4.294)	-0.768*** (-3.196)	-0.487* (-1.905)
L_{gr}						0.693*** (3.497)	0.770*** (3.798)	0.690*** (3.452)
ln(L/N)							5.450* (1.933)	7.544*** (2.643)
CBR				-4.188*** (-4.917)	-3.584 (-1.023)			
CBR15				-0.994** (-2.122)				
CBR20					1.053 (0.636)			
CDR				-1.301 (-1.024)	-0.941 (-0.561)			
Dns			-0.452 (-0.499)	-1.377** (-2.257)	1.000 (0.286)		0.327 (0.360)	-0.362 (-0.393)

(continued)

Table 5.3. Continued

	Barro	Early KS	Augmented KS	KS Comp. 15 years	KS Comp. 20 years	BW Trns	BCM Trns	BCM TrnsEx
	(1)	(2)	(3)	(4)	(5)	(6)	(7)	(8)
$\ln(N)$			5.250**	8.547***	0.448			5.592***
			(2.578)	(4.473)	(0.045)			(2.748)
year 70	-1.825***	-1.115	0.862	1.984**		-1.035	-1.140*	0.938
	(-3.167)	(-1.566)	(0.828)	(2.141)		(-1.502)	(-1.659)	(0.928)
year 80	-2.849***	-1.384	1.628	1.791		-2.065**	-2.079**	1.221
	(-3.314)	(-1.360)	(1.058)	(1.213)		(-2.055)	(-2.086)	(0.790)
year 90	-4.422***	-1.986	1.926	1.741	0.779	-3.066***	-3.285***	0.931
	(-4.037)	(-1.589)	(0.984)	(0.914)	(0.613)	(-2.451)	(-2.637)	(0.476)
Constant	36.078***	33.198***	11.330	12.726	75.796	27.142***	31.240***	10.389
	(8.387)	(7.301)	(1.182)	(1.457)	(1.343)	(5.708)	(5.996)	(1.137)
Adjusted R^2	0.938	0.934	0.936	0.957	0.696	0.938	0.939	0.942
P value, Year Dummies	0.000	0.199	0.407	0.000	0.543	0.007	0.003	0.060
P value, $N_{gr} = -1$						0.395	0.336	0.047
P value, $L_{gr} = 1$						0.124	0.258	0.124
P value, $\ln(Y/N) = -\ln(L/N)$							0.351	0.482
No. of obs	187	188	188	186	93	188	188	188

Note: The dependent variable is Y/N_{gr}. The full sample includes 47 prefectures, three decennial periods (1960–70, 1970–80, 1980–90), and one quinquennial period (1990–95).

* means significant at 10%,

** means significant at 5%, and

*** means significant at 1%. t-Values are reported in parentheses below the coefficient estimates.

Model 4 shows that the current birth rate has a significantly negative effect on economic growth. Contrary to our hypothesis, the birth rate lagged by 15 years also has a significantly negative effect on growth in output per capita. The coefficient for the birth rate lagged by 15 years is smaller than that of the current birth rate, but we cannot find a positive effect of past births (i.e., current labor force size) on economic growth. It may take a long time for children to enter the labor market because of the importance placed on higher education in Japan. When we estimate the effect of the birth rate lagged by 20 years in Model 5, the coefficient is positive but not significant. Given the high level of university enrollment, 20 years may not be enough of a lag. Moreover, many Japanese do not live in the same prefecture where they were born. It would therefore be advisable to consider the effects of migration.

In Models 6 and 7, population growth has a negative effect on economic growth, whereas labor force growth has a positive effect. According to Bloom and Williamson's (1998) hypothesis, the coefficients of population growth and labor force growth should be -1 and $+1$, respectively. We find that the coefficient of labor force growth is greater than that of population growth in Models 7 and 8. Except for the population growth rate in Model 8, we cannot reject the hypothesis that the coefficient of the growth rate of population is -1 and the coefficient of the growth rate of the labor force is $+1$. Models 7 and 8 show that a large share of the employed population within the total population has a positive and significant effect on economic growth.

Thus, the results indicate that labor force is an important source of economic growth. The importance of age distribution is questionable, however (Table 5.A3). When we use data on the working-age population instead of the employed population, the effect of the working-age population on growth is either significantly negative or negative but not significant. This result contradicts Kelley and Schmidt's hypothesis and results. One possible problem with our estimation is multicolinearity; growth rates of the population and the working-age population are highly correlated. We must bear in mind that not all of the working-age population is employed. It includes the unemployed, students, and homemakers as well as the gainfully employed. Models 7 and 8 show that the share of the working-age population in the total population has a positive effect on economic growth, a result that implies that the working-age population itself is an important source of economic growth.

Table 5.4 presents our results from FEM using panel data from Chinese provinces. In all specifications, the coefficient of output per capita is positive and statistically significant. This means that conditional convergence cannot be observed by considering only demographic

Table 5.4. Estimated results from FEM: Chinese provinces

	Barro	Early KS	Augmented KS	KS Comp, 15 years	KS Comp, 20 years	BW Trns	BCM Trns	BCM TrnsEx
	(1)	(2)	(3)	(4)	(5)	(6)	(7)	(8)
$\ln(Y/N)$	4.486*** (3.528)	5.451*** (4.556)	5.368*** (4.381)	3.929*** (3.321)	4.075*** (3.278)	5.446*** (4.477)	5.384*** (4.369)	5.315*** (4.191)
$\ln(\text{TFR})$	−2.533 (−1.484)							
N_{gr}		−1.799*** (−3.648)	−2.178*** (−3.994)			−1.796*** (−3.537)	−2.136*** (−3.907)	−2.116*** (−3.802)
L_{gr}						0.005 (0.035)	0.025 (0.155)	0.041 (0.239)
$\ln(L/N)$							−2.664 (−1.239)	−3.287 (−1.057)
CBR				−0.954 (−1.229)	−1.541** (−1.995)			
CBR15				1.445*** (3.199)				
CBR20					0.948** (2.135)			
CDR				12.834*** (2.947)	9.727*** (2.140)			

Dns			8.663	−0.782	3.362		7.077	6.519
			(1.620)	(−0.152)	(0.554)		(1.302)	(1.116)
ln(N)			4.081	−0.300	−0.175			−2.291
			(0.766)	(−0.054)	(−0.029)			(−0.280)
year 80	−2.031	−2.790***	−3.927***	−0.085	−1.011	−2.786***	−3.253***	−2.832
	(−1.593)	(−2.705)	(−2.666)	(−0.061)	(−0.716)	(−2.666)	(−3.085)	(−1.539)
year 90	−5.120**	−7.079***	−9.123***	−1.474	−3.708	−7.060***	−7.928***	−7.114*
	(−2.196)	(−3.364)	(−3.130)	(−0.507)	(−1.286)	(−3.217)	(−3.593)	(−1.942)
Constant	−16.446**	−21.728***	−63.629	−24.495	−22.542	−21.720***	−27.137***	−4.793
	(−2.251)	(−3.254)	(−1.148)	(−0.425)	(−0.364)	(−3.220)	(−3.363)	(−0.060)
Adjusted R^2	0.419	0.516	0.524	0.546	0.498	0.507	0.524	0.515
P value, Year Dummies	0.040	0.002	0.003	0.335	0.133	0.005	0.002	0.043
P value, $N_{gr} = -1$						0.123	0.043	0.051
P value, $L_{gr} = 1$						0.000	0.000	0.000
P value, $\ln(Y/N) = -\ln(L/N)$							0.240	0.552
No. of Obs	86	86	86	86	86	86	86	86

Note: The dependent variable is Y/N_{gr}. The full sample includes 29 provinces and two decennial periods (1970–80, 1980–90) and one quinquennial period (1990–95). See also note for Table 5.3.

variables.[6] In Model 1, the total fertility rate has a negative effect on economic growth, but the coefficient is not statistically significant. In Models 2, 3, 6, 7, and 8, population growth has a negative and significant effect on economic growth. The coefficients of population density are not significant in any specification. In Models 4 and 5, the current birth rate has a negative effect and the birth rate lagged by 15 or 20 years has a positive effect on economic growth. Current births are a burden on economic growth, but later they contribute to the labor force and to economic growth. As we have seen, this result is inconsistent with that for Japan. Because migration between provinces is less common in China than is migration between prefectures in Japan, a person born in a province of China tends to become a source of economic growth in the same province. Models 6 to 8 show that the growth rate of employed labor does not have a significant effect on economic growth in China. The share of employed population in the total population slows economic growth, contrary to our hypothesis. The working population is an important source of economic growth, but the quality of labor could also be important. Further analysis of this issue is needed.

Results estimated by OLS using Japanese data with regional dummies do not differ very much from those obtained by FEM. Those results are not reported here but are available upon request. In the case of China, we estimated the equation by OLS using the dummy variable for coastal areas. The results are presented in Table 5.A4. They indicate that population size has a significant positive effect on economic growth.

In estimating how much demographic change has contributed to economic growth in Japan and China, we considered both coefficient size and the magnitude of relevant changes in our demographic variables. Kelley and Schmidt (2001) calculated interperiod changes in the mean value of each demographic variable. Multiplying the mean and estimated coefficient, they calculated the demographic impacts on changes in output per capita from decadal changes. Table 5.A5 presents their estimated demographic impacts on changes in output per capita from decadal changes. In the same way as Kelley and Schmidt, we have calculated demographic effects on economic growth in the prefectures of Japan and the provinces of China. Tables 5.5 and 5.6 present the overall quantitative impacts of various components of demographic change on economic growth in Japan and China, respectively. Kelly and Schmidt's results indicate that demographic trends such as declining population growth,

---

[6] Huang (2004), however, finds that conditional convergence holds for the data sets from 1988 to 2000. It is possible that after the economic reform of 1978, income disparity among regions declined and the income of the Chinese provinces tended to converge. Hence, we need further analysis using other time periods.

Table 5.5. *Demographic impacts on changes in* Y/N_gr *from decadal changes: Japan*

Model	Year	Demographic Impacts		ln(TFR)	N_{gr}	L_{gr}	ln(L/N)	CBR	CBR15	CBR20	CDR	Dns	ln(N)
		w/ CDR	w/o CDR										
Part 1: Period means													
	1960s			0.753	0.382	1.299	−0.745	1.633	2.520	—	0.757	0.481	7.418
	1970s			0.719	0.950	0.510	−0.723	1.640	1.692	—	0.706	0.558	7.489
	1980s			0.598	0.483	0.683	−0.735	1.203	1.709	1.633	0.695	0.607	7.563
	1990s			0.448	0.216	0.633	−0.692	0.975	1.404	1.640	0.766	0.629	7.586
Part 2: Inter-period changes in means													
	1960s			−0.034	0.568	−0.790	0.022	0.006	−0.828	—	−0.050	0.077	0.070
	1970s			−0.121	−0.467	0.173	−0.012	−0.437	0.017	—	−0.011	0.049	0.074
	1980s			−0.150	−0.267	−0.050	0.044	−0.227	−0.305	0.006	0.071	0.022	0.023
Part 3: Impact of inter-period changes in demography													
(1)	1960s	0.217		0.217	—	—	—	—	—	—	—	—	—
	1970s	0.771		0.771	—	—	—	—	—	—	—	—	—
	1980s	0.957		0.957	—	—	—	—	—	—	—	—	—
	Average	0.649											
(2)	1960s	−0.191		—	−0.191	—	—	—	—	—	—	—	—
	1970s	0.157		—	0.157	—	—	—	—	—	—	—	—
	1980s	0.090		—	0.090	—	—	—	—	—	—	—	—
	Average	0.019											
(3)	1960s	0.272		—	−0.062	—	—	—	—	—	−0.035	0.368	—
	1970s	0.419		—	0.051	—	—	—	—	—	−0.022	0.390	—
	1980s	0.139		—	0.029	—	—	—	—	—	−0.010	0.120	—
	Average	0.277											

(continued)

Table 5.5. Continued

Model	Year	Demographic Impacts w/ CDR	w/o CDR	ln(TFR)	N_{gr}	L_{gr}	ln(L/N)	CBR	CBR15	CBR20	CDR	Dns	ln(N)
(4)	1960s	1.355	1.290	–	–	–	–	-0.027	0.823	–	0.066	-0.106	0.599
	1970s	2.395	2.380	–	–	–	–	1.829	-0.017	–	0.015	-0.067	0.635
	1980s	1.328	1.421	–	–	–	–	0.952	0.303	–	-0.093	-0.030	0.195
	Average	1.693	1.697										
(5)	1960s	0.133	0.085	–	–	–	–	-0.023	–	–	0.047	0.077	0.031
	1970s	3.378	1.648	–	–	–	–	1.565	–	1.719	0.011	0.049	0.033
	1980s	0.786	0.847	–	–	–	–	0.815	–	0.007	-0.067	0.022	0.010
	Average	1.432	0.860										
(6)	1960s		-1.021	–	-0.473	-0.547	–	–	–	–	–	–	–
	1970s		0.510	–	0.389	0.120	–	–	–	–	–	–	–
	1980s		0.188	–	0.223	-0.035	–	–	–	–	–	–	–
	Average		-0.108										
(7)	1960s		-0.897	–	-0.436	-0.608	0.122	–	–	–	–	0.025	–
	1970s		0.441	–	0.358	0.134	-0.067	–	–	–	–	0.016	–
	1980s		0.411	–	0.205	-0.038	0.237	–	–	–	–	0.007	–
	Average		-0.015										
(8)	1960s		-0.288	–	-0.277	-0.545	0.169	–	–	–	–	-0.028	0.392
	1970s		0.652	–	0.227	0.120	-0.093	–	–	–	–	-0.018	0.416
	1980s		0.544	–	0.130	-0.034	0.328	–	–	–	–	-0.008	0.128
	Average		0.303										
AVG. EIGHT MODELS		1.562	0.460										

Table 5.6.   Demographic impacts on changes in Y/N_{gr} from decadal changes: China

Model	Year	Demographic Impacts w/ CDR	w/o CDR	ln(TFR)	N_{gr}	L_{gr}	ln(L/N)	CBR	CBR15	CBR20	CDR	Dns	ln(N)
Part 1: Period means													
	1970s			1.315	2.009	2.559	−1.713	2.527	3.113	3.207	0.706	0.269	10.021
	1980s			0.903	1.382	3.008	−1.712	1.900	3.162	3.286	0.619	0.298	10.163
	1990s			0.828	1.084	1.106	−1.760	1.596	1.964	2.458	0.657	0.336	10.296
Part 2: Inter-period changes in means													
	1970s			−0.411	−0.626	0.449	0.001	−0.627	0.049	0.079	−0.088	0.029	0.142
	1980s			−0.075	−0.298	−1.901	−0.048	−0.305	−1.198	−0.828	0.038	0.037	0.133
Part 3: Impact of inter-period changes in demography													
(1) Barro	1970s	1.042		1.042	—	—	—	—	—	—	—	—	—
	1980s	0.190		0.190	—	—	—	—	—	—	—	—	—
	Average	0.616											
(2) Early KS	1970s	1.127		—	1.127	—	—	—	—	—	—	—	—
	1980s	0.536		—	0.536	—	—	—	—	—	—	—	—
	Average	0.831											
(3) Augmented KS	1970s	2.193		—	1.364	—	—	—	—	—	—	0.251	0.578
	1980s	1.517		—	0.649	—	—	—	—	—	—	0.325	0.543
	Average	1.855											

(continued)

Table 5.6. Continued

Model	Year	Demographic Impacts w/ CDR	w/o CDR	ln(TFR)	N_{gr}	L_{gr}	ln(L/N)	CBR	CBR15	CBR20	CDR	Dns	ln(N)
(4) KS Comp, 15 years	1970s	-0.522	0.604	—	—	—	—	0.599	0.070	—	-1.126	-0.023	-0.042
	1980s	-1.016	-1.509	—	—	—	—	0.291	-1.730	—	0.492	-0.029	-0.040
	Average	-0.769	-0.453										
(5) KS Comp, 20 years	1970s	0.261	1.114	—	—	—	—	0.967	—	0.075	-0.853	0.097	-0.025
	1980s	0.161	-0.212	—	—	—	—	0.469	—	-0.785	0.373	0.126	-0.023
	Average	0.211	0.451										
(6) BW Trns	1970s		1.127	—	1.124	0.002	—	—	—	—	—	—	—
	1980s		0.525	—	0.535	-0.010	—	—	—	—	—	—	—
	Average		0.826										
(7) BCM Trns	1970s		1.550	—	1.337	0.011	-0.004	—	—	—	—	0.205	—
	1980s		0.982	—	0.637	-0.047	0.127	—	—	—	—	0.265	—
	Average		1.266										
(8) BCM TrnsEx	1970s		1.203	—	1.325	0.018	-0.005	—	—	—	—	0.189	-0.325
	1980s		0.650	—	0.631	-0.078	0.157	—	—	—	—	0.244	-0.305
	Average		0.926										
AVG. EIGHT MODELS		-0.279	0.790										

fertility, and mortality; changing age distributions; and rising density and population size have had remarkable effects on economic growth. On average across the eight models over 30 years, demographic change increases output per capita by 0.64 points.[7] Declines in fertility and mortality have contributed around half of these effects. Kelley and Schmidt's results are striking in that the combined demographic impacts across the eight models are similar. Population size and density induce economic growth, but these effects are relatively small. In most models the demographic effects decline over time.

In Japan, declining fertility played an important role in economic growth (Table 5.5). The crude birth rate netted of infant deaths increased slightly during the 1960s. The net birth rate decreased further during the 1980s. (The crude birth rate itself declined after the post–World War II baby boom ended.) High fertility means a high youth-dependency burden, and so a decline in fertility causes economic growth. Population size has a larger effect on economic growth than in the case of world panel data. Paradoxically, declines in both fertility and population growth contributed to Japan's economic growth. In the 1980s, however, the growth of the employed population decreased, and the contribution of population size to economic growth also declined. Throughout our model, demographic effects on growth are seen to be greatest in the 1980s. Compared with the results based on world-panel data, our results differ profoundly in the various models, and those differences indicate a need for further attention in future research.

In China overall, demographic changes contributed remarkably to economic growth (Table 5.6). In the 1970s the crude birth rate and the population growth rate declined dramatically, reducing the dependency burden. (The crude birth rate for China is not netted of infant deaths.) The effects of population density and population size vary greatly in the different models. Because the estimated effect of the crude death rate on economic growth is positive and significant, contrary to our hypothesis, the demographic effects of the crude death rate are not realistic. If we ignore the effects of the crude death rate, the demographic effects on economic growth are seen to have been greater in the 1970s than in the

---

[7] A controversial issue is whether we should include mortality changes in the calculation. Kelley and Schmidt included life expectancy at birth in all their estimations. Barro (1997) used life expectancy primarily as a proxy for health. The crude death rate or life expectancy could imply characteristics other than demographic ones, but ignoring mortality downplays the effects of demographic change. In their analysis, Kelley and Schmidt calculated demographic effects with and without mortality changes separately. In future research, it would be desirable to estimate a model that included life expectancy at birth.

1980s in all the models. The growth of the labor force declined in the 1980s as a result of lower birth rates in the preceding decade. If the fertility decline continues, we can expect neither a constant increase in the size of the labor force nor continued positive economic effects of population size.

5.3. Conclusion

Our analysis confirms that demographic characteristics have played an important role in the economic growth of Japan and China. After World War II, many Asian countries experienced rapid demographic transition. In both Japan and China, fertility declined dramatically in the latter half of twentieth century, reducing their youth-dependency burdens and stimulating economic growth. Now, however, low fertility poses a serious problem. Our analysis, based on regional data, suggests that a decreasing share of employed population can have a negative influence on economic growth in both countries. Increasing the relative size of the labor force population will be desirable for future economic growth. Increased fertility can therefore be beneficial over the long term. But it impedes economic growth in the short term because of the cost of raising children. Nowadays it takes longer for children to enter the labor force than in the past because they spend more years in school. When we discuss the contribution of population to development, we should consider not only the size of the labor force but also the quality of labor, the labor force participation of women and the elderly, and unemployment.

Our analysis indicates that a large population accumulates knowledge and promotes economies of scale, thus becoming a great source of economic growth. Our findings suggest that a moderate increase in population growth would be beneficial to Japan and China. In both countries, the total fertility rate is much lower than the replacement level, which means that their populations will eventually begin to shrink unless fertility increases. Because children are an economic burden in the short run, it will be difficult to increase fertility in a small geographic area. Addressing the problem of low fertility over the long term and throughout each country requires careful planning.

Our analysis needs further refinement of the empirical specifications. In contrast to Kelley and Schmidt's results, our results are very sensitive to the data specifications. More discussion of the theoretical model is also indicated because our results for China do not support the convergent-pattern hypothesis. Despite these problems, our study provides a better understanding of the effects of demographic variables and demographic change on economic growth in Japan and China.

Appendix 5.1

Footnote 5 mentions several studies by Yamaguchi and his colleagues that found the total effect of population growth on per capita income growth to be positive in Japan. Those results are consistent with the positive effect of population size on per capita income growth reported in this chapter. Here, we explain those earlier results in more detail.

General equilibrium growth accounting for the Japanese economy

Yamaguchi and his colleagues used general equilibrium growth accounting methods to obtain their results. (For more detail, see Yamaguchi and Binswanger 1975; Yamaguchi 1982; Yamaguchi and Kennedy 1984a,b.) Figure 5.A1 shows the historical average growth rates of the eight endogenous variables (agricultural and nonagricultural outputs, agricultural and nonagricultural capital, agricultural and nonagricultural labor, relative price and per capita income) as the sum of all the contributions of each exogenous variable in each decade. There are nine exogenous variables, but only five principal ones—agricultural technical change, nonagricultural technical change, total capital, total labor, and population—are shown in Figure 5.A1 to avoid complicating the picture.

Table 5.A1.   Definitions of variables used in the analysis

Variable	Definition
TFR	Total fertility rate
L	Thousands of employed population
WA	Thousands of working age population
Y	Gross prefectural/provincial domestic product (real)
L_{gr}	Percentage change in employed population
N_{gr}	Percentage change in population size
WA_{gr}	Percentage change in population aged 15–64
CBR	Crude birth rate (per 100 population).
CBR15	Crude birth rate lagged 15 years
CBR20	Crude birth rate lagged 20 years
CDR	Crude death rate (per 100 population)
Dns	Thousands of population per square kilometer
N	Thousands of population.

Figure 5.A1.   Contribution of population, technical change and others to eight endogenous variables

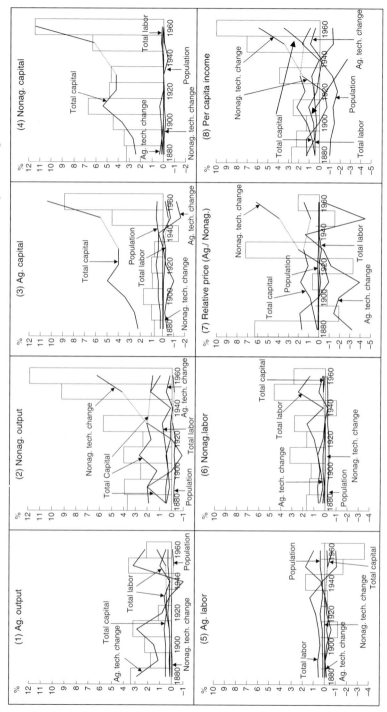

Table 5.A2.　Kelley and Schmidt's estimated results from world panel data (abbreviated)

	Barro	Early KS	Augmented KS	KS Comp. 15 years	BW Trns	BCM Trns	BCM TrnsEx
	(1)	(2)	(3)	(4)	(6)	(7)	(8)
$\ln(Y/N)$	-1.50*** (-6.01)	-1.27*** (-5.00)	-1.35*** (-5.50)	-1.20*** (-5.02)	-1.06*** (-4.13)	-1.27*** (-5.08)	-1.28*** (-5.18)
$\ln(TFR)$	-2.52*** (-6.02)						
N_{gr}		-0.53*** (3.64)	-0.41*** (-2.85)		-1.47*** (-4.61)	-1.37*** (-4.49)	-1.27*** (-4.14)
WA_{gr}					0.95*** (3.31)	1.41*** (4.79)	1.31*** (4.46)
$\ln(WA/N)$						9.52*** (4.42)	8.54*** (3.94)
CBR				-1.54*** (-4.53)			
CBR15				0.23 (0.69)			
CDR				-1.71*** (3.62)			
Dns			0.57*** (3.04)	0.36 (1.93)		0.21 (1.15)	0.31 (1.70)
$\ln(N)$			0.27*** (3.20)	0.18** (2.13)			0.18** (2.22)
Adjusted R^2	0.55	0.52	0.55	0.58	0.58	0.59	0.58
P value, $N_{gr} = -1$					0.137	0.232	0.388
P value, $L_{gr} = 1$					0.850	0.172	0.302
P value, $\ln(Y/N) = -\ln(L/N)$						0.000	0.000
No. of Obs	344	344	344	344	344	344	344

Note: Abstracted from Kelley and Schmidt (2001). The dependent variable is Y/N_{gr}. Kelley and Schmidt did not estimate model 5, and they estimated one other model that is not reported here.

Table 5.A3.   *Effect of working-age population: Japan*

	BW Trns	BCM Trns	BCM TrnsE
	(6)	(7)	(8)
ln(Y/N)	-2.667^{***}	-3.649^{***}	-7.720^{***}
	(-3.071)	(-3.773)	(-6.093)
ln(TFR)			
N_{gr}	-0.137	-0.052	0.634^{**}
	(-0.720)	(-0.209)	(2.301)
WA$_{gr}$	-0.168	-0.127	-0.323^{***}
	(-1.500)	(-1.115)	(-2.830)
ln(WA/N)		8.259^{**}	11.807^{***}
		(2.524)	(3.750)
Dns		-0.482	-1.664^{*}
		(-0.534)	(-1.888)
ln(N)			9.756^{***}
			(4.574)
year 70	-1.992^{**}	-1.482	1.303
	(-2.168)	(-1.598)	(1.232)
year 80	-2.675^{**}	-1.630	2.766^{*}
	(-2.013)	(-1.176)	(1.717)
year 90	-3.577^{**}	-2.391	3.345^{*}
	(-2.188)	(-1.403)	(1.653)
Constant	27.832^{***}	38.578^{***}	-4.311
	(4.825)	(5.367)	(-0.374)
Adjusted R^2	0.935	0.937	0.945
P value, Year Dummies	0.078	0.038	0.022
P value, $N_{gr} = -1$	0.000	0.000	0.000
P value, WA$_{gr} = 1$	0.000	0.000	0.000
P value, ln(Y/N) $= -$ln(WA/N)		0.126	0.146
No. of Obs	188	188	188

Note: The dependent variable is Y/N_{gr}. See also note for Table 5.3.

First, we consider per capita income (panel 8 of Figure 5.A1). For this dependent variable, nonagricultural technical change has the largest effect on the whole. Its contribution, however, varies widely over the decades. In contrast, the contribution of agricultural technical change is fairly stable and almost of the same magnitude as the contribution of total labor, on average. The contribution of agricultural technical change is also relatively large in the early stage of Japan's economic development. As mentioned previously, total labor contributed positively to per capita income growth. The contribution of capital is somewhat larger than that

Table 5.A4. *Estimated results from OLS: Chinese provinces*

	Barro	Early KS	Augmented KS	KS Comp. 15 years	KS Comp. 20 years	BW Trns	BCM Trns	BCM TrnsEx
	(1)	(3)	(2)	(4)	(5)	(6)	(7)	(8)
ln(Y/N)	-0.414 (-0.961)	-0.258 (-0.674)	0.306 (0.459)	1.181* (1.699)	0.785 (1.145)	-0.231 (-0.584)	0.248 (0.371)	0.389 (0.589)
ln(TFR)	-0.797 (-0.993)							
N_{gr}		-0.746* (-1.918)	-0.531 (-1.251)					
L_{gr}						-0.749** (-1.934)	-0.545 (-1.266)	-0.511 (-1.246)
ln(L/N)						0.085 (0.506)	0.076 (0.474)	0.081 (0.513)
CBR				-0.813 (-1.336)	-0.848 (-1.330)		-0.332 (-1.540)	1.285 (0.694)
CBR15				1.114*** (3.398)				
CBR20					0.580** (2.402)			
CDR				7.695*** (3.720)	6.841*** (3.356)			
Dns			-0.462 (-0.532)	-1.072 (-1.568)	-1.012 (-1.291)		-0.293 (-0.360)	-0.710 (-0.725)

(continued)

Table 5.A4. *Continued*

	Barro	Augmented KS	Early KS	KS Comp, 15 years	KS Comp, 20 years	BW Trms	BCM Trms	BCM TrmsEx
	(1)	(2)	(3)	(4)	(5)	(6)	(7)	(8)
$\ln(N)$		0.367*		0.537**	0.474**			1.691
		(1.679)		(2.384)	(2.070)			(0.883)
Coast	1.840***	1.490***	1.702***	1.796***	1.727***	1.710***	1.514***	1.459***
	(3.763)	(2.897)	(3.375)	(4.196)	(3.835)	(3.432)	(2.935)	(2.898)
year 80	2.134***	1.584**	1.885***	1.414**	1.608***	1.825***	1.629**	1.319*
	(4.077)	(2.315)	(3.534)	(2.382)	(2.628)	(3.258)	(2.358)	(1.661)
year 90	3.510***	2.194*	2.960***	2.199**	1.918*	3.038***	2.456**	1.910
	(4.488)	(1.845)	(3.539)	(2.152)	(1.798)	(3.652)	(2.196)	(1.459)
Constant	8.922***	1.352	8.518***	−13.245*	−8.029	8.146***	4.575	−10.369
	(2.873)	(0.246)	(3.604)	(−1.824)	(−1.154)	(3.119)	(1.089)	(−0.601)
Adjusted R^2	0.522	0.544	0.539	0.621	0.589	0.535	0.538	0.537
P value, Year Dummies	0.000	0.071	0.002	0.059	0.033	0.001	0.062	0.258
P value, $N_{gr} = -1$						0.519	0.295	0.237
P value, $L_{gr} = 1$						0.000	0.000	0.000
P value, $\ln(Y/N) = -\ln(L/N)$							0.878	0.425
No. of Obs	86	86	86	86	86	86	86	86

Note: The dependent variable is Y/N_{gr}. The full sample includes 29 provinces and two decennial periods (1970–80, 1980–90) and one quinquennial period (1990–95). "Coast" is the dummy variable for coastal provinces: Beijing, Liaoning, Tianjin, Hebei, Shandong, Jiangsu, Shanghai, Zhejiang, Fujian, and Guangdong. See also note for Table 5.3.

Table 5.A5. Demographic impacts on changes in Y/N_{gr} from decadal changes: World panel data

Model	Year	Demographic Impacts		ln(TFR)	ln(e_0)	N_{gr}	WA_{gr}	ln(WA/N)	CBR	CBR15	CDR	Dns	ln(N)
		w/ CDR	w/o CDR										
Part 1: Period means													
	1960s			1.65	3.97	2.28	2.04	−0.59	3.39	3.41	1.12	0.13	9.06
	1970s			1.52	4.04	2.13	2.37	−0.60	3.27	3.42	0.99	0.16	9.27
	1980s			1.34	4.10	2.00	2.34	−0.57	3.02	3.27	0.88	0.19	9.48
	1990s			1.18	4.16	1.40	1.64	−0.54	2.77	3.02	0.81	0.22	9.68
Part 2: Inter-period changes in means													
	1960s			−0.13	0.07	−0.14	0.33	−0.01	−0.12	0.01	−0.13	0.03	0.21
	1970s			−0.18	0.07	−0.13	−0.03	0.03	−0.25	−0.15	−0.11	0.03	0.21
	1980s			−0.16	0.06	−0.60	−0.70	0.03	−0.25	−0.25	−0.07	0.03	0.20
Part 3: Impact of inter-period changes in demography													
(1) Barro	1960s	0.66	0.33	0.33	0.32	—	—	—	—	—	—	—	—
	1970s	0.76	0.45	0.45	0.31	—	—	—	—	—	—	—	—
	1980s	0.64	0.40	0.40	0.25	—	—	—	—	—	—	—	—
	Average	0.68	0.39										
(2) Early KS	1960s	0.53	0.08	—	0.45	0.08	—	—	—	—	—	—	—
	1970s	0.51	0.07	—	0.44	0.07	—	—	—	—	—	—	—
	1980s	0.67	0.32	—	0.34	0.32	—	—	—	—	—	—	—
	Average	0.57	0.16										

(continued)

Table 5.A5. Continued

Model	Year	Demographic Impacts w/ CDR	Demographic Impacts w/o CDR	ln(TFR)	ln(e_0)	N_{gr}	WA_{gr}	ln(WA/N)	CBR	CBR15	CDR	Dns	ln(N)
(3) Augmented	1960s	0.58	0.13	–	0.44	0.06	–	–	–	–	–	0.02	0.06
KS	1970s	0.56	0.13	–	0.43	0.05	–	–	–	–	–	0.02	0.06
	1980s	0.66	0.32	–	0.34	0.25	–	–	–	–	–	0.02	0.05
	Average	0.60	0.19										
(4) KS Comp,	1960s	0.66	0.41	–		–	–	–	0.36	0.00	0.23	0.01	0.04
15 years	1970s	0.55	0.36	–		–	–	–	0.34	–0.03	0.19	0.01	0.04
	1980s	0.57	0.45	–		–	–	–	0.46	–0.06	0.12	0.01	0.04
	Average	0.59	0.41										
(6) BW	1960s	0.91	0.52	–	0.38	0.21	0.31	–	–	–	–	–	–
Trms	1970s	0.54	0.17	–	0.37	0.19	–0.02	–	–	–	–	–	–
	1980s	0.52	0.22	–	0.30	0.88	–0.66	–	–	–	–	–	–
	Average	0.69	0.31										
(7) BCM	1960s	0.91	0.56	–	0.35	0.20	0.46	–0.11	–	–	–	0.01	–
Trms	1970s	0.76	0.42	–	0.34	0.18	–0.04	0.27	–	–	–	0.01	–
	1980s	0.40	0.13	–	0.27	0.82	–0.98	0.29	–	–	–	0.01	–
	Average	0.69	0.37										
(8) BCM	1960s	0.92	0.56	–	0.36	0.18	0.43	–0.10	–	–	–	0.01	0.04
TrmsEx	1970s	0.78	0.43	–	0.35	0.17	–0.03	0.24	–	–	–	0.01	0.04
	1980s	0.43	0.15	–	0.28	0.76	–0.92	0.26	–	–	–	0.01	0.04
	Average	0.71	0.38										
AVG. SEVEN MODELS		0.65	0.32										

Note: Abstracted from Kelley and Schmidt (2001). Numbers of the models correspond to those in Table 5.1. ln(e_0) is life expectancy at birth.

of labor, however. Population has, of course, a negative effect on per capita income; but its net contribution, which is the sum of the contributions of population and of labor, has a much smaller negative value. In the ordinary model, which treats labor and population together, we can obtain only the net contribution of population. This model, in contrast, allows us to evaluate the contributions of population and labor independently and to see the effect of the labor participation rate as well.

To understand how population and labor contributed to per capita income growth in Japan, we need to see the growth accounting for sectoral output and input, shown in panels 1 to 7. With respect to agricultural output (panel 1), the largest contribution is agricultural technical change, followed in order of importance by total labor, total capital, and population. The contribution of nonagricultural technical change has a zero or negative value in each decade. Note that population growth makes a positive contribution. For the variable labeled nonagricultural output (panel 2), nonagricultural technical change makes the largest contribution, but the contribution varies widely. Total capital, total labor, and agricultural technical change follow in order of importance. Population growth makes a small negative contribution.

As we have already noted, agricultural technical change tends to push resources out of agriculture (making a negative contribution to agricultural labor and a positive contribution to nonagricultural labor), whereas nonagricultural technical change tends to pull resources into nonagriculture (making a negative contribution to agricultural labor and a positive contribution to nonagricultural labor). The asymmetrical effect of technical change is due to the low price and income elasticities for agricultural goods (see Appendix 5.2). Therefore, agricultural technical change is seen to have made a positive contribution to the growth of nonagricultural output, especially in the 1910s and 1920s, when its contribution was larger than that of nonagricultural technical change, which contributed negatively to agricultural output.

From these growth accountings shown in panels 1 through 7, we can see that population growth increases agricultural output and inputs (capital and labor) and decreases nonagricultural output and inputs. As a result, per capita income decreases because agricultural productivity, including agricultural labor productivity, is lower than nonagricultural productivity. On the other hand, labor growth causes output and input in both sectors to increase and also increases per capita income. The net contribution of population, which is the sum of the contributions of population and labor, is negative if we do not consider population's and labor's contributions to technical change. We consider this point next.

The direct, indirect, and total effects of population and labor on per capita income in Japan

Yamaguchi and his colleagues set out to measure the effect of population and labor on per capita income through technical change. They considered this effect to be an indirect contribution to per capita income. To measure the total contribution (including both positive and negative effects) of population and labor growth on per capita income in Japan over the period from 1880 to 1970, they used a two-sector general equilibrium growth accounting model. The model treated population and labor growth as separate variables so that the contributions of each to per capita income growth could be estimated separately.

The first step was to estimate the direct effect of population and labor growth on per capita income growth (Table 5.A6). The next step was to estimate the indirect effect and contribution via population and labor's influence on technical change in each sector. Three alternative methods were employed: the residual method, the Verdoorn method, and the factor-augmenting rate method. Each of those methods yielded consistent results.

Next, Yamaguchi and his colleagues derived the total effect of population and labor growth on per capita income growth by combining their direct and indirect contributions. With respect to per capita income growth, the total contribution of population cum labor growth tended to be negative in the decades 1880–1930 and positive in the decades 1930–70, with the exception of 1940–50 (see Table 5.A6). Over the period 1880–1970, however, population and labor growth together tended on average to make a positive contribution to per capita income growth under the residual method (0.35% per year), the factor-augmenting rate method (0.29% per year), and the Verdoorn method (0.01% per year).

We have included the results of their sensitivity analysis to show how growth rate multiplier values are affected by changes in the parameters (see Yamaguchi and Kennedy 1984a). Each of the three methods used to estimate the indirect contribution of population plus labor growth to per capita income growth was necessarily arbitrary and involved certain assumptions. However, the fact that each of the three very different methods yielded consistent results provides fairly substantial evidence that population combined with labor growth made a positive contribution to per capita income in Japan over the period 1880–1970, especially after 1930. This means that a large population has a positive effect on per capita income growth.

Table 5.A6. *Total contribution of population cum labor growth to per capita income growth: Japan, 1880–1970* (% per year)

Decade	Direct Contribution to Per Capita Income Growth (CEPop_D)	Indirect Contribution to Per Capita Income Growth (CEPop_I)			Total Contribution to Per Capita Income Growth (COPop_T)		
	(1)	Residual Method (2)	Verdoorn Method (3)	Factor Augmenting Rate Method (4)	Residual Method (5) (1)+(2)	Verdoorn Method (6) (1)+(3)	Factor Augmenting Rate Method (7) (1)+(4)
1880–90	−0.59	0.55	0.38	0.99	−0.04	−0.21	0.40
1890–1900	−0.66	0.66	0.40	0.97	0.00	−0.26	0.31
1900–10	−1.10	0.38	0.18	1.00	−0.72	−0.92	−0.10
1910–20	−0.95	0.65	0.34	0.97	−0.30	−0.61	0.02
1920–30	−1.11	0.97	0.59	0.93	−0.14	−0.52	−0.18
1930–40	−0.20	1.74	1.01	0.93	1.54	0.81	0.73
1940–50	−1.56	0.15	0.07	0.91	−1.41	−1.49	−0.65
1950–60	0.43	2.56	1.88	0.93	2.99	2.31	1.36
1960–70	−0.21	1.44	0.98	0.89	1.23	0.77	0.68
Average	−0.65	1.01	0.65	0.95	0.35	0.01	0.29

Appendix 5.2

To clarify the asymmetrical effect of technical change, a brief explanation of growth accounting for capital and labor, the two agricultural and nonagricultural inputs, may be helpful. Our discussion here refers to Figure 5.A1.

The first input is capital. For agricultural capital stock (panel 3 of Figure 5.A1), the largest contributor is, of course, total capital. Other contributions are fairly small. In this case, population makes a small positive contribution. The contributions of technical change in both sectors are negative. As we stated before, technical change pushes and pulls agricultural factor inputs into the nonagricultural sector. For nonagricultural capital stock (panel 4 of Figure 5.A1), the largest effect and contributor is, again, total capital. Agricultural technical change, nonagricultural technical change, and total labor follow with markedly smaller contributions. Finally, population has a negative effect, making an opposite contribution to that of technical change.

Labor is the other input. For agricultural labor (panel 5 of Figure 5.A1), total labor makes the largest contribution, followed by population. The rest of the variables have a negative effect, pushing and pulling agricultural labor into the nonagricultural sector. For nonagricultural labor (panel 6 of Figure 5.A1), total labor again has the largest effect. Agricultural technical change, total capital, and nonagricultural technical change follow in importance. This result corresponds to the pushing and pulling effect of technical change. Population obviously makes a positive contribution to agricultural inputs, as noted above. For relative price (agricultural price/ nonagricultural price), shown in panel 7 of Figure 5.A1, nonagricultural technical change produces the largest positive effect, and agricultural technical change the largest negative effect. The contributions of the other variables are very small except for the fairly large contribution of total capital.

References

Barro, Robert J. 1997. "Determinants of economic growth: A cross-country empirical study". Development Discussion Paper No. 579. Cambridge, MA: Harvard Institute for International Development.
Barro, Robert J. and Xavier Sala-i-Martin, 1995. *Economic Growth*. New York: McGraw-Hill.
Bloom, David E., David Canning, and Pia N. Malaney. 1999. "Demographic change and economic growth in Asia". CID (Center for International Development at Harvard University) Working Paper No. 15, Cambridge, MA.

Bloom, David E. and Jeffery G. Williamson. 1998. "Demographic transitions and economic miracles in emerging Asia". *World Bank Economic Review* 12(3): 419–55.

Cai Fang, Wang Dewen, and Du Yang. 2002. "Regional disparity and economic growth in China: The impact of labor market distortions". *China Economic Review* 13: 197–212.

Chen, Jian and Fleisher, Belton M. 1996. "Regional income inequality and economic growth in China". *Journal of Comparative Economics* 22: 141–164.

China. Academy of Social Sciences. Population Research Center. Various years. *Almanac of China's population.* Beijing.

China. State Statistical Bureau. Various years. *China Statistical Yearbook.* Beijing: China Statistics Press.

Huang Wei. 2004. *Chugoku ni okeru jinko to keizai no keiryoteki-bunseki: Chugoku no paneru deta niyoru jissho bunseki* (Econometric analysis of population and economy in Japan: Empirical analysis of Chinese panel data). Master's thesis, Graduate School of Economics, Kobe University (in Japanese).

Japan. National Institute of Population and Social Security Research 2005. *Ippan Jinko Tokei (General Population Statistics) http://www.ipss.go.jp/syoushika/tohkei/Popular/Popular2005.asp?chap=0* (August 28, 2005).

Japan. Ministry of Public Management, Home Affairs, Posts and Telecommunications. Statistical Bureau. Various years. *Japan Statistical Yearbook,* Japan.

Kelley, Allen C. and Robert M. Schmidt. 1994. "Population and income change: Recent evidence". World Bank Discussion Paper 249. Washington, DC: World Bank.

———. 1995. "Aggregate population and economic growth correlations: The role of the components of demographic change". *Demography* 32(4): 543–55.

———. 2001. "Economic and demographic change: A synthesis of models, findings, and perspectives", in: Nancy Birdsall, Allen C. Kelley, and Steven Sinding, editors. *Population matters: Demographic change, economic growth, and poverty in the developing world,* pp. 67–105. New York: Oxford University Press.

Kinugasa, Tomoko. 2002. Contribution of demographic variables on economic growth: Empirical analysis of Japanese prefecture data. *Kokumin Keizai Zasshi (Journal of Economics and Business Administration)* 186(4): 95–108 (in Japanese).

Yamaguchi, Mitoshi. 1982. "The source of Japanese economic development: 1880–1970". *Economic Studies Quarterly* 33(2): 126–46.

Yamaguchi, Mitoshi, and Hans. P. Binswanger. 1975. "The role of sectoral technical change in development: Japan, 1880–1965". *American Journal of Agricultural Economics* 57(2): 269–78.

Yamaguchi, Mitoshi, and George Kennedy. 1984a. "Contribution of population growth to per capita income and sectoral output growth in Japan, 1880–1970". *Developing Economies* 22(3): 237–63.

———. 1984b. "A graphic model of the effects of sectoral technical change: The case of Japan, 1880–1970". *Canadian Journal of Agricultural Economics* 32(1): 71–92.

Yao, Shujie, and Zhang Zongyi. 2001. "Regional growth in China under economic reforms". *Journal of Development Studies* (December): 167–86.

CHAPTER 6

Job Opportunities for Older Workers: When Are Jobs Filled with External Hires?

Robert Hutchens

Any assessment of job opportunities for older people must grapple with employer hiring behavior. Employers seem to avoid hiring new older workers for jobs that older workers can obviously do. In the event of a job opening, the employer either shifts a current employee (young or old) into the job, or hires a new young worker. Why do employers behave this way?

This type of employer behavior is a problem because it can lead to a labor market with restricted job opportunities for older workers. In fact, there is evidence of such restricted opportunities. Consider the effects of job loss. In the United States, workers over age 55 are somewhat less likely to become unemployed than workers below this age, yet compared with the young these older workers "have the lowest reemployment probabilities, the longest time to reemployment, high probabilities of part-time employment, and the largest wage losses" (Hirsch, Macpherson, and Hardy 2000, 402). Indeed, Chan and Stevens (2001, 484) find that, for displaced workers (for example, workers who lost their jobs because of a plant closing), "four years after job losses at age 55, the employment rate of displaced workers remains 20 percentage points below the employment rate of similar nondisplaced workers." Even after controlling for a list of factors that influence labor supply (e.g., marital status, pensions, wealth holdings), Chan and Stevens find lower employment rates for older displaced workers. A plausible interpretation would be this: If you lose your job when you are in your 50s or 60s, it can be difficult to find similar work. You may be better off simply going into retirement.

A similar phenomenon occurs in Japan. According to a recent OECD study, the incidence of long-term unemployment rises with age in Japan. Among unemployed persons over age 50 in 2002, the fraction who had been unemployed for more than a year was 36.1%; among those over age 60, the fraction was 39.6%. The comparable number at ages 25–49 was 29.9% (OECD 2004, table 2.5). Moreover, there is evidence that during

POPULATION CHANGE, LABOR MARKETS, AND SUSTAINABLE GROWTH
VOLUME 281   ISSN 0573-8555/DOI 10.1016/S0573-8555(07)81006-6

the 1990s, reduced demand combined with an increase in the age of mandatory retirement from 55 to 60 contributed to reduced employment of older (ages 60–64) wage and salary workers (Mitani 2002, 25).

From a policy perspective, restricted job opportunities are a major concern. In the United States, the fraction of the population aged 50 and older is projected to increase from 30 to 36 percent over the next 30 years (computed from US Census Bureau 2002, Table NP-T3). This has led to calls for policies that expand labor force participation of older Americans. Not only will later retirement reduce financial pressure on the US social security system, but also it could conceivably address labor market shortages arising from smaller numbers of young workers. (see, for example, Committee for Economic Development 1999 and, for a particularly insightful discussion, Burtless and Quinn 2001). A similar phenomenon is occurring in Japan. The fraction of the labor force over age 50 is destined to grow, and efforts are underway to institute policies that encourage increased labor force participation in the older population (OECD 2004). Certainly one way to bring about this increase is to create enhanced job opportunities for older workers, and the governments of both the United States and Japan are currently pursuing that goal.

This chapter uses new data on jobs from a sample of establishments to examine employer-hiring behavior. By studying hiring behavior, we can gain a better understanding of why some jobs seem to be closed to older workers, and thereby a better understanding of job opportunities for older workers.

For purposes of studying the hiring of older workers, a survey of establishments has both advantages and disadvantages. A key advantage is that such data can provide information on employer policies, and those policies can then be related to characteristics of the workplace. At least in the United States, a disadvantage to establishment-level data is that it may be difficult to obtain truthful answers to questions about hiring older workers. For example, one would like to ask an employer whether he or she is willing to hire a 55-year-old worker for a specific job. Given laws prohibiting age discrimination, an employer in the United States may hesitate to say anything but "yes" to such a question. Although the firm may, in reality, avoid hiring older workers, no spokesperson for the firm would actually *say* that in an interview. Such an answer could conceivably be interpreted as indicating age discrimination and thereby somehow used in a lawsuit.

This chapter avoids the problem of less than truthful responses by focusing on whether the firm fills a specific job from the "inside" or the "outside." Employers can candidly discuss this topic without fear of age discrimination lawsuits. An employer fills a job from the inside when an existing employee is promoted or shifted into the job. A job is filled from the outside when a new worker (young or old) is hired into the job.

The study contributes to the literature by presenting evidence indicating that older workers often hold jobs that are simply not filled from the outside, and by testing hypotheses for why that is. Thus, one reason why there are jobs for which firms employ but do not hire older workers is that the firms do not hire *any* outside worker for those jobs. While there may be qualified outsiders (both young and old) who could do the job, that opportunity never arises. The job is open only to insiders.

6.1. The literature

Much of the economic literature on barriers to hiring older workers is built on the concept of quasi-fixed costs. In a classic article, Walter Oi (1962) argued that the labor input is quasi-fixed; that is, its total cost is partially variable and partially fixed.

The total discounted costs, C, of hiring an additional worker is the sum of the present value of expected wage payments, the hiring cost, H, and training expense, K.

$$C = \sum_{0}^{T} W_t (1 + r)^{-t} + H + K, \tag{6.1}$$

where W_t is the expected wage in the t-th period, r denotes the rate at which future costs are discounted, and T denotes the expected period of employment. (Oi 1962, 539).

Firms that have large fixed costs—such as Oi's hiring and training costs—will tend to employ but not hire older workers. To see this, consider a world where a new generation of Z income-maximizing workers enters the workforce every period. The members of each generation work for two periods and retire. Assume these workers are equally productive, that productivity does not grow over the life cycle, and that young and old are perfect substitutes in production. Thus, at any point in time there are $2Z$ equally productive workers in the labor market, Z of whom are young workers in their first period of work, and Z of whom are older workers.

To begin with, assume that all firms in this market have zero fixed costs; wages are their only labor cost. Such firms and workers would presumably form a spot market, since neither has reason for a long-term relationship. Moreover, since old and young workers are equally productive and impose no fixed costs on the firms, the wages of young and old will be equal and firms will be indifferent toward hiring one rather than the other.

Now suppose that a new firm, which perhaps produces a different product, enters this competitive labor market. This firm incurs fixed cost F each time it hires a worker. For example, in Oi's framework above, F is the sum of hiring and training costs. If it hires old workers it pays F every period. If it hires young workers and retains them for their full two-period working life, it pays F only every other period. Since young and old are paid the same wage, this firm minimizes costs by hiring only young workers. This is true even if young and old are equally productive and perfect substitutes in production. Although the firm employs old workers—workers who were young when hired and are completing the second period of their working life—it does not hire them.

The idea that fixed costs lead the firm to avoid hiring older workers is central to the theoretical argument in an earlier study of mine (Hutchens 1986), which argues that delayed payment contracts—contracts that discourage worker shirking and malfeasance by shifting compensation to the end of the contract—create a form of fixed cost. Much as with the hiring and training costs in Oi (1962), these fixed costs lead firms to hire primarily young (long-term) workers. After making that argument, I presented empirical evidence that was largely based on an index of the form

$$I(i,j) = \frac{\%\ \text{of recently hired workers in industry}\ i\ \text{and occupation}\ j\ \text{that are over age}\ k}{\%\ \text{of all workers in industry}\ i\ \text{and occupation}\ j\ \text{that are over age}\ k}$$

where age k was set at 55. Small values of the index reveal jobs that employ but do not hire older workers. The study found that jobs with small values of the index tended to have the characteristics of delayed-payment contracts; that is, long tenure with the firm, pensions, mandatory retirement, and high wages for older workers.

The subsequent empirical literature is largely consistent with the result in Hutchens (1986). Heywood, Ho, and Wei (1999) used data from establishments in Hong Kong to test the hypothesis that delayed payment contracts are associated with establishments that employ but do not hire older workers.[1] They computed the above index with age k set at 35 for each establishment, and took that as their dependent variable in multivariate models. They found that establishments with pensions and lengthy job tenures tended to

---

[1] Hong Kong is attractive for this purpose because it does not have the kinds of anti-discrimination legislation invoked by Scott, Berger, and Garen (1995), who argue that such rules cause pensions to be associated with reduced hiring of older workers. Evidence in Garen, Berger, and Scott (1996) is consistent with that. Among other things, Heywood, Ho, and Wei (1999) argue essentially that even without such rules, pensions are associated with reduced hiring of older workers.

have lower values of the index. Similarly, in a study that provides some of the most comprehensive empirical work on the topic, Hirsch, Macpherson, and Hardy (2000) examined data on occupations in the United States. After pooling data on 494 detailed occupations in a series of Current Population Survey data sets from the period 1983–98, those authors set age k at 50, computed the above index for each occupation, and used that as their dependent variable in multivariate models. Their analysis indicates that, among other things, occupations with pensions and steep wage profiles tend to employ, but not hire, older workers.

Another branch of the literature on hiring older workers is built on the idea of fixed costs, but unlike the studies mentioned above (and like Oi 1962), focuses on hiring and training costs. For example, Hu (2003) argues not only that specific training is a form of fixed cost, but also that such investments increase with firm size. This leads to the prediction that larger firms will tend to hire relatively young workers. Another example is a study by Scott, Berger, and Garen (1995), who argue that health insurance and pensions create a form of fixed costs. Although their theory is more complicated than that sketched above, they too predict that an increase in such fixed costs will cause the firm to increase its hiring of young workers.

These predictions regarding training and health insurance receive a degree of empirical support. Hu (2003) draws data on white-collar workers in the United States from the Current Population Survey and finds that, other things being equal, larger firms tend to hire younger workers. Heywood, Ho, and Wei (1999) find that establishments with more skilled workforces tend to employ but not hire older workers. In both cases, the authors interpret their results as potentially linked to the effect of specific training. With regard to health insurance, Scott, Berger, and Garen (1995) obtain the result that the presence of employer-provided health insurance tends to decrease hiring of workers between ages 55 and 64. Hirsch, Macpherson, and Hardy (2000), however, find essentially no support for that finding.

It is important to acknowledge that not all empirical results in the literature can be explained in terms of fixed costs. For example, Hirsch, Macpherson, and Hardy (2000) find that firms where employees often use computers tend to employ but not hire older workers. While that tendency could conceivably be due to fixed costs (e.g., specific training), there is no way to know whether that is the case.

6.2. Theory and hypotheses

It is useful to think about the probability that an employer hires a new older worker after making two decisions. The first decision is whether or not to fill the job with a new hire from the outside—that is, to fill the job with a worker of any age who is not currently employed by the firm. The second decision is conditional on the first: Given that the firm fills the job with a new hire from the outside, does the firm hire an older worker? As such, one can write the probability of hiring a new older worker into job j as the product of a marginal probability and a conditional probability:

$$\Pr(\text{OHire in } j) = \Pr(\text{OHire in } j \mid \text{Hire in } j)\, \Pr(\text{Hire in } j)$$

where

Pr(OHire in j) is the probability of hiring an outside older worker into job j,
Pr(Hire in j) is the probability of hiring an outside worker (young or old)
    into job j, and
Pr(OHire in j | Hire in j) is the probability of hiring an outside older worker
    conditional on hiring an outside worker into job j.

The economic theory that underlies much of the empirical literature on hiring older workers focuses primarily on the conditional probability, Pr(OHire in j | Hire in j). Indeed, the argument about fixed costs in the literature surveyed above takes that form; assuming that a firm fills a job from the outside, what effect do fixed costs have on the firm's propensity to hire old versus young workers? That question and the theory that addresses it are the basis for the empirical work in Hutchens (1986); Heywood, Wo, and Wei (1999); Scott, Berger, and Garen (1995); and Hu (2003).

This focus on the conditional probability is somewhat troubling. Several authors have used firm-level personnel records to show that some jobs are more likely to be filled from the inside than others. (See, for example, Baker, Gibbs, Holmstrom 1994, Table II; Lazear and Oyer 2004, Table 1.) A firm may employ but not hire an older worker for a specific job simply because it does not hire outside workers—young or old—for the job. Alternatively stated, one good reason why Pr(OHire in j) may differ across jobs is that the marginal probability, Pr(Hire in j), differs across jobs. This section considers theoretical arguments for why some jobs may or may not be filled with an outside hire. The arguments are, of course, linked to the subsequent empirical work.

A good place to start is to examine the extent to which the above ideas about fixed costs provide an explanation for why some jobs are filled with an outside hire. Consider the argument in the opening paragraphs of my literature review. Once again, assume that a new firm enters a labor market populated by firms that use a technology for which young and old are perfect substitutes in production, and that have no fixed costs. As before, each new generation of Z workers is available to work for two periods, and workers are identical in all respects except that some entered the labor market in the current period (the young) while others entered in the previous period (the old).

Now, unlike the situation described in the opening paragraphs of the literature review, suppose that the new firm employs $N + 1$ workers in a hierarchy involving two types of jobs. One type of job is called a "regular" job or R-job; both young (first period) and old (second period) workers are equally productive in this job. Assume the firm employs N workers in R-jobs. The second type of job is called a "management" job or M-job; old workers are more productive than young workers in this job.[2] The firm has only one M-job. Assume that the firm's technology is such that vacancies in either type of job are quite costly to the firm; thus in every period the firm employs one manager and N "regular" employees. The firm's problem is to decide whether to fill its $N + 1$ jobs with inside or outside workers. In particular, if it fills some or all of the R-jobs with young workers in period $t - 1$, then the firm has the option of "promoting" one of those workers into the M-job in period t. When will the M-job be filled from the inside, and when will it be filled with an outside hire?

To begin with, we wish to examine whether the above ideas about fixed costs provide an explanation for why some jobs are filled from the inside. Suppose this firm incurs a fixed cost F_R (F_M) when a worker starts the R-job (M-job). For example, the fixed cost could be a form of specific training that is useful in that job. Would such fixed costs affect the firm's propensity to promote its previous period's R-job worker to the M-job? Generally speaking, the answer is no. For example, suppose both F_R and F_M are positive and F_M is independent of F_R. Then to promote a previous period's R-job worker into the M-job implies costly turnover in the R-job. To minimize the cost of R-job workers, the firm should always hire young workers into the R-job and retain them in that job for two periods.

More rigorously, let the firm choose between two strategies: (1) in every period hire one outside old worker into the M-job, as well as $N/2$ young workers into the R-job under a two-period contract every period; (2) in every period promote one inside worker (who in the previous period was a young worker in the R-job) into the M-job, and hire $(N/2) + 1$ young workers into the R-job. Under the first strategy, the expenditure per period

---

[2] This could simply be a consequence of age. For example, the society may have a tradition of honoring and following the lead of older people. Thus, even though young and old are otherwise identical, the old are better managers; an identical young person cannot lead as effectively.

on fixed costs is $(NF_R)/2 + F_M$. Under the second strategy, this cost is $(NF_R)/2 + F_R + F_M$. The first strategy is less costly than the second.

Of course, there is a case in which fixed costs can cause the firm to fill the M-job from the inside. This case arises when F_M for outsiders is larger than F_M for insiders. For example, suppose that $F_M = \theta$ for a worker hired from the outside, whereas $F_M \leq \theta - F_R$ if a previous period's R-job worker is promoted to the M-job. This could happen if specific training costs incurred in the R-job reduce similar costs in the M-job. In this case, a promotion can be less costly than an outside hire, and the cost-minimizing firm will thereby avoid the outside hire. In this case, fixed costs influence the above marginal probability, Pr(Hire in j).

Is this a realistic case? Is it, for example, realistic to assume that the cost of training an insider to do a management job is substantially less than the cost of training an outsider for the same job? Since the answer is not obvious *a priori*, we should view this as an interesting hypothesis. Thus,

Hypothesis 1: *Jobs with large fixed costs, such as specific training, are particularly likely to be filled from the inside, ceteris paribus.*

Another reason why a firm may prefer insiders to outsiders is that a job requires some difficult-to-observe worker characteristic, and the firm's information on that characteristic is asymmetric in the sense that its information is better for insiders than for outsiders. To see this, suppose that workers are heterogeneous in a characteristic "A" that is productive in the M-job but not in the R-job. For example, A could represent leadership skills, integrity, or a capacity for intense work. Assume that the firm cannot observe A when hiring from the outside; for outsiders the firm only knows $E(A)$, the expected value of A. The firm can, however, obtain accurate information on A_i—the value of A for individual i—by observing the worker in the R-job for one period. Thus, by observing its regular workers, the firm can determine whether a worker is an effective leader, is trustworthy, or tends to shirk. In this case, given N young workers in the R-job in period $t - 1$, a risk-neutral firm will prefer to fill the M-job with an insider when $\max_{i = 1, N}\{A_i\} > E(A)$. Thus, due to asymmetric information, insiders may be preferred to outsiders.

An important and growing literature examines employer behavior when the employer has better information on insiders versus outsiders. At the heart of this literature lies the firm's assignment problem. The firm has various jobs with different skill requirements, and workers are heterogeneous in their skills. The firm's problem is to assign workers to jobs so as to maximize profit. If the firm has complete information on the characteristics of inside and outside workers, then there is no preference for insiders. If, as is more likely, the firm has better information on the characteristics of inside workers, then vacancies are likely to be filled from the inside. Much of the recent theoretical work on job assignment and promotion assume this type of asymmetric information (see Valsecchi 2000 for a useful review); but only a handful of articles (e.g., Demougin and Siow 1994; Novos 1995, and Waldman 2003) explicitly consider outside hires, and they do not provide guidance on the types of jobs that are likely to be filled from the inside.

Tournament theory provides another explanation for why jobs are filled internally, rather than with outside hires. Once again, however, the theory does not provide much guidance on what types of jobs will be filled from the outside. The literature on promotion tournaments is large and growing (see Prendergast 1999 for a useful review). Here the firm faces a different kind of information problem: it can observe an *ordinal* ranking of employees from best to worst rather than a *cardinal* measure of each employee's performance. In order to induce optimal effort, the firm fashions a tournament whereby the best performer is promoted to a higher-paying job. From the perspective of this chapter, tournament theory provides an explanation for why some jobs are often filled internally: some jobs are prizes in the tournament. To fill them from the outside is to reduce the incentives of the tournament (Chan 1996; Chen 2005). Other jobs may be primarily filled from the inside because the firm has a long-term implicit contract with its workers, and therefore provides jobs to losers in the tournament. Unfortunately, the theory gives little guidance about the characteristics of jobs that are prizes, jobs that go to losers, and how and why such jobs differ from jobs that are filled from the outside.

One set of jobs where informational asymmetries may be particularly important is jobs with delayed payment contracts. Suppose the firm has a job in which worker shirking and malfeasance are particularly costly to the firm. As Lazear (1979, 1981) posits, in order to discourage such behavior, the firm uses delayed compensation. Suppose, in addition, that workers are heterogeneous in their propensity to shirk or steal from the firm; that is, some workers are more likely to shirk or steal than others. Since delayed payments are costly to the firm (Hutchens 1986), the firm can reduce both the cost of delayed payments and the likelihood of shirking and malfeasance by filling the job with a particularly honest and hardworking employee. (It is reasonable to assume that a worker with a very low propensity to shirk or steal can be induced to forgo shirking and malfeasance with minimal delayed compensation. And less delayed compensation implies a lower fixed cost of the form analyzed in my 1986 study.) If there are informational asymmetries whereby the firm has better information on insiders than outsiders (if information on the propensity to shirk or steal takes the form of the variable A above), then the best worker for a job with a delayed payment contract may well be an insider.[3] For purposes of the subsequent empirical work, it is useful to state this as a hypothesis.

Hypothesis 2: *Jobs with the characteristics of delayed payment contracts, such as defined-benefit pensions, high wages, and long job tenures, are particularly likely to be filled from the inside, ceteris paribus.*

Asymmetries in the firm's information on insiders versus outsiders also imply a hypothesis about the size of the firm. To see this, consider two firms. The first firm, the small firm, has one M-job and one R-job. The second firm, the large firm, has one M-job and 100 R-jobs. Both fill the M-job with an insider when $\max_{i=1,N}\{A_i\} > E(A)$. Other things being equal, this condition is less likely to be met in the small firm. When the small firm observes A_i for its one R-job worker, it may be disappointed. The worker's ability to do the M-job may be so low that the firm would rather fill the M-job with an outside worker of unknown ability; a random draw from the outside would be better than promotion of an untalented insider. This is less likely for the large firm, since it has more employees in the R-job. In a sense, the large firm has more chances at finding an R-job employee who can perform well in the M-job. Thus, given informational asymmetries, large firms are less likely to fill jobs from the outside, *ceteris paribus.*

Of course, firm size may also influence fixed costs and the presence of delayed payment contracts. Large firms tend to have higher survival probabilities than small firms (Idson 1996), and long-term relationships are thereby more feasible in large firms. Consequently, jobs involving fixed costs and delayed-payment contracts should be more likely to arise in large firms. The point of the above argument is that firm size should have an independent effect on whether a job is filled with an outside hire. Even after controlling for fixed costs and delayed payment contracts, larger firms should be more likely to fill jobs from the inside. Thus,

Hypothesis 3: *Jobs in large firms are more likely to be filled from the inside than jobs in small firms, ceteris paribus.*

An empirical test of the third hypothesis is reasonably straightforward. One simply needs a measure of firm size. The subsequent empirical work uses information on the number of employees in the establishment as well as the larger organization. The other two hypotheses require proxies for

---

[3] These arguments are similar to those in Aoki (1988, 1990). Aoki's J-firm not only uses delayed compensation, but also uses screening mechanisms to weed out low-productivity workers. Implicit in Aoki's discussion is the idea that, at least for some components of productivity, the firm has better information on insiders than outsiders.

fixed costs as well as delayed-payment contracts. Since the hypotheses will be tested in data on jobs from a survey of establishments, the testing requires some discussion.

A test of the first hypothesis requires proxies indicating whether or not a job involves fixed costs. Here, I focus on a particularly important form of fixed costs: specific training. Three proxies will be used to indicate whether a job involves specific training: the number of months required for a newly hired worker to learn the job, whether the job rarely involves employer-sponsored training, and whether the person who currently fills the job has skills that are easily transferred to other organizations. All of these variables are described in the subsequent section. Consistent with the first hypothesis, firms should be more likely to hire an outsider into a job that is quickly learned, that involves little employer-sponsored training, and that requires skills that are easily transferred to other employers.

A test of the second hypothesis requires proxies for delayed compensation. Three proxies drawn from information on the person who currently fills the job are used here, specifically, the length of the person's tenure with the firm, whether the person has a defined-benefit pension, and the person's wage. Consistent with the second hypothesis, larger values of these variables are expected to be associated with a lower likelihood of hiring an outsider into the job.[4] Of course, while these variables may reveal the presence of delayed compensation, they do not speak to the question of whether the delayed compensation is due to shirking and malfeasance, as depicted by Lazear (1979, 1981). For example, a longer tenure with the firm and a higher wage could conceivably be due to specific training. The same issue is discussed in Hutchens (1986, 1987).

6.3. The data

Unlike much of the previous research on hiring older workers, the present study uses data from establishment interviews. Thanks to a grant from the Sloan Foundation, between June 2001 and November 2002, the University of Massachusetts Center for Survey Research conducted telephone interviews in a representative sample of 950 establishments in the continental

---

[4] The data pertain to jobs currently held by older workers. Under a delayed-payment contract, older workers should receive relatively high wages in such jobs, ceteris paribus. Under a delayed-payment contract a defined-benefit pension is more likely than a defined-contribution pension because it is easier to fashion a defined-benefit pension so that a worker who is dismissed for shirking or malfeasance suffers a loss in future pension benefits.

US on the topic of phased retirement by white-collar workers. My collea-gue Karen Grace-Martin and I used the data to analyze why establishments differ in their policies toward phased retirement (Hutchens and Grace-Martin 2006). This chapter uses the same survey to examine employer hiring behavior.

At the outset it is useful to define an establishment. An establishment is a single physical location at which business is conducted or services or industrial operations are performed. An establishment may or may not be part of a larger organization (such as a business with several addresses). For purposes of studying hiring behavior, establishment-level data are arguably better than data collected from the larger organization. In con-trast to, say, a survey of upper-level executives at corporate headquarters, establishment-level respondents are more likely to know how policy is actually implemented. To obtain detailed information in a relatively brief interview, the survey focused on white-collar workers. The sample was restricted to establishments not engaged in either agriculture or mining, with 20 or more employees, and at least two white-collar employees aged 55 or more. The last restriction insured that questions about phased retirement were relevant to the establishment's current situation.[5]

The sample universe was the Dun and Bradstreet Strategic Marketing Record for December 2000, a comprehensive listing of establishment addresses in the United States. The main source of these data is credit inquiries, although information is also obtained from the US Postal Service, banks, newspapers, yellow pages, and other public records. (Kalleberg et al. 1990 provide a particularly useful introduction to these data, along with a discussion of their advantages and disadvantages.) To insure adequate numbers of large establishments, the sample was stratified by establishment size.

The survey was conducted by telephone. The survey research firm first contacted the establishment and asked to speak with the person who was best able to answer questions about flexible work schedules and employee benefits, in many cases a human resource manager or benefits manager. Interviews were conducted with a CATI (Computer-Assisted Telephone Interviewing) system, thereby permitting an interview to be completed over several phone calls. Although this technology simplified the inter-view process, new technologies on the respondents' side (in particular,

---

[5] Given the restrictions on the sample, the results cannot be compared with a benchmark survey. There exists no comparable national survey of establishments that includes infor-mation on the demographics of the establishment's workforce. We have, however, com-pared the industry, region, and union characteristics of this sample with the Health and Retirement Survey sample of older white-collar workers in establishments with more than 20 employees. The results are remarkably similar.

answering machines) complicated matters. The median number of telephone calls required to complete an interview was 10 with 10% of the interviews requiring 30, or more calls to complete.

The overall response rate was 61%. Most of the unit nonresponses occurred when screening establishments for eligibility (e.g., having at least two white-collar employees age 55+), and before respondents knew the purpose of the survey. Interviews were completed in 89% of the establishments that were successfully screened. This is on a par with other establishment-level telephone surveys.

After asking a series of question about the characteristics of the establishment and its human resource and pension policies, the interviewer proceeded as follows:

So far, we have been talking about general policies at your establishment. I'd now like to ask about more specific situations. In order to answer these questions, it is easiest to talk about an actual person who does an actual job in your establishment

To begin with, I would like you to give me the first names of three men [or three women] age 55 or over who are full-time white-collar employees in your establishment. If it would make you more comfortable, you can give me fictitious names, but please think of specific employees. You should know the work of these employees reasonably well. For example, they may be people you supervise. If possible, it would be best if these three employees have different job titles.

This question was randomized on gender. Roughly half of the employers were asked to select three men, while the other half were asked to select three women. Of course, if the respondent did not know of three older men (women) in the establishment, we accepted the other gender.

Given the three first names, we then randomly selected one of the names and asked questions about the characteristics of the selected worker, the nature of that worker's job, and what the firm would do if the worker left. Particularly important for the present study was the following question, subsequently denoted as Q1:

Q1. If [NAME] were to leave her/his job, we'd like to know how likely it is that the job would be filled with a *new hire*, as opposed to someone already employed by your establishment. On a scale from 1 to 5 where *1 means not at all likely* and *5 means very likely*, how likely is it that [NAME]'s job would be filled with a new hire?

1. Not at all likely	# responses = 129/814	(15.8%)
2.	= 125/814	(15.4%)
3.	= 186/814	(22.9%)
4.	= 131/814	(16.1%)
5. Very likely	= 236/814	(29.0%)
6. Job probably wouldn't be replaced	= 1/814	(0.1%)
7. Don't know/Not sure	= 6/814	(0.7%)

Representatives of 814 establishments answered this question. In most cases, those who did not refused to provide information on a selected individual. The percentages in parentheses indicate the distribution of responses.

Answers to the question provide data on the marginal probability, Pr(Hire in j). The survey did not ask a question about the conditional probability Pr(OHire in j | Hire in j). As noted above, by admitting that a younger worker would be preferred to an otherwise equivalent older worker, an employer could open up a hornet's nest of legal liability. Since honest reporting was unlikely in response to the conditional question, we decided not to ask it. Thus, this study focuses on the marginal probability, for which the survey provides high-quality information.

Table 6.1 presents an overview of the data. Column 1 presents averages within the sample of establishments where the answer to Q1 was 4 or 5, and column 3 presents a similar average within the sample of establishments where the answer to Q1 was 1 or 2. The standard deviations of these averages are in columns 2 and 4. Thus, the first entry in column 1 indicates that for those establishments where the selected worker's job would likely be filled with a new hire, 28% of the selected workers were managers. The corresponding number in column 3 is 44%, and, as indicated by the asterisk, this difference between columns 1 and 3 is statistically significant at a .05 level. Of course, this result is no surprise; firms often prefer to select managers from the ranks of existing employees. Although managers are sometimes hired from the outside, that is rather unusual. Note that the phenomenon does not arise in the second row. Jobs held by professionals (accountants, engineers, lawyers) are relatively *more* likely to be filled from the outside.

Panel B of Table 6.1 presents data on the demographic characteristics of the selected worker. While health and gender are not significantly different in columns 1 and 3, there are differences in age, tenure in the establishment, and education. As one would expect, the average tenure is shorter for selected workers in jobs that are filled from the outside. In contrast, the average education is larger for these workers. This education

Table 6.1. Descriptive statistics on jobs by whether job is filled with an outside hire

| | Employer Response to Question about Whether Job is Likely to be Filled with an Outside Hire (Q1) | | | | Fraction Missing in Sample (5) |
| | "Yes" (Q1 = 4, 5) | | "No" (Q1 = 1, 2) | | |
	Mean[a] (1)	Stand Error (2)	Mean[a] (3)	Stand Error (4)	
A. Occupation of the selected worker's job					
1. Manager	0.28*	0.02	0.44	0.03	0.00
2. Professional	0.48*	0.03	0.31	0.03	0.00
3. Sales	0.06	0.01	0.04	0.01	0.00
4. Clerical	0.18	0.02	0.21	0.03	0.00
B. Demographic characteristics of selected worker (SW)					
5. Age	58.43*	0.19	58.90	0.27	0.00
6. Education (years)	15.09*	0.10	14.69	0.13	0.02
7. Health (0=worst possible, 10=best possible)	7.61	0.10	7.79	0.11	0.04
8. Gender (1=male; 0=female)	0.48	0.03	0.50	0.03	0.00
9. Job tenure in establishment (years)	13.24*	0.47	16.63	0.59	0.01
C. Characteristics of selected worker's job					
10. SW's salary (in thousands of $)	53.81*	2.23	69.72	5.40	0.09
11. Number of hours worked by SW in a typical week	42.56	0.43	43.00	0.47	0.01
12. SW covered by a defined benefit pension (1=yes; 0=no)	0.34*	0.03	0.47	0.03	0.02
13. SW's job is covered by union contract (1=yes; 0=no)	0.13	0.02	0.15	0.02	0.00

(continued)

Table 6.1. Continued

	Employer Response to Question about Whether Job is Likely to be Filled with an Outside Hire (Q1)				
	"Yes" (Q1 = 4, 5)		"No" (Q1 = 1, 2)		Fraction Missing in Sample (5)
	Mean[a] (1)	Stand Error (2)	Mean[a] (3)	Stand Error (4)	
14. There is rarely employer-sponsored training in SW's job 1 = yes (rarely); 0 = no	0.20	0.02	0.22	0.03	0.01
15. Are SW's skills transferable to other organizations? 1 = not at all; 3 = very	2.48*	0.03	2.34	0.04	0.01
D. What if the job is filled with an outside hire?					
16. Number of months for a new hire to learn SW's job?	11.93*	0.89	14.33	1.08	0.03
17. Ideal education for the new hire. 1 = high school grad; 4 = graduate work or degree	2.86	0.05	2.91	0.06	0.06
18. Ideal amount of experience for the new hire (years)	5.04*	0.18	5.99	0.25	0.02
19. How desirable to fill job with a recent graduate? 1 = not at all desirable; 5 = very desirable	2.44*	0.06	1.78	0.07	0.01
E. Characteristics of the establishment					
20. Size of establishment	225*	25	336	62	0.00
21. Size of organization	3865*	882	6657	1373	0.05
22. Establishment is part of a larger organization	0.34*	0.02	0.44	0.03	0.00

Industry of establishment				
23. Construction	0.02	0.01	0.02	0.00
24. Manufacturing	0.15*	0.02	0.23	0.00
25. Transportation, communications, and utilities	0.04*	0.01	0.06	0.00
26. Wholesale and retail trade	0.11	0.02	0.09	0.00
27. Finance	0.05	0.01	0.05	0.00
28. Health, education, and social services	0.14	0.02	0.15	0.00
29. Other services	0.42*	0.03	0.28	0.00
30. Public administration	0.07*	0.01	0.13	0.00
Region of establishment				
31. East	0.18	0.02	0.15	0.00
32. Central	0.30	0.02	0.28	0.00
33. South	0.33	0.02	0.31	0.00
34. West	0.19*	0.02	0.26	0.00

[a] Column 1 indicates the fraction of those establishments that responded "yes" to Q1 that had the row characteristics, and column 3 indicates the fraction of those establishments that responded "no" to Q1 that had the row characteristics. Thus, the occupation, industry, and region categories sum to 1 in both columns 1 and 3.

* The difference between the means in columns 1 and 3 is statistically significant at a .05 level.

result is consistent with the above result on professionals: highly educated professionals are often in jobs that are filled from the outside.

Panel C of Table 6.1 presents information on salient characteristics of the selected worker's job. There are clear differences in compensation. Selected workers in jobs that are filled from the outside tend to be paid less and are less likely to have a defined-benefit pension. Although not shown in this table, the pensions in jobs filled from the outside tend to be defined-contribution pensions. Note also that average weekly hours are roughly the same in columns 1 and 3; the difference in compensation is evidently not simply a consequence of people working longer hours. When selecting workers for discussion, the respondents were asked to focus on full-time workers. (It should also be noted that a check on health-insurance coverage between columns 1 and 3 jobs reveals no difference.) Although the next two variables in panel C—union status and training—have similar means in columns 1 and 3, the final variable in panel C indicates differences in something like specific training. Respondents were asked,

> How transferable are the skills involved in doing [NAME]'s job to other organizations? Would you say not at all transferable, somewhat transferable, or very transferable?

For jobs that were filled from the outside, skills were perceived to be significantly more transferable.

Panel D of Table 6.1 presents data on filling the selected worker's job with an outside hire. The survey posed the following questions, which correspond to variables 16–19 in Table 6.1.

> About how long do you think it would take someone hired from outside your establishment to *master the skills* and *gain the knowledge* necessary to be fully comfortable performing [NAME]'s current job duties?

> If [NAME] were to leave her/his position and the job was filled with a new hire, what would be the ideal level of education for this new hire?

> 1. High school graduate or GED

> 2. Technical diploma or degree

> 3. College degree

> 4. Graduate work or degree

If [NAME] were to leave her/his position and the job was filled with a new hire, what would be the *ideal number of years of experience* for this new hire?

If [NAME] were to leave her/his position and the job was filled with a new hire, we'd like to know how desirable it would be to fill the job with a *recent graduate*. On a scale from 1 to 5, where *1 means not at all desirable* and *5 means very desirable*, how likely is it that [NAME]'s job would be filled with a recent graduate?

Survey respondents indicated that jobs that were filled from the outside took somewhat less time to learn (variable 16) than those that were filled from the inside. Table 6.1 indicates that for jobs that were filled from the inside, employers did not seek a significantly higher level of education (variable 17). They did, however, want a higher level of experience (variable 18) in such jobs. Consistent with this result, employers were much less likely to fill such jobs with a new graduate (variable 19).

This result on "experience" is both unexpected and paradoxical. In searching for a new job, older workers have one clear advantage over younger workers: they have more experience. The Table 6.1 result on "experience" suggests that an older worker's experience is, in fact, of limited benefit; when an employer wants to put an experienced worker in a job, the employer prefers to not hire a new outside worker. Rather, the employer tends to fill the job from the inside. Such employers may, instead, go outside to hire workers into different entry jobs at the bottom of a job ladder and concentrate on hiring young workers. This result is explored further in the subsequent multivariate analysis.

The final block of rows in Table 6.1 (Block E) presents information on the characteristics of the selected individual's establishment. With regard to organization size, in those cases where an establishment did not belong to a larger organization, organization size equaled establishment size. As expected, smaller establishments and smaller organizations were more likely to fill jobs from the outside. Note also the industry results: establishments in manufacturing, public administration, and transport, communications, and utilities tended to fill jobs from the inside; establishments in "other" services (services other than health, education, and social services) tended to fill from the outside.

The results in Table 6.1 strongly suggest that an employer's propensity to fill a job with an outside hire not only varies between establishments but also between jobs in establishments. These cross-tabulations indicate that some jobs, particularly those with more generous compensation, are more likely to be filled from the inside. There remains the issue of whether such results remain valid in multivariate models.

6.4. Multivariate results

Table 6.2 presents ordered probit models of the employer's response to Q1. For this ordered probit the dependent variable ranges from a low value of one to a high value of five, and estimation involves selecting parameters $\alpha_1, \alpha_2, \ldots, \alpha_4$ (referred to as "cut points") and β in a model of the form

$$P_1 = \Phi(\alpha_1 + \beta' \mathbf{x})$$

$$P_2 = \Phi(\alpha_2 + \beta' \mathbf{x}) - \Phi(\alpha_1 + \beta' \mathbf{x})$$

$$P_3 = \Phi(\alpha_3 + \beta' \mathbf{x}) - \Phi(\alpha_2 + \beta' \mathbf{x})$$

$$P_4 = \Phi(\alpha_4 + \beta' \mathbf{x}) - \Phi(\alpha_3 + \beta' \mathbf{x})$$

$$P_5 = 1 - \Phi(\alpha_4 + \beta' \mathbf{x}),$$

where $P_1, P_2, \ldots P_5$ are the probabilities corresponding to the five values of the dependent variable, $\Phi()$ is the cumulative standard normal distribution function, and $\mathbf{x}$ is a vector of explanatory variables. Models were estimated after observations with missing data were deleted from the sample.

The first model in Table 6.2 includes variables indicating the selected worker's occupation and level of education. These variables essentially act as controls for the nature of the job, and are thus included in the subsequent models. The negative coefficient on the manager occupation variable indicates that managerial jobs tend to not be filled from the outside. Note, however, from the associate t-statistic that the coefficient is not statistically significant at conventional levels. Indeed, the only statistically significant coefficient in this first model is the positive coefficient on years of education. Thus, as the education requirements of a job increase, the job is more likely to be filled from the outside.

Model 2 introduces three proxies for specific training: the number of months for a newly hired worker to learn the job, whether the person who currently fills the job has skills that are easily transferred to other organizations, and whether the job rarely involves employer-sponsored training. From the first hypothesis, we expect outside hires to be more likely in jobs that require few months to learn, that involve skills that are easily

Table 6.2. *Employer response to question about whether job is likely to be filled with an outside hire (Q1)*

(Models estimated with ordered probit; dependent variable ranges from 1 [Not likely] to 5 [Very likely])

Variable Name	Model 1		Model 2		Model 3	
	Coeff.	t	Coeff.	t	Coeff.	t
Occupation[a] and education of the selected worker (SW)						
Occupation is manager	−0.3131	(1.5)	−0.3660	(1.8)	−0.2172	(1.0)
Occupation is professional	0.0033	(0.0)	−0.0250	(0.1)	0.1410	(0.7)
Occupation is clerical	−0.0686	(0.3)	−0.1682	(0.8)	−0.0606	(0.3)
Education (years)	0.0608	(2.7)	0.0616	(2.7)	0.0720	(3.1)
Proxies for specific training						
There is rarely employer-sponsored training in SW's job			−0.0312	(0.3)	−0.0470	(0.5)
Number of months for a new hire to learn SW's job			−0.0095	(3.1)	−0.0066	(2.1)
SW's skills are very transferable to other organizations			0.1510	(2.3)	0.1470	(2.2)
Proxies for delayed payment contracts						
SW covered by a defined benefit pension					−0.2133	(2.5)
SW's job tenure in establishment (years)					−0.0144	(3.1)
SW's salary (in thousands of $)					−0.0017	(2.7)
Ideal experience and education of a new hire						
Ideal experience (years)						
Ideal education (1 = high school; 4 = graduate school)						
Establishment and organization size (number employees)						
Organization size						
Organization size squared						
Establishment size						
Establishment size squared						
Industry and region dummies included	No		No		No	
Cutpoints						
Cut 1	−0.8664		−0.6768		−0.8794	
Cut 2	−0.3251		−0.1225		−0.3064	
Cut 3	0.2736		0.4832		0.3148	
Cut 4	0.7168		0.9275		0.7656	
Log likelihood	−1084.40		−1076.90		−1063.18	
Pseudo R square	0.01		0.02		0.03	
N	695		695		695	

(continued)

Table 6.2. *Continued*

Variable Name	Model 4 Coeff.	t	Model 5 Coeff.	t	Model 6 Coeff.	t
Occupation[a] and education of the selected worker (SW)						
Occupation is manager	−0.0589	(0.3)	−0.0644	(0.3)	−0.1746	(0.8)
Occupation is professional	0.2991	(1.4)	0.2859	(1.3)	0.1813	(0.8)
Occupation is clerical	−0.1054	(0.5)	−0.0873	(0.4)	−0.1745	(0.7)
Education (years)	−	−	−	−	−	−
Proxies for specific training						
There is rarely employer-sponsored training in SW's job	−0.0546	(0.5)	−0.0704	(0.7)	−0.0472	(0.4)
Number of months for a new hire to learn SW's job	−0.0050	(1.6)	−0.0045	(1.4)	−0.0051	(1.6)
SW's skills are very transferable to other organizations	0.1653	(2.4)	0.1729	(2.5)	0.1694	(2.4)
Proxies for delayed payment contracts						
SW covered by a defined benefit pension	−0.2093	(2.3)	−0.1730	(1.9)	−0.1999	(2.1)
SW's job tenure in establishment (years)	−0.0170	(3.5)	−0.0156	(3.2)	−0.0158	(3.2)
SW's salary (in thousands of $)	−0.0013	(2.0)	−0.0013	(2.0)	−0.0012	(1.8)
Ideal experience and education of a new hire						
Ideal experience (years)	−0.0315	(2.4)	−0.0320	(2.4)	−0.0304	(2.2)
Ideal education (1 = high school; 4 = graduate school)	0.0748	(1.3)	0.0792	(1.4)	0.0838	(1.4)
Establishment and organization size						
Organization size (thousands of employees)			−0.0168	(2.9)	−0.0163	(2.8)
Organization size squared			0.0001	(2.3)	0.0001	(2.2)
Establishment size (thousands of employees)			−0.0637	(0.8)	−0.0658	(0.9)
Establishment size squared			0.0020	(0.8)	0.0021	(0.8)
Industry and region dummies included	No		No		Yes	
Cutpoints						
Cut 1	−1.0299		−1.0510		−0.8561	
Cut 2	−0.4397		−0.4563		−0.2570	
Cut 3	0.1723		0.1606		0.3677	
Cut 4	0.6167		0.6105		0.8231	
Log likelihood	−984.40		−978.87		−973.66	
Pseudo R square	0.03		0.04		0.04	
N	644		644		644	

[a.] The missing occupation is sales.

transferred to other organizations, and that rarely involve employer-sponsored training. At least for the first two variables, the results in Model 2 are consistent with those predictions. Interestingly, however, the coefficient on employer-sponsored training has an unexpected sign and is not statistically significant. Of course, that may simply reveal that the other two variables are better proxies for specific training. Alternatively, this variable may not adequately measure employer-sponsored training. The relevant training may have occurred in previous jobs at the firm before the selected worker moved to his or her current job.

Model 3 in Table 6.2 introduces three proxies for delayed-payment contracts: the selected worker's wage, tenure with the firm, and a variable indicating that the worker has a defined-benefit pension. From the second hypothesis, jobs with delayed-payment contracts are expected to be filled from the inside. As such, the three proxies are expected to have negative coefficients. The results in Model 3 fully accord with that hypothesis.

As noted above, the three proxies for delayed-payment contracts may not necessarily reveal the delayed-payment contracts described in Lazear (1979, 1981). They could conceivably be associated with specific training or other forms of fixed cost. Note, however, that the coefficients on the measures of specific training in the model are largely unaffected by inclusion of these proxies.

The fourth model introduces the employer's assessment of the ideal education and experience of a new hire for the job currently occupied by the selected worker. Note that when these variables are entered, the actual education of the selected worker is dropped from the model. Note also that the number of observations falls with this model. This is because several respondents answered, "Don't know" to the question about ideal education.

As was the case in Table 6.1, the ideal experience variable is negatively and significantly related to the employer's propensity to fill the job with a new outside worker. There is, then, evidence that an older worker's experience is of limited value when looking for a new job. When employers want an experienced worker, they tend to fill the job from the inside.

One can only speculate about the economic forces that underlie this unexpected result. A possible explanation focuses on asymmetric information. Perhaps when respondents say that several years of experience would be ideal, what they are really saying is that the ideal person for this job should have qualities that are revealed only with time—for example, leadership skills, the ability to "get things done," or integrity. It is interesting that the word "experience" is often used this way in the world of national politics. An "experienced" politician has survived a series of challenging tests and thereby revealed qualities that are valued in a leader. Perhaps the same is true within the firm.

If "experience" really means qualities that are revealed only with time, then an outsider may be at a disadvantage in relation to an insider. The firm arguably has better information on such hard-to-observe qualities for insiders. Indeed, it may use rank-order tournaments to obtain information on such traits. By this interpretation, the result on "ideal experience" in Model 4 reveals a paradox. Those jobs for which older workers *should* have a comparative advantage—jobs where years of experience are of value—are paradoxically jobs for which firms do not hire outside older workers. Although there are undoubtedly outside older workers who can perform well in the jobs, firms tend to fill such jobs with *inside* older workers.

Model 5 introduces measures of establishment size and organization size. Consistent with the third hypothesis, larger establishments and organizations are more likely to fill the job from the inside, *ceteris paribus*. (For most of the establishments and organizations in the sample, the quadratic is decreasing. It reaches a minimum at an establishment size of 16,364 and an organization size of 96,377.) Only the result for organization size is statistically significant, however, at conventional levels. Note that the other variables in the model—the proxies for specific training and for delayed compensation—do not change dramatically when firm-size variables are included. This result is consistent with the argument associated with the third hypothesis; that is, these measures of establishment and organizational size are not simply proxies for specific training or delayed-payment contracts. Asymmetric information may also play a role here. Larger firms may be less likely to fill jobs from the outside because they know there is an insider who has better productivity characteristics than the average outsider.

Finally, Model 6 introduces a vector of industry and region dummies. The results reinforce the conclusion that there is evidence in support of the three initial hypotheses. Jobs that are embedded in large organizations, that involve specific training, and that have characteristics of delayed-payment contracts tend to be filled from the inside. Inclusion of the industry and region dummies has little effect on the estimated coefficients.

6.5 Conclusion

Older workers bring many positive attributes to the job. Not only do they have a reputation for excellent work habits (AARP 2000), but they can also draw on a lifetime of experiences. As such, it is interesting that older workers have difficulty finding new jobs. In particular, employers appear not to hire older workers for jobs that are currently held by older workers, jobs that older workers can obviously do.

Of course, some of this could be due to prejudice and age discrimination. The point of the economic literature on this topic is that other forces may also be at work. Barriers to hiring older workers could be not only age discrimination, but also economic phenomena associated with the activities of the firm.

This chapter argues that one reason why older people are not hired for jobs currently held by older workers is that the jobs are often filled from the inside. The employer simply does not fill the job with a new worker— either young or old. The empirical evidence indicates that jobs currently held by older workers are more likely to be filled from the inside when they involve fixed costs associated with specific training, they involve delayed-payment contracts, they require a more experienced worker, and the job is embedded in a large organization.

Although the previous literature on why older workers are employed but not hired for some jobs has been based largely on a theory of fixed costs, this study suggests that other explanations need to be considered. In particular, asymmetric information on the characteristics of inside versus outside workers may provide a useful theoretical basis for predicting when jobs will be filled from the inside.

The empirical result on "ideal experience" may be particularly revealing. One would think that older workers would have a comparative advantage in jobs that require several years of experience. Yet, this study finds that such jobs are precisely the kinds of jobs that employers tend to fill from the inside. Although there may well be outside older workers who are qualified to do such jobs, they do not have an opportunity to compete for them. The employer prefers to fill such jobs with insiders.

From a governmental policy perspective, this result provides support for policies that encourage retention of older workers. The governments of both the United States and Japan are trying to increase the labor force participation of older people. One way to do that is by reducing hiring barriers and creating greater job opportunities for older workers. Another way to proceed is to encourage the retention of older workers in their career jobs. There are advantages in emphasizing retention. If a specific job is the highest and best use of a worker's labor when he is 50 years old, then that is likely to still be true when he or she is 63 or 65. Moreover, as indicated in this study, an employee's "experience" may be of value primarily to the current employer. While other employers have jobs for which experience is important, they do not hire outside older workers for those jobs.

In this regard, aspects of Japan's 2004 legislation on employment of older persons may provide a useful model to other countries (Japan Institute for Labour Policy and Training 2004). The legislation contains several provisions that encourage employers to maintain the employment of current older workers. Moreover, in the event that an older worker is laid off for economic reasons, the employer must assist that person in finding new employment by providing documents about his or her professional experiences and skills. The legislation thus not only emphasizes retention, but also helps improve market information on workers who are not retained. Such policies increase the likelihood that an experienced older person will work for an employer who values that experience.

References

American Association of Retired Persons (AARP). (2000). *American Business and Older Employees.* Washington, DC.

Aoki, Masahiko (1988). *Information, Incentives, and Bargaining in the Japanese Economy.* Cambridge: Cambridge University Press.

———. 1990. "Toward an economic model of the Japanese firm". *Journal of Economic Literature* 28(1): 1–27.

Baker, George, Michael Gibbs, and Bengt Holmstrom. 1994. "The internal economics of the firm: Evidence from personnel data". *The Quarterly Journal of Economics* 1099(4): 881–919.

Burtless, Gary and Joseph F. Quinn. 2001. "Retirement trends and policies to encourage work among older Americans". in: Peter P. Budetti, Richard V. Burkhauser, Janice M. Gregory, and H. Allan Hunt, eds, *Ensuring Health and Income Security for an Aging Workforce*, Kalamzoo, MI: W.E. Upjohn Institute. 375–415.

Chan, Sewin and Ann Huff Stevens. 2001. "Job loss and employment patterns of older workers". *Journal of Labor Economics* 19(2): 484–521.

Chan, William 1996. "External recruitment versus internal promotion". *Journal of Labor Economics* 14(4): 555–70.

Chen, Kong-Pin 2005. "External recruitment as an incentive device". *Journal of Labor Economics* 23(2): 259–278.

Committee for Economic Development. 1999. *New Opportunities for Older Workers.* New York.

Demougin, Dominique and Aloysius Siow. 1994. "Careers in ongoing hierarchies". *American Economic Review* 84(5): 1261–77.

Garen, John, Mark Berger, and Frank Scott. 1996. "Pensions, non-discrimination policies, and the employment of older workers". *Quarterly Review of Economics and Finance* 36(4): 417–28.

Heywood, John S., Lok-Sang Ho, and Xiangdong Wei. 1999. "Determinants of hiring older workers: Evidence from Hong Kong". *Industrial and Labor Relations Review* 52(3): 444–59.

Hirsch, Barry T., David A. Macpherson, and Melissa A. Hardy. 2000. "Occupational age structure and access for older workers". *Industrial and Labor Relations Review* 53(3): 401–18.

Hu, Luojia 2003. "The hiring decisions and compensation structures of large firms". *Industrial and Labor Relations Review* 56(4): 663–81.

Hutchens, Robert M. 1986. "Delayed payment contracts and a firm's propensity to hire older workers". *Journal of Labor Economics* 4(4): 439–57.

———. 1987. "A test of Lazear's theory of delayed payment contracts". *Journal of Labor Economics* 5(4): S153–S170.

Hutchens, Robert M. and Karen Grace-Martin. 2006. "Employer willingness to permit phased retirement: Why are some more willing than others?". *Industrial and Labor Relations Review* 59(4): 525–46.

Idson, Todd L. 1996. "Employer size and labor turnover". *Research in Labor Economics* 15: 273–304.

Japan Institute for Labour Policy and Training. 2004. *Law Concerning Stabilization of Employment of Older Persons (Law 68 of May 25, 1971)* amended on 11 June 2004, 47. http://www.jil.go.jp/english/laborinfo/library/documents/llj_law16.pdf.

Kalleberg, Arne, Peter Marsden, Howard Aldrich, and James Cassell. 1990. "Comparing organizational sampling frames". *Administrative Science Quarterly* 35: 658–88.

Lazear, Edward P. 1979. "Why is there mandatory retirement?". *Journal of Political Economy* 87(6): 1261–84.

———. 1981. "Agency, earnings profiles, productivity, and hours restrictions". *American Economic Review* 71(4): 606–20.

Lazear, Edward P. and Paul Oyer. 2004. "Internal and external labor markets: A personnel economics approach". *Labour Economics* 11(5): 527–54.

Mitani, Naoki. 2002. Employment of older workers in Japan: Employment policies and labor demand. Paper presented at the Conference on Population Change, Labor Market Transition, and Economic Development in Asia, Taipei, Taiwan, 7–9 December.

Novos, Ian E. 1995. "Imperfections in labor markets and the scope of the firm". *International Journal of Industrial Organization* 13: 387–410.

Oi, Walter. 1962. "Labor as a quasi-fixed factor". *Journal of Political Economy* 70(6): 538–55.

Organization for Economic Co-operation and Development (OECD). 2004. *Ageing and Employment Policies: Japan.* Paris.

Prendergast, Canice. 1999. "The provision of incentives in firms". *Journal of Economic Literature* 37(1): 7–63.

Scott, Frank A., Mark C. Berger, and John E. Garen. 1995. "Do health insurance and pension costs reduce the job opportunities of older workers?". *Industrial and Labor Relations Review* 48(4): 775–91.

United States (US). Census Bureau, Population Division, Population Projections Branch. 2002. National population projections. Washington, D.C. http://www.census.gov/population /www/projections/natdet-D2.html.

Valsecchi, Irene 2000. "Job assignment and promotion". *Journal of Economic Surveys* 14(1): 31–51.

Waldman, Michael 2003. "Ex ante versus ex post optimal promotion rules: The case of internal promotion". *Economic Inquiry* 41(1): 27–41.

CHAPTER 7

Skills, Wages, and the Employment
of Older Workers

Naoki Mitani

Given the rapid aging of Japan's population, the employment of older workers has become a worrisome issue for Japanese society. Promoting employment opportunities for older workers, particularly those 60–64 years old, is especially important because almost all firms have a mandatory retirement age of 60, but the eligibility age for receiving the public pension is being raised gradually from 60 in 2000 to 65 in 2025. More precisely, the eligibility age for receiving the basic payment (fixed part) of the pension benefits will be raised to 65 by 2013, and that for receiving the salary-related benefit will be raised gradually from 60 to 65 by 2025.

The government has been coping with the issue of employment of older workers for some 25 years. Given the extremely low ratio of job offers to job applicants for older workers, the basic strategy has been to raise the mandatory retirement age and to promote continuous employment after the mandatory retirement age in the same company. Continuous employment is defined as employment after the mandatory retirement age and includes re-employment and extended employment. Nonetheless, recent studies have revealed that, under Japan's strict employment-protection legislation, middle-aged and older workers are substituting for young workers in employment, so that maintaining the employment of older workers has negative effects on the employment of young workers. With high youth unemployment, the question of how to implement employment measures that benefit older workers without harming young workers is receiving greater attention.

I am grateful to Professor Hajime Imamura of Toyo University, Dr. Hwang Soo-Kyeong of the Korea Labor Institute, Professor Isao Ohashi of Hitotsubashi University, and the participants of the Kansai Labor Forum for their comments on earlier versions of this chapter. Thanks are also due to the Japan Institute for Labour Policy and Training for permission to use their data.

POPULATION CHANGE, LABOR MARKETS, AND SUSTAINABLE GROWTH
VOLUME 281   ISSN 0573-8555/DOI 10.1016/S0573-8555(07)81007-8

The employment of different age groups, mandatory retirement practices, and the internal wage structure within a firm are closely interrelated.

It is well known that the employment/population ratio varies by occupation. Highly skilled workers tend to continue working until reaching older ages, whereas low-skilled workers are more likely to retire earlier from the labor market. The patterns of retirement across occupations are not straightforward, however, because there are transaction costs within the firm and also institutional factors, such as the mandatory retirement age. The optimal retirement age may differ among occupations. Certainly, it is not always 65, the eligible age derived from the budget considerations of the Public Pension System (Ohashi 1998). Analysis of the employment of older workers by occupation is also important because the structural changes have created a generation-specific occupational distribution, with a higher proportion of older workers in low-skilled occupations and a higher proportion of younger workers in professional and technical occupations.

This chapter analyzes the employment of older workers and the internal wage structure, focusing on skill profiles and occupational groups classified by the required skills. It uses data from a survey of firms, in which the employers provided information on skill profiles, wage profiles, and desirable wages for their employees.

I begin by considering some theoretical predictions based on a simple deferred-payment system. Next, I analyze the relationship between the changing patterns of skills over a person's working age and some indices of employment of older workers. Then, I present an analysis of the slope of the wage profile and the wage differentials in relation to the skill profiles and occupational groups. This is followed by an analysis of the substitution or complementary relationship between older workers and young workers, using the hiring rate of new school leavers. The concluding section summarizes the results.

7.1. Theoretical considerations

In a competitive labor market, where there is no transaction cost[1] and the relationship between an employer and the employee is short-term, employment and wages are simultaneously determined so that the value of marginal product or skill is equal to the wage. However, if there exist transaction costs and the employment relationship is long-term owing to the specificity of a worker's skills, one should take into account other

---

[1] Here, "transaction costs" include such costs as the difficulties of monitoring the skills and performance of a worker or to verify them in a court of law, the difficulties of motivating a worker to make sufficient efforts, and the costs stemming from the specificity of skills (Williamson 1985).

aspects of employment such as human capital accumulation through on-the-job training and incentive contracts (or the wage system) to explain the relationship between skill, wages, and employment.

Figure 7.1 shows a typical relationship between skill, wage, and mandatory retirement age in the latter case. Wages and skill rise as the worker ages. Given the low turnover of employees in Japan, the steeper age–skill profile suggests that firms invest more in firm-specific human capital. These firms are more likely to hire younger workers than older workers, because the investments represent fixed costs regardless of employment duration and younger workers have longer horizons over which the firms can recoup their investments (see Chapter 6). In other words, firms are more likely to hire older workers in occupations requiring low-level skills or involving simple tasks than for jobs requiring higher-level skills.

In addition, to minimize the transaction costs stemming from the difficulty of measuring workers' skills or performance, the firm may adopt a deferred-payment system (Lazear 1979, 1981). In such a system, wages lower than the skill (or the value of marginal product) are paid to younger workers, whereas wages higher than the skill (or the value of marginal product) are paid to older workers. If workers' efforts are lower than promised, then they will be fired. Under this arrangement, a worker is obliged to work hard and there is less moral hazard. But mandatory retirement is necessary to balance the underpayment and overpayment of workers. Of course, a deferred-payment system is not the only cause of wage growth during workers' careers in firms that incur transaction costs. Job assignments and promotions, as well as specific human capital accumulation and efficiency wages, are also important factors explaining

Figure 7.1. Skill, wage, and retirement age

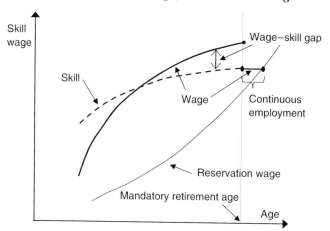

wage growth (see, for example, Gibbons and Waldman 1999). Nonetheless, the effects of the deferred-payment system are in evidence in Japan, as we shall see.

Simple considerations suggest the following:

First, a steeper skill profile is associated with a steeper age–wage profile. Since skill is a proxy for the value of marginal product, wages rise along with the accumulation of skills, or human capital, over an employee's working-age span. Nonetheless, the slope of the wage profile cannot be fully explained by the patterns of skill development over age; also explaining it is the existence of transaction costs, proxies for which may be the attributes of the skills required and the organization of the workplace.[2]

Second, extending the mandatory retirement age will flatten the slope of the wage profile, whereas eliciting more efforts from individual workers, to compensate for a decline in their efforts due to the decline in the rise of wages as workers age, will widen the wage differential. Figure 7.1 suggests that the slope of the wage profile must flatten to balance the underpayment of a younger worker and the overpayment of an older worker when the mandatory retirement age is extended, provided that the starting wage for the young worker is fixed or the worker has already spent enough time to be underpaid under this contract. In effect, Mitani (2003) has found some evidence that is consistent with this prediction. Okunishi (2001) contends that a flexible wage structure, such as a flatter wage profile and a larger wage differential, is necessary to promote the employment of older workers.

Third, the employment of older workers after they reach the mandatory retirement age (so-called "continuous employment") will be greater if the wage–skill gap shown in Figure 7.1 is smaller. At this point, the wages that the firm would like to pay are equal to the workers' skill level, as the underpayment and overpayment of wages are balanced when workers reach the mandatory retirement age. A larger wage–skill gap would induce a greater reduction in wages for those working after the mandatory retirement age, and consequently it would be more likely to induce older workers to retire from the labor market. In addition, a larger wage–skill gap suggests that firms are likely to invest more in firm-specific human capital and to hire younger workers, as mentioned above.

Fourth, the employment of older workers may adversely affect the hiring of young workers under the strict employment-protection legislation. Within the internal labor market, workers move up the job ladder

---

[2] A discrepancy between wages and the value of marginal product also arises from the existence of firm-specific skills (Becker 1964). The costs due to the specificity of the skills may be considered part of the transaction costs.

over their careers (Doeringer and Piore 1971). When a vacancy is created by the retirement of an older worker, a worker in the lower rank is promoted to this vacancy unless it is filled from the external labor market. In turn, the newly created vacancy is filled by a worker in the lower ranks, and finally a vacancy is created at the entry level or in the lowest ranks typically filled by a young worker. Thus, a reduction in the number of retiring older workers reduces the number of hired young workers. This effect is stronger when the internal labor market is more closed or when the fixed costs due to the specificity of the skills are greater. The growing financial burden on firms stemming from the increasing number of older workers under strict employment-protection legislation induces the firms to suppress the hiring of young workers, especially during an economic recession. Several studies have found such negative effects of the employment of older workers on youth employment (e.g., Mitani 2001; Genda 2004). The negative effects may be mitigated if the wage–skill gap is small, because a smaller wage–skill gap suggests that the net wage costs (the wages minus the value of marginal product) needed to maintain the employment of older workers are smaller and that this in turn allows the firm to hire more young workers.

7.1.1. The Data

The problem for empirical analysis is that usually data on skill profiles and skill–wage gaps are not available. In this case, however, it is possible to test the predictions outlined above using data from Japanese firms that provide some information on them. The data used in the analysis are derived from an establishment survey called the "Survey on the Future Use of Middle-Aged and Older Workers in the Company" (simply "the survey" hereafter), conducted by the Japan Institute for Labour Policy and Training among firms with 30 or more employees in February 2004. A questionnaire was sent to 10,126 firms, of which 1704 (or 16.8%) replied. The survey collected data on changing patterns of skills over working age by occupation and the firms' retirement policies, together with information on the slope of the wage profile and wage differentials within the firms. The descriptive statistics are shown in Table 7.A1 in the appendix.

7.2. Skill profiles, occupational groups, and employment indices of older workers

Figures 7.2 and 7.3 show the age–wage profiles and the wage differentials derived from the survey data. From them, we can make the following observations. First, both actual and desirable wages increase gradually

Figure 7.2.   Age–wage profile

(40–49 = 100)

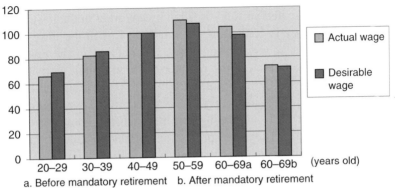

a. Before mandatory retirement   b. After mandatory retirement

Figure 7.3.   Actual and desirable wage differentials

(annual salaries among regular employees
with the same age and tenure)

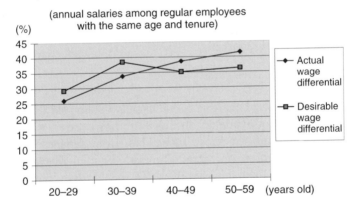

with age to the peak ages of 50–59 years and then decrease gradually. Second, the desirable wages are higher than the actual wages before employees reach ages 40–49, but the relationship is reversed for older workers. If the desirable wages correspond to productivity, these patterns are consistent with the deferred-wage hypothesis shown in Figure 7.1. Third, the actual wage differential increases gradually with age, but the desirable wage differential is highest for employees 30–39 years old, after which age group it decreases somewhat and levels off.

The survey inquired about the changing patterns of skills for the three most common occupations in each firm, as shown in Figure 7.4. With this information, it was possible to estimate the average skill profile for each occupation, based on scores obtained by the ordered probit model. The method I used is as follows. The dependent variable was a dummy variable with a value of 2 for the "rising" age–skill profile, a value of

Figure 7.4.   Types of age–skill profile: (a) Rising, (b) Flat, and (c) Declining (as defined in the questionnaire)

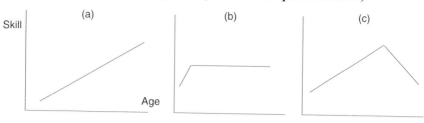

1 for the "flat" profile, and a value of 0 for the "declining" profile, in which skill declines from a certain age. The explanatory variables were the occupation dummies, the firm-size dummies (fewer than 100 employees, 100–999 employees, and 1000 or more employees), and the hiring rate. I estimated the value of the linear part (= the score) in the normal distribution density function for each occupation. I divided the occupations equally into three groups: "rising," "flat," and "declining," by descending order of the average score for each occupation.

Table 7.1, which provides an overview of the changing patterns of skills over age by occupation, shows that the occupations with rising skill profiles were mostly professional and technical, such as scientific researchers, architects, and engineers. Among the occupations with flat profiles were sales workers and service workers. Among occupations with declining profiles were production workers and laborers, such as production workers in manufacturing, transport laborers, and cleaners. Workers were supposed to maintain their occupational skills and to be able to work until older ages, progressing from rising to flat and to declining skill profiles during their working lives.

Nonetheless, the average skill profiles are not necessarily consistent with the ages at which workers can perform. The survey collected information about "the age at which the worker's skill is the highest," "the age at which the worker can work normally," and "the age until which the worker can work ordinarily with some consideration"—which I call the "peak age," the "normal age," and the "consideration age," respectively. Later, I call all of these ages the "turning ages" of the "declining" skill-profiles. Table 7.1 shows that these ages were not so high for the "rising" occupations, although there were some exceptions, such as physicians, dentists, and pharmacists. Rather, the age until which the worker could work ordinarily with some consideration was higher for the occupations with "flat" or "declining" profiles, such as cleaners and caretakers.

These discrepancies become clearer with the use of indices that show the extent of employment of older workers. Those indices were (1) the

Table 7.1. *Age-skill profile and the ages at which workers are able to work, by occupation*

No.	Occupation	Average Skill Profile	Rank of Score	Score (= Xb)	Skill Profile = "Declining" Type		
					Age at Which a Worker can Work Best	Age Until Which a Worker can Work Normally	Age Until Which a Worker can Work with Consideration
1	Scientific researchers	"rising"	6	0.029	40.0	53.6	61.5
2	Agricultural, food processing technicians	"flat"	16	−0.287	42.8	51.8	61.3
3	Architects, civil and surveying engineers	"rising"	4	0.101	45.6	55.8	62.0
4	Information-processing engineers	"declining"	29	−0.887	38.5	47.5	54.6
5	Physicians and dentists	"rising"	2	0.145	46.7	55.5	66.1
6	Nurses	"declining"	23	−0.651	41.7	52.5	61.1
7	Pharmacists	"rising"	10	−0.100	43.3	57.7	66.7
8	Social and welfare workers	"flat"	21	−0.479	41.6	51.7	60.0
9	Managers and officials	"rising"	1	0.341	48.5	56.9	62.8
10	General clerical workers	"rising"	7	0.015	44.3	56.2	62.5
11	Clerical workers in planning	"flat"	12	−0.214	42.5	52.6	58.1
12	Accounting clerks	"rising"	3	0.111	47.2	58.0	62.4
13	Clerical workers in production-related	"rising"	8	0.015	44.4	57.3	62.8
14	Clerical workers in sales	"rising"	9	−0.009	44.0	54.5	60.7
16	Clerical workers in transportation	"rising"	5	0.051	43.2	55.7	63.4
17	Computer operators	"declining"	27	−0.782	39.0	49.6	56.8
18	Shop sales workers	"flat"	15	−0.281	41.4	52.2	59.7

				Xb			
19	Buyers and salespersons	"flat"	11	−0.143	43.2	53.3	60.0
20	Food- and beverage-preparing workers	"flat"	19	−0.383	43.3	53.8	60.5
21	Restaurant service workers	"flat"	18	−0.378	39.5	50.2	58.4
22	Caretakers	"flat"	17	−0.330	50.0	62.8	68.3
23	Protective workers	"declining"	31	−0.951	48.6	58.6	64.6
24	Motormen	"declining"	26	−0.687	48.3	58.3	63.3
25	Automobile drivers	"declining"	32	−1.031	43.2	55.7	62.9
26	Communication workers	"flat"	14	−0.265	46.7	56.0	61.7
27	Mining workers	"flat"	28	−0.785	53.3	62.3	66.7
28	Production-processing workers	"declining"	25	−0.677	42.3	54.4	61.9
29	Stationary-engine, construction-machinery operators, and electrical workers	"declining"	22	−0.500	45.4	55.7	60.7
30	Construction workers	"declining"	30	−0.948	45.2	56.1	63.2
31	Transport laborers	"declining"	33	−1.086	42.4	54.3	62.4
32	Cleaners	"declining"	24	−0.666	49.4	59.4	66.1
33	Other workers	"flat"	20	−0.399	42.6	53.2	59.9
	Total		13	−0.232	43.4	54.4	61.4

Note: Score = value of Xb, obtained by the order-probit model, with the dependent variable being the type of age–skill profile ("rising" = 2, "flat" = 1, "declining" = 0). See Figure 7.4 for the type of age–skill profile in the questionnaire used in this exercise, which is different from the "average skill profile" of each occupation in Table 7.1.

proportion of firms whose mandatory retirement age was 61 or over; (2) the proportion of firms that provided continuous employment after the mandatory retirement age for all employees who wanted it; (3) the proportion of workers aged 60 or over; (4) the proportion of middle-aged and older workers (those aged 50 or over); and (5) the proportion of firms whose retention rate of workers from the baby-boom generation (i.e., those born during 1947–49) was greater than 60%.

According to Table 7.2, in which the five highest figures of the indices are shown in bold-faced letters, the indices for the employment of older workers (ages 60 or over) are not high for professional and technical occupations with rising average skill profiles, but are high for flat or declining average profile occupations such as cleaners, caretakers, protective service workers, and automobile drivers. Similarly, the retention rate of the baby-boom generation is high for some professional and technical occupations such as agricultural food-processing technicians, and managers, and it is also high for some clerical and production occupations such as computer operators, stationary-engine workers, construction-machinery operators, and electrical workers. In sum, there seems to be no consistent relationship between the index and average skill profile.

These findings are also confirmed by econometric analysis. Tables 7.3 and 7.4 show the estimation results of the econometric models (probit or OLS), in which the dependent variables are indices of employment of older workers and the explanatory variables are skill-profile dummies, firm-size dummies, the slope of the age–wage profile (annual wages of workers in their 50s divided by those of workers in their 20s), the wage differential (equal to the maximum minus the minimum of wages of workers in their 40s when the average wages of those in their 40s are normalized to 100), and the wage gap (equal to actual wages minus desirable wages).

According to the results shown in Table 7.3, skill-profile dummies have little significant effect on the employment indices of older workers, except for the flat skill profile, which has a negative significant coefficient for the mandatory-retirement-age dummy, suggesting that the rising-profile occupations are more likely than the flat-profile occupations to have a mandatory retirement age of 61 or over. In contrast, the wage-structure variables have rather significant coefficients. The slope of the wage profile is negatively significant for the dummy for the mandatory retirement age of 61 or over and that for the continuous employment for all employees. It has a positive significant effect on the retention rate of the baby-boom generation. The wage differential is negatively correlated with the dummy for the mandatory retirement age of 61 or over. The wage gap has only negative effects on the proportion of workers aged 60 or over.

Table 7.2.   *Older workers' employment indices by occupation*

No.	Occupation (the most common)	Mandatory Retirement Age	Mandatory Retirement Age > 60 Years	Continuous Employment of all Retirees Who Want it	Proportion 50+ Years Old	Proportion 60+ Years Old	Retention Rate of the Baby-Boom Generation ≥60%
1	Scientific researchers	60.6	11.8	5.9	26.1	2.8	52.9
2	Agricultural, forestry and fishers. food- processing technicians	60.1	8.0	**32.0**	32.1	3.8	**80.0**
3	Architects, civil and surveying engineers	60.3	10.8	8.3	29.3	5.4	57.5
4	Information-processing engineers	60.0	1.7	13.3	10.9	0.9	26.7
5	Physicians and dentists	65.0	100.0	0.0	31.6	6.6	100.0
6	Nurses	60.6	12.7	14.3	18.6	4.3	36.5
7	Pharmacists	60.2	11.1	0.0	10.4	1.1	22.2
8	Social and welfare workers	60.6	14.3	0.0	19.0	4.0	42.9
9	Managers and officials	60.4	7.1	17.9	35.1	3.6	**64.3**
10	General clerical workers	60.8	15.8	5.3	25.4	3.7	52.6
11	Clerical workers in planning	60.3	5.9	17.6	22.6	2.2	52.9
12	Accounting clerks	60.2	**20.0**	6.7	20.5	3.1	46.7
13	Clerical workers in production-related	60.0	0.0	0.0	36.3	4.4	23.1
14	Clerical workers in sales	60.2	6.2	11.0	23.2	3.1	53.1
15	Workers in bill collecting and meter reading	60.0	0.0	0.0	16.0	1.3	33.3
16	Clerical workers in transportation	60.3	9.1	9.1	42.3	7.8	36.4
17	Electric computer operator	60.4	**20.0**	20.0	43.5	**11.2**	**60.0**

(continued)

Table 7.2. Continued

No.	Occupation (the most common)	Mandatory Retirement Age	Mandatory Retirement Age > 60 Years	Continuous Employment of all Retirees Who Want it	Proportion 50+ Years Old	Proportion 60+ Years Old	Retention Rate of the Baby-Boom Generation ≥60%
18	Shop sales workers	60.1	4.4	15.8	19.4	2.0	45.6
19	Buyers and salespersons	60.0	2.8	13.0	20.0	2.2	47.2
20	Food- and beverage-preparing workers	60.0	6.3	12.5	27.8	5.6	31.3
21	Restaurant service workers	60.1	8.5	13.6	25.3	3.1	18.6
22	Caretakers	61.3	12.5	**37.5**	63.0	**29.0**	25.0
23	Protective workers	60.9	**27.8**	**33.3**	52.3	**16.9**	44.4
24	Motormen	60.0	**25.0**	25.0	41.8	2.3	50.0
25	Automobile drivers	60.5	12.2	**32.8**	39.6	6.3	35.9
26	Communication workers	60.0	0.0	0.0	18.8	3.8	0.0
27	Mining workers	60.0	0.0	0.0	34.3	1.6	50.0
28	Production-processing workers	60.2	6.0	20.6	31.1	3.9	54.0
29	Stationary-engine, construction-machinery operators and electrical	60.2	4.2	12.5	29.0	5.9	**70.8**
30	Construction workers	60.7	**23.7**	15.8	35.3	9.7	50.0
31	Tranport laborers	60.5	9.5	19.0	29.1	4.1	42.9
32	Cleaners	61.9	**42.3**	**23.1**	51.5	**18.7**	23.1
33	Other workers	60.5	12.8	11.2	25.7	3.5	**63.2**
	Total	60.3	9.0	16.5	28.0	4.4	48.4

Table 7.3. Skill profiles and older workers' employment indices

Explanatory Variable	Dependent Variable							
	Mandatory Retirement Age ≥61 years		Continuous Employment for all Retirees		Retention Rate of Baby-Boom Generation ≥60%		Proportion of Older Workers Aged 60+	
	Probit		Probit		Probit		OLS	
	coef.	$P > \lvert z \rvert$	coef.	$P > \lvert z \rvert$	coef.	$P > \lvert z \rvert$	coef.	$P > \lvert z \rvert$
(base = skill profile "rising")								
skill profile "flat"	-0.2753*	0.068	0.1709	0.189	0.0221	0.841	0.0011	0.797
skill profile "declining"	-0.1678	0.253	0.1391	0.285	-0.1097	0.312	0.0064	0.287
(base = f_size (1–99))								
f_size (100–999)	-0.2178*	0.068	-0.1353	0.151	0.0266	0.746	-0.0197**	0.000
f_size (1000+)	0.0926	0.641	-0.0372	0.821	0.1025	0.470	-0.0293**	0.000
w_slope	-0.0049*	0.075	-0.0071**	0.002	0.0090**	0.000	-0.0001	0.251
w_differential (40–49)	-0.0062**	0.008	-0.0018	0.276	-0.0013	0.329	-0.0002**	0.008
wage gap (50–59)	-0.0008	0.871	0.0052	0.194	-0.0004	0.898	-0.0006**	0.001
constant	-0.7441**	0.000	-0.6926**	0.000	-0.1659	0.218	0.0655**	0.000
Number of obs	1144		1158		1087		Number of obs	1118
LR chi²	19.17		17.51		28.92		F(8, 426)	8.3
Prob > chi²	0.008		0.014		0.000		Prob > F	0.000
Pseudo R²	0.031		0.017		0.019		R-squared	0.050
Log likelihood	-300.7		-508.1		-730.3		Adj R-squared	0.0

Table 7.4. *Turning ages of skill profiles and older workers' employment indices*

(establishments with declining skill profile only)

Explanatory Variable	Dependent Variable							
	Mandatory Retirement Age ≥61 Years		Continuous Employment for all Retirees		Retention Rate of Baby-Boom Generation ≥60%		Proportion of Older Workers Aged 60+	
	Probit		Probit		Probit		OLS	
	coef.	$P > \|z\|$	coef.	$P > \|z\|$	coef.	$P > \|z\|$	coef.	$P > \|z\|$
peak_age	0.0086	0.620	-0.0108	0.434	0.0057	0.626	0.0011*	0.097
normal_age	-0.0050	0.850	0.0094	0.645	-0.0027	0.876	-0.0011	0.287
consideration_age	0.0162	0.538	0.0557**	0.011	0.0233	0.170	0.0032**	0.002
(base = f_size (1–99))								
f_size (100–999)	-0.3185*	0.095	-0.2739*	0.076	-0.0054	0.967	-0.0161**	0.037
f_size (1000+)	-0.4903	0.280	0.1287	0.626	0.2164	0.364	-0.0298**	0.031
w_slope	-0.0088*	0.054	-0.0119**	0.001	0.0078**	0.009	-0.0001	0.662
w_differential (40–49)	-0.0062*	0.096	-0.0009	0.726	0.0003	0.890	-0.0002	0.151
wage gap (50–59)	-0.0114	0.207	0.0139**	0.048	0.0023	0.687	-0.0008**	0.016
constant	-1.7702*	0.075	-3.8600**	0.000	-1.7934**	0.007	-0.1132**	0.003
Number of obs	447		451		427		Number of obs	435
LR chi²	17.01		34.62		15.44		$F(8, 426)$	6.10
Prob > chi²	0.030		0.000		0.051		Prob > F	0.000
Pseudo R^2	0.071		0.083		0.026		R-squared	0.103
Log likelihood	-111.8		-191.9		-287.0		Adj R-squared	0.086

The picture is similar in Table 7.4, where skill-profile dummies are replaced by the turning ages of skill profiles in the explanatory variables. The figures are for only the establishments where skill profiles are declining. The turning ages have no significant effects on the employment of older workers, except in the case of the consideration age for continuous employment for all employees and the proportion of older workers aged 60 or over.

Skills required for an occupation may provide information on the longevity of the skill level of the occupation, as each skill has a specific pattern of growth and decline over a worker's age. The survey listed five levels and inquired about the level required for each of 13 skills in the major three occupations of the respondent firms. (The 13 skills are shown in Table 7.A3 in the appendix.) With this information, it was possible to classify the 33 occupations into five groups using cluster analysis. I used the measure of similarity/dissimilarity as the levels required for the 13 skills in each occupation. The five occupational groups were production workers, professional workers, technicians and engineers, clerical and service workers, and salespersons (see Table 7.A2 in the appendix). The production workers group required more physical strength than the other groups. The professional workers group needed a high level of professional knowledge, the technicians and engineers group required a high level of professional knowledge and also technical skill, the clerical and service workers group required a lower skill level for all skills, and the salespersons group needed a high level of professional knowledge and the ability to negotiate, as well as the ability to sell and provide customer care (see Table 7.A3 in the appendix).

Compared with production workers, the professional workers were more likely, and salespersons less likely, to have the mandatory retirement age of 61 years old or over (Table 7.5). It is noteworthy that the effect of the slope of the wage profile on the mandatory retirement age of 61 years or over is surmounted by that of the professional group. Professional workers and technicians and engineers were less likely than the other groups to have continuous employment. The clerical and service group tended to have a higher proportion of older workers (aged 60 or over), whereas the salespersons group tended to have a lower proportion of older workers. The retention rate of the baby-boom generation was likely to be lower for professionals and the clerical and service group.

Several inferences can be drawn from these results. First, the occupational group classified by the skill levels required, not the skill profile or the turning ages of the skill profile, affected the mandatory retirement age of 61 or over. This suggests that occupation-specific attributes such as the skill composition and the organization of the workplace affect the mandatory

Table 7.5. Occupational group and older workers' employment indices

Explanatory Variable	Dependent Variable							
	Mandatory Retirement Age ≥61 Years Probit		Continuous Employment for all Retirees Probit		Retention Rate of Baby-Boom Generation ≥60% Probit		Proportion of Older Workers Aged 60+ OLS	
	coef.	P > |z|	coef.	P > |z|	coef.	P > |z|	coef.	P > |z|
(base = production workers gr.)								
Professional gr.	0.4944**	0.017	−0.5335**	0.019	−0.4363**	0.012	−0.0007	0.941
Technicians and engineers	0.1026	0.508	−0.3060**	0.019	0.0342	0.758	−0.0017	0.773
Clerical and service gr.	0.1223*	0.462	−0.0096	0.941	−0.5592**	0.000	0.0232**	0.000
Salespersons gr.	−0.3168*	0.07	−0.1757	0.143	−0.0934	0.370	−0.0138**	0.015
(base = f_size (1–99))								
f_size (100–999)	−0.2668**	0.029	−0.0943	0.321	0.0505	0.543	−0.0196**	0.000
f_size (1000+)	0.0192	0.925	0.0048	0.977	0.2145	0.134	−0.0312**	0.000
w_slope	−0.0032	0.263	−0.0063**	0.007	0.0071**	0.000	0.0000	0.997
w_differential (40–49)	−0.0052**	0.027	−0.0020	0.231	−0.0021	0.130	−0.0002**	0.033
wage gap (50–59)	−0.0012	0.818	0.0051	0.210	−0.0011	0.759	−0.0006**	0.001
constant	−1.0228**	0	−0.4825**	0.000	0.0204	0.865	0.0622**	0.000
Number of obs	1144		1158		1087		1118	
LR chi^2	29.46		26.75		55.66		$F_{(8, 426)}$ 9.52	
Prob > chi^2	0.001		0.002		0.000		Prob > F 0.000	
Pseudo R^2	0.048		0.026		0.037		R-squared 0.072	
Log likelihood	−295.5		−503.5		−717.0		Adj R-squared 0.0642	

retirement age. Second, continuous employment after mandatory retirement was most common in low-skill, low-wage occupations. Third, the proportion of workers aged 60 or over was most prevalent in small firms with small wage gaps. Fourth, the retention rate of the baby-boom generation before the mandatory retirement age was greater for production workers, salespersons, and technicians and engineers than for the other occupational groups. This finding may imply that, for those groups, employment security is higher before the mandatory retirement age because of the high transaction costs to the organization of replacing them.

7.3. Slopes of the wage profile and wage differentials

The findings reported in the previous section suggest that the wage profile and the wage differential within the firm play important roles in the employment of older workers even after they reach the mandatory retirement age. A flatter wage profile and a large wage differential are assumed to be associated with a higher mandatory retirement age. Faced with increasing wage costs due to the aging of the workforce, many firms have introduced pay-for-performance systems to elicit greater efforts from their workers and thereby to strengthen the link between performance and compensation (see, for example, Ohashi and Nakamura 2002 on the recent reforms of the pay system in Japan). This recent reform of the wage system from seniority-based wages to performance-based wages is expected to result in flatter wage profiles and larger wage differentials.

This section focuses on an analysis of the slope of the wage profile and the wage differentials in relation to the skill profiles and occupation groups. It could be argued that it is not suitable to use simultaneously the skill profiles and occupational groups as explanatory variables, since the two are closely related. Their relationship is not so close as to be of concern, however, because the occupational groups were obtained by cluster analysis, in which I classified 33 occupations into five groups, and skill profiles for the same occupation can differ among firms. In addition, I estimated the regression separately, including only one of them in turn, either the skill profiles or the occupation groups.

The regression of the slope of the age–wage profile produced the following results. Skill profiles were positively associated with the wage slopes, as predicted. Tables 7.6 and 7.7 show that the rising-profile occupations had the steepest wage profiles, followed by those of the declining-profile occupations, and the flat-profile occupations had the flattest wage profiles. Compared with production workers, the wage profiles of salespersons and, to a lesser extent, technicians and engineers were

Table 7.6. Regression of the slop of wage profile (1)

(OLS, dependent variable = slope of wage profile = wages at ages 50–59 – wages at ages 20–29; wages at ages 40–49 = 100)

	Coef.	$P > |t|$	Coef.	$P > |t|$	Coef.	$P > |t|$
(base = skill profile "rising")						
skill profile "flat"	−4.4659**	0.005			−3.3869**	0.033
skill profile "declining"	−3.8497**	0.015			−2.6923*	0.091
(base = production workers gr.)						
Professional gr.			0.6804	0.874	0.0726	0.987
Technicians and engineers gr.			3.9983**	0.041	3.5814*	0.068
Clerical and service gr.			−5.1580**	0.027	−5.2003**	0.026
Salespersons gr.			7.2765**	0.000	6.7220**	0.001
hiring_rt	−24.9412**	0.000	−23.0434**	0.001	−23.1062**	0.001
(base = f_size (1–99))						
f_size (100–999)	5.2016**	0.000	4.7411**	0.000	4.9338**	0.000
f_size (1000 +)	15.1103**	0.000	14.2250**	0.000	14.5366**	0.000
constant	51.1699**	0.000	47.3843**	0.000	48.8196**	0.000
13 industry dummies	Yes		Yes		Yes	
Number of obs	1320		1320		1320	
F (18, 1301)	11.71		12.08		11.21	
Prob > F	0.000		0.000		0.000	
R-squared	0.139		0.157		0.160	
Adj R-squared	0.128		0.144		0.146	

Table 7.7.   Regression of the slope of wage profile (2)

(OLS, dependent variable = slope of wage profile = wages at ages 50–59 − wages at ages 20–29; wages at ages 40–49 = 100)

	Coef.	P > |t|	Coef.	P > |t|	Coef.	P > |t|	Coef.	P > |t|
(base = skill profile "rising")								
skill profile "flat"	−3.3778**	0.033	−3.3595**	0.034	−3.0670*	0.058	−3.3681**	0.033
skill profile "declining"	−2.7016*	0.090	−2.6522*	0.096	−1.7861	0.271	−2.7052*	0.089
(base = production workers gr.)								
Professional gr.	0.0891	0.984	−0.0719	0.987	0.6952	0.875	−0.0636	0.988
Technicians and engineers gr.	3.5802*	0.069	3.4699*	0.078	3.9742**	0.049	3.4536*	0.079
Clerical and service gr.	−5.1809**	0.027	−4.9465**	0.035	−5.3992**	0.025	−5.1829**	0.026
Salespersons gr.	6.6949***	0.001	6.6403***	0.001	6.7475***	0.001	6.5774***	0.001
pay for performance	0.2777	0.812						
proportion of 50+			−3.2575	0.334				
retention rate of baby-boom generation ≥ 60%					3.4730**	0.004		
hiring rate	−23.1087**	0.001	−24.0215**	0.001	−21.1060**	0.007	−32.8009**	0.000
(base = f_size (1–99))								
f_size (100–999)	4.9129***	0.000	4.8169***	0.000	5.5276***	0.000	4.6620***	0.000
f_size (1000+)	14.4881***	0.000	14.3002***	0.000	14.7041***	0.000	14.0667***	0.000
constant	48.7531**	0.000	50.1548**	0.000	42.4884**	0.000	49.0441**	0.000
13 industry dummies	Yes		Yes		Yes		Yes	
Number of obs	1320		1320		1234		1320	
F (18, 1301)	10.72		10.77		11.39		10.94	
Prob > F	0.000		0.000		0.000		0.000	
R-squared	0.160		0.160		0.178		0.163	
Adj R-squared	0.145		0.146		0.162		0.148	

steeper, whereas those of the clerical and service group were flatter. The pay-for-performance dummy and the proportion of workers aged 50 or over have no significant coefficient. The high retention rate of the baby-boom generation was positively associated with the high slope of the age–wage profile. Finally, the hiring rate had negative and significant effects on the wage slope. This implies that the hiring rate is a proxy for the turnover rate of the workforce, and that the higher the turnover rate, the flatter is the age–wage profile.

Regarding the wage differentials, the analysis reveals the following results (Tables 7.8 and 7.9). The declining-skill-profile occupations were more likely to have greater wage differentials than the rising-skill-profile occupations. The salespersons group had larger wage differentials than the other groups. Firms with high hiring rates tended to have larger wage differentials than other firms. The introduction of pay-for-performance systems induced larger wage differentials, whereas a larger proportion of employees aged 50 years or over was negatively associated with wage differentials.

The wage gap, defined as the difference between the actual wage and the wage desired by the employer, may be a measure of the flexibility of wages or the internal wage structure. The gap was found to be highest in the declining-skill-profile occupations, and it was higher among production workers and the technicians and engineers group than in the other occupational groups (Table 7.10).

7.3. Displacement effects of older workers on new school leavers

Finally, I examined the substitution/complement relationship between older and young workers by considering the hiring rate of new school leavers. On one hand, I predicted that if older workers and young workers were substitutes for each other, the number of young workers hired was likely to be smaller in firms with higher proportions of older workers, and hence the number of new school leavers who were hired would also be smaller. On the other hand, if the wage adjustment was flexible, so that the wage gap was smaller for older workers, then I predicted that the hiring rate of new school leavers would be high. Table 7.11 shows that the hiring rate of new school leavers was lower in firms where the proportion of employees aged 50 years or over was higher or the wage gap was greater. Thus, the estimation results were consistent with the predictions.

The analysis reveals that the employment of older workers was a substitute for youth employment, but that this effect was mitigated by the smaller wage gap of older workers. The wage gap was greater for the occupations with declining-skill profiles, production workers, and the

Table 7.8. Regression of wage differential (1)

(OLS, dependent variable = wage differential (ages 40–49) = max − min annual wage, average = 100)

	Coef.	$P > \lvert t \rvert$	Coef.	$P > \lvert t \rvert$	Coef.	$P > \lvert t \rvert$
(base = skill profile "rising")						
skill profile "flat"	0.4811	0.833			1.3008	0.571
skill profile "declining"	3.7448	0.101			4.6037**	0.046
(base = production workers gr.)						
Professional gr.			−7.8758	0.177	−6.9832	0.232
Technicians and engineers gr.			1.9098	0.498	2.4151	0.394
Clerical and service gr.			−3.3412	0.315	−3.0004	0.367
Salespersons gr.			5.5868*	0.055	6.4163**	0.029
hiring_rt	25.827**	0.004	27.6876**	0.002	27.2621**	0.002
(base = f_size (1–99))						
f_size (100–999)	4.3107**	0.012	4.3838**	0.010	4.1818**	0.014
f_size (1000+)	25.3189**	0.000	25.0218**	0.000	25.0237**	0.000
constant	27.2670**	0.006	26.2927**	0.010	24.5181**	0.017
13 industry dummies	Yes		Yes		Yes	
Number of obs	1239		1239		1239	
F (18, 1301)	6.67		6.38		6.06	
Prob > F	0.000		0.000		0.000	
R-squared	0.090		0.095		0.099	
Adj R-squared	0.07		0.080		0.083	

Table 7.9. Regression of wage differential (2)

(OLS, dependent variable = wage differential (ages 40–49) = max − min annual wage, average = 100)

	Coef.	P > |t|	Coef.	P > |t|	Coef.	P > |t|	Coef.	P > |t|
(base = skill profile "rising")								
skill profile "flat"	1.5155	0.507	1.4321	0.532	1.6013	0.499	1.3061	0.569
skill profile "declining"	4.4126*	0.055	4.7043**	0.041	4.9651**	0.037	4.6016**	0.047
(base = production workers gr.)								
Professional gr.	−6.8350	0.240	−7.8896	0.177	−7.6293	0.206	−7.0028	0.230
Technicians and engineers gr.	2.3513	0.404	1.8954	0.503	2.5126	0.391	2.3981	0.397
Clerical and service gr.	−2.7375	0.408	−2.0592	0.538	−3.3444*	0.336	−2.9790	0.370
Salespersons gr.	5.7734**	0.049	6.0180**	0.040	5.3246*	0.078	6.3946**	0.030
pay-for-performance proportion of 50+	5.5634**	0.001						
retention rate of baby-boom generation ≥ 60%			−11.3352**	0.015	−1.2385	0.474		
hiring rate	27.9859**	0.002	25.2083***	0.005	22.2479**	0.024	25.0632**	0.017
(base = f_size (1–99))								
f_size (100–999)	3.8575***	0.023	3.7201**	0.030	5.1287***	0.004	4.1064**	0.017
f_size (1000+)	24.0610***	0.000	24.3010***	0.000	25.3568***	0.000	24.8921***	0.000
constant	22.8914***	0.025	28.5379***	0.006	16.0297*	0.091	24.5195***	0.017
13 industry dummies	Yes		Yes		Yes		Yes	
Number of obs	1239		1239		1151		1239	
F (18, 1301)	6.34		6.08		5.42		5.8	
Prob > F	0.000		0.000		0.000		0.000	
R-squared	0.107		0.103		0.0100		0.099	
Adj R-squared	0.090		0.086		0.081		0.082	

Table 7.10. Wage gap by skill profiles and occupational group

Skill Profile	Wage Gap
"rising"	1.4
"flat"	2.2
"declining"	3.5
Occpational group	
Production workers gr.	3.2
Professional workers gr.	2.8
Technicians and engineers gr.	3.0
Clerical and service workers gr.	1.3
Salespersons gr.	2.6
Total	2.7

Note: Wage gap = actual wage − desirable wage. Wages are normalized as those of workers in their 40s = 100.

technicians and engineers group. The substitution effects of employment of older workers may be higher for those occupations.

7.4. Conclusion

The employment of older workers was not necessarily determined by the pattern of the age–skill profiles or the turning age of the skill profile. A mandatory retirement age of over 60 was not explained by these covariates but rather by the occupational group classified by levels of skills required. In particular, the professional workers group had a significantly higher mandatory retirement age than the other occupational groups. This suggests that the retirement age is determined by occupation-specific attributes such as the skill composition and the organization of the workplace. Continuous employment after mandatory retirement was most common in low-skill, low-wage but physically easy occupations. A higher proportion of workers aged 60 or over was most prevalent in small firms that had small wage gaps.

Although skill profiles explained the internal wage structure (the slope of the wage profile and wage differentials) fairly well as predicted, occupational type again had a large influence. The salespersons group and the technicians and engineers group tended to have steeper wage profiles and larger wage differentials than professional workers. This suggests that in those occupations, because of the asymmetry of information and the nonverifiability of performance, transaction costs tend to be large and deferred-payment systems are more strictly applied. It is too early to judge whether the recent

Naoki Mitani

Table 7.11. Regression of the hiring ratio of new school leavers

(dependent variable = hiring ratio of new school leavers = new school leavers/number of employees)

	Coef.	$P > \lvert t \rvert$	Coef.	$P > \lvert t \rvert$	Coef.	$P > \lvert t \rvert$	Coef.	$P > \lvert t \rvert$
wage gap (50–59)	-0.0002*	0.062	-0.0003**	0.015	-0.0002**	0.050	-0.0002**	0.018
proportion of 50+			-0.0518**	0.000	-0.0408**	0.000	-0.0404**	0.000
mandatory retirement age	-0.0015	0.176	-0.0001	0.915	-0.0015*	0.057	-0.0015*	0.070
retention rate of baby-boom generation ≥ 60%	-0.0032	0.240	-0.0008	0.766	0.0036	0.059	0.0029	0.133
hiring rate					0.2509**	0.000	0.2544**	0.000
w_slope							0.0001**	0.013
(base = f_size (1–99))								
f_size (100–999)	0.0079**	0.005	0.0052*	0.063	0.0074**	0.000	0.0070**	0.000
f_size (1000+)	0.0253**	0.000	0.0222**	0.000	0.0161**	0.000	0.0147*	0.000
constant	0.1164*	0.100	0.0519	0.459	0.1066**	0.031	0.0974*	0.052
13 industry dummies	Yes		Yes		Yes		Yes	
Number of obs	1130		1130		1124		1111	
F (18, 1111)	4.86		7.07		30.49		29.19	
Prob > F	0.000		0.000		0.000		0.000	
Adj R-squared	0.058		0.093		0.344		0.348	

reform of the Japanese wage system toward pay for performance will promote a more flexible wage system and the employment of older workers, because pay for performance is associated with steeper wage profiles.

Finally, the relationship between the employment of older workers and the hiring rate of new school leavers seems to be one of substitution, in the sense that the hiring rate was lower in firms with higher proportions of older workers. But this negative effect of the employment of older workers was mitigated by the flexibility of wages among older workers and small wage gaps. The negative effect may be larger for occupations that have declining-skill profiles and for production workers and technicians and engineers.

References

Becker, Gary S. 1964. *Human Capital: A Theoretical and Empirical Analysis, with Special Reference to Education*. New York: National Bureau of Economic Research and Columbia University Press.

Doeringer, Peter B. and Michael J. Piore. 1971. *Internal Labor Markets and Manpower Analysis*. Lexington, MA: D. C. Heath and Company.

Genda, Yuji 2004. *Job Creation in Japan*. Tokyo: Nihon-Keizai-Shinbun-Sya (in Japanese).

Gibbons, Robert and Michael Waldman. 1999. "Careers in organizations: Theory and evidence". in: Orley, Ashenfelter and David Card, eds, *Handbook of Labor Economics*, Vol. 3, Amsterdam: ELSEVIER SCIENCE B.V., 2373–437.

Lazear, Edward P. 1979. "Why is there mandatory retirement?" *Journal of Political Economy* 87(6): 1261–84.

———— 1981. "Agency, earnings profiles, productivity, and hours restrictions". *American Economic Review* 71(4): 606–20.

Mitani, Naoki. 2001. "Employment policy of older workers and labor demand (Koureisha koyou seisaku to roudou-jyuyou)". in: T. Inoki and F. Ohtake, eds, *Economic Analysis of Employment Policy (Koyouseisaku no keizai bunseki)*. Tokyo: Tokyo University Press, 339–77.

———— 2003. "Changes in age-wage profiles and the extension of mandatory retirement age (Nenrei-chingin profile no henka to teinen enchou)". *Journal of Economics and Business Administration (Kokumin Keizai Zasshi)* 187(2): 33–50.

Ohashi, Isao. 1998. "Theoretical analysis of mandatory retirement and pension schemes (Teinen taishoku to nenkin seido no rironteki bunseki)". *Japanese Journal of Labour Studies (Nihon Roudou Kenkyu Zasshi)* (456): 11–20.

Ohashi, Isao, and Jiro Nakamura. 2002. "Wage systems and labor markets in Japan: A perspective (Nihon no chingin seido to roudoushijyou: Tenbou)". *Economic Review (Keizai-Kenkyu)* 53(2): 97–116.

Okunishi, Yoshio 2001. "The aging and the direction of the reform of the employment system: From the mandatory retirement at 60 years old to the mandatory retirement over 60 years old. (Koureika to koyouseido kaikaku no houkousei: 60 sai teinensei kara post 60 sai teinensei he)". in: Atsushi Seike, ed., *Employment Policy in the Era of Employment over the Working Life (Shougai geneki jidai no koyou seisaku)*. Tokyo: Nihon-Hyouron Sha, 40–84.

Williamson, Oliver E. 1985. *The Economic Institutions of Capitalism*. New York: Free Press.

Naoki Mitani

Table 7.A1. Descriptive statistics

Variable	Description	Obs	Mean	Std. Dev	Min	Max
Clerical and service gr.	Occupation group dummy	1704	0.1719	0.3774	0	1
consideration_age	Age until which a worker can work normally with some consideration	620	61.1855	6.1011	23	80
continuous employment for all retirees	Dummy variable	1704	0.1649	0.3712	0	1
f_size (1000 +)	Firm-size dummy	1704	0.1004	0.3006	0	1
f_size (100–999)	Firm-size dummy	1704	0.4343	0.4958	0	1
hiring rate	Ratio of the hired during previous year to all regular employees	1563	0.0805	0.0917	0	1
hiring ratio of new school leavers	Ratio of hired new school leavers to all regular employees	1571	0.0257	0.0493	0	0.769
mandatory retirement age		1675	60.3105	1.2271	55	70
mandatory retirement age $\geq$ 61 years old	Dummy variable	1681	0.0779	0.2681	0	1
normal_age	Age at which a worker can work normally	652	53.8635	6.9815	25	70
pay for performance	Dummy variable	1704	0.3680	0.4824	0	1
peak_age	Age at which a worker's skill is the highest	655	42.8855	7.0444	25	65
Professional gr.	Occupational-group dummy	1704	0.0651	0.2468	0	1
proportion of 50 +	Proportion among employees	1610	0.2797	0.1903	0	1
proportion of 60 +	Proportion among employees	1610	0.0439	0.0789	0	0.899
retention rate of "mass generation" $\geq 60\%$	Dummy variable	1566	0.5262	0.4995	0	1
Salespersons gr.	Occupational-group dummy	1704	0.2424	0.4286	0	1
skill profile "declining"	Dummy variable	1704	0.4085	0.4917	0	1
skill profile "flat"	Dummy variable	1704	0.3903	0.4880	0	1
Technicians and engineers gr.	Occupation group dummy	1704	0.2142	0.4104	0	1
w_differential (40–49)	Wage differential	1314	38.5807	29.1482	0	210
w_slope	Slope of age-wage profile	1405	43.9388	21.7818	−30	150
wage gap (50-59)	Actual wages minus desirable wages	1293	2.6481	11.7269	−90	80

Table 7.A2. *Occupation groups by cluster analysis based on the skills required*

Occupation	Occupational Group	No.
Mining workers		27
Production-processing workers	Production	28
Stationary-engine, construction-machinery operators and electrical workers	workers group	29
Construction workers		30
Carrying laborers		31
Scientific researchers		1
Physicians and dentists	Professional	5
Nurses	workers group	6
Pharmacists		7
Social and welfare workers		8
Agricultural, forestry and fishers, food- processing technicians		2
Architects, civil and surveying engineers	Technicians and	3
Information-processing engineers	engineers group	4
General clerical workers		10
Food- and beverage-preparing workers		20
Other workers		33
Accounting clerks		12
Clerical workers in production-related		13
Workers in bill collecting and meter reading		15
Clerical workers in transportation		16
Electric computer operator	Clerical and	17
Restaurant service workers	service workers group	21
Caretakers		22
Protective workers		23
Motormen		24
Automobile drivers		25
Cleaners		32
Managers and officials		9
Clerical workers in planning		11
Clerical workers in sales		14
Shop sales workers	Salespersons group	18
Buyers and salespersons		19
Communication workers		26

Table 7.A3. **Skill levels required, by skill and occupational group**

Skills Required	Production Workers gr.	Professional Workers gr.	Technicians and Engineers gr.	Clerical and Service Workers gr.	Salespersons gr.	Total
			Occupational group			
Professional knowledge	2.4	3.9	3.4	2.5	3.1	3.0
Understanding	2.3	3.5	2.7	2.2	2.9	2.6
Planning and development ability	1.1	2.6	2.3	1.1	2.6	1.8
Ability for sales and customer care	1.0	2.4	2.0	2.0	3.0	2.1
Judgment	2.3	3.5	2.7	2.5	3.0	2.8
Ability to manage	2.0	2.5	2.2	1.6	2.5	2.1
Ability to coordinate	1.8	2.5	2.3	1.7	2.6	2.1
Ability to negotiate	1.3	2.2	2.3	1.7	3.0	2.1
Ability to train persons	2.0	3.1	2.4	1.7	2.6	2.2
Physical strength	2.6	2.3	2.2	2.0	2.0	2.2
Power of concentration	2.6	3.4	2.7	2.4	2.5	2.6
Eyesight and hearing ability	2.4	2.7	2.1	2.2	1.9	2.2
Technical skill	2.9	3.6	3.0	2.5	2.3	2.8

Note: Skill levels range from 1 to 5.

CHAPTER 8

Work-Life Balance Measures and Gender Division of Labor

Akira Kawaguchi

Recently work-life balance (WLB) measures have been attracting attention in Japan. WLB measures are programs that promote the reconciliation of conflicts between workplace and family responsibilities. They include the provision of on-site childcare centers, maternity leave systems, parental-leave systems, and flexitime systems. There are several reasons for the current interest in them. First, the labor force participation of women with children is increasing, particularly as it has become more socially acceptable for women to re-enter the labor force after childbirth. Second, the fertility rate has been declining in Japan over the past 30 years. The government has implemented many countermeasures to alleviate declining fertility. At the core of the countermeasures is the harmonization of work and childcare. Third, traditionally large family households consisting of three generations or more are declining. This decline has resulted in an absence of extended-family members to help with childcare responsibilities when parents are working. Moreover, the number of single-parent families is rising. All of these changes have increased the need for WLB measures.

In Japan, as in many advanced countries, male workers seldom take advantage of WLB measures. Sakamoto (2002) posits four reasons for this: (1) male workers do not know they are entitled to take childcare leave; (2) male workers do not need to take leave because the mother usually stays at home and takes care of the children; (3) the loss of income is larger for households when the man takes leave than when the woman takes leave; and (4) workplace practices prevent male workers from taking the leave.[1]

I am grateful to Rebecca Cassells and an anonymous referee for helpful comments and to Kimitaka Nishitani for his excellent research assistance.

[1] Sakamoto also mentions that "very few male workers can take long childcare leave." This is not a reason for the low rate of leave-taking, however, but rather a reason for workers to take short leaves.

In this chapter, I discuss reasons for the low acceptance rates of WLB measures by male workers. I argue that one of the most important reasons is that employers are reluctant to offer WLB measures to male workers. Male workers place priority on market work, whereas female workers give priority to family care. Hence, male workers seldom quit the labor force or reduce their labor market participation because of family matters. More often it is female workers who reduce their labor force participation when the need for childcare or housekeeping increases.

As family responsibilities do not reduce the labor force participation of male workers, there is little incentive for firms to offer male workers WLB measures.[2] On the one hand, the improvement of male workers' productivity through WLB measures is limited. On the other, solving conflicts between work and family will reduce female quit rates and increase female labor force participation.[3] Hence, firms have a greater incentive to offer WLB measures to female workers than to male workers.[4]

I also argue that a positive externality exists where WLB measures are provided for male workers. When WLB measures are provided for male workers, they reduce the quit rates of the workers' spouses. For example, in a household where both the husband and the wife are working and the regular work hours of the husband are long and childcare leave is limited, it is often the wife who must take care of the children. Consequently, the probability that the wife will quit her job increases. If, on the other hand, a husband can use flexitime and a childcare leave system, it becomes less difficult for the wife to harmonize work and family responsibilities and less likely that she will leave her job. As a result, the firm that offers male workers WLB measures gains little benefit but contributes to a reduced quit rate among the wives of its employees.

The existence of an externality implies a suboptimal level of WLB measures at Nash equilibrium. I hypothesize that actions taken to

---

[2] I do not deny that there are possible benefits to firms in offering WLB measures for male workers. Hammer et al. (2005) found that WLB measures increased male workers' job satisfaction. This in turn might have increased their productivity.

[3] The psychology literature distinguishes between work-to-family conflict and family-to-work conflict. In the former case, demands of the workplace hinder family life, whereas in the latter case family demands interfere with work in the labor market. See, for example, Netemeyer, Boles, and McMurrian (1996). In this chapter, I focus on the family-to-work conflict.

[4] WLB measures for male employees could also have indirect social implications, by harmonizing the family home as husbands take on more responsibility for the care of their children and the running of the household. These in turn could have positive social effects by reducing divorce rates and social problems such as domestic violence and depression. These implications, however, lie beyond the scope of this chapter.

increase male take-up rates of WLB measures will increase the total profit of firms.

In the following section I present some statistics that characterize WLB measures in Japan. Next comes an empirical discussion of the effect of WLB measures in a husband's firm on the probability of his wife's quitting. I then describe a theoretical model and discuss the reasons for and consequences of the low acceptance rate of WLB measures by male workers. Finally, I offer some concluding remarks.

8.1. Work-life balance meaures in Japan

The WLB measures provided to workers in Japan are very few compared with those in other developed countries. The OECD (2001) has devised an indicator of work–family reconciliation policies and ranked 18 OECD countries according to the indicator. The indicator is based on childcare coverage for children less than 3 years of age, maternity-pay entitlement, flexitime work, voluntary part-time work, and voluntary family leave in firms. Japan is ranked 17th out of the 18 OECD countries. Sweden is at the top of the ranking, and Denmark follows. Southern European countries, such as Italy, Portugal, Spain, and Greece, are at the bottom of the ranking.

Many Japanese women resign after becoming pregnant or giving birth. Figure 8.1 illustrates the changes in the female employment rate

Figure 8.1. Proportion of working women by age of youngest child: Japan, 1987–2002

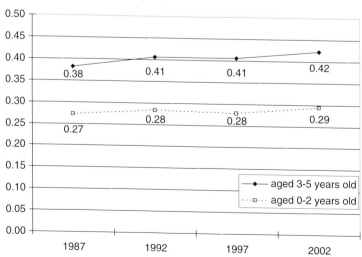

(defined as the total number of employed females divided by the total female population) by age of youngest child between 1987 and 2002. During that period, the Childcare Leave Law was enacted (in 1991). Figure 8.1 shows that the employment rate of women with young children did not increase substantially over the period. The employment rate of women whose youngest child was 0–2 years old increased by only 2 percentage points between 1987 and 2002, suggesting that the Childcare Leave Law has had a limited effect on female labor force participation.

Figure 8.2 shows that the female acceptance rate for childcare leave over roughly the same period has been rising substantially, particularly since 1996. It grew by more than 25 percentage points between 1996 and 2004. It is also noteworthy that although the female acceptance rate for childcare leave has been increasing, the female labor force participation rate has not.

At first glance, these two phenomena seem to contradict each other, but upon further analysis it can be seen that this is not the case. The childcare leave acceptance rate is defined as the number of workers who take childcare leave divided by the number of workers who are entitled to take the leave. Those women who left the labor force after becoming pregnant or giving birth were not entitled to childcare leave. Therefore, the figures for female leave acceptance and for female labor force participation indicate that the number of women who take childcare leave is

Figure 8.2. Acceptance rate of childcare leave: Japan, 1993–2004

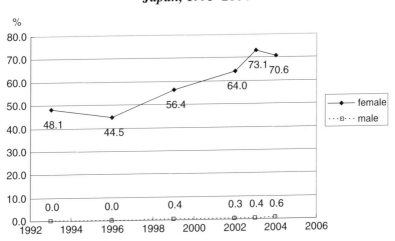

Source: Bureau of Statistics (2005, table 190).

increasing, but the number of women who leave the labor market after pregnancy or childbirth remains static.

Another striking feature of Figure 8.2 is the large gender gap in childcare leave acceptance rates. The male acceptance rate remained less than 1% between 1993 and 2004. The low acceptance rate of childcare leave by male workers does not imply that there is no demand for such leave by male workers. Sato and Takeishi (2004, 28), citing a Nippon Life Insurance Research Institute survey of 500 male workers interviewed in 2002, reported that 55% of the respondents who had children wanted to take childcare leave but could not, and 36% of the sample wanted to take childcare leave if they had a child in the future. There was a large gap between the number of males who wished to take childcare leave and the actual rate of childcare leave in the same sample.

Figures 8.3 and 8.4 show the attitudes of executives, personnel managers, and employees toward childcare leave for male and female workers, based on the study by Sato and Takeishi (2004). They show, first, a substantial gap between the attitudes of employers and employees, and, second, a particularly large gap in attitudes toward childcare leave for male and female employees. Whereas 34% of employees supported childcare leave for male colleagues, only 11% of executives supported childcare leave for male workers. The corresponding figures for the childcare leave of female workers were 70% and 36%.

Figure 8.3. Attitudes toward childcare leave taken by male employees: Japan, 2002

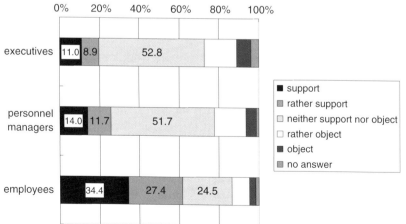

Source: Sato and Takeishi (2004, 40–41).

Figure 8.4. *Attitudes toward childcare leave taken by female employees: Japan, 2002*

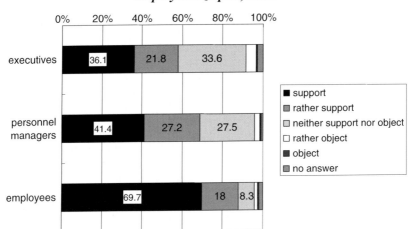

Source: Sato and Takeishi (2004, 40–41).

The reluctance of employers to offer WLB measures to male workers can be interpreted as follows. Men tend to place priority on performing market work, while women give preference to family care. As a result, family responsibilities affect female labor force participation more than male labor force participation. Declining quit rates, however, offer several benefits to firms: they make it possible for the firms to conduct more training and improve productivity, they increase the commitment of workers to the firms, and in doing so they attract more talented workers to the firms. These benefits should be greater for female workers than for male workers.

While the WLB measures offered to male workers may not affect male quit rates, they may reduce the quit rates of their spouses and increase the spouses' productivity. That is, the WLB measures for male workers may not benefit the firms that provide the WLB measures, but may benefit the firms where their spouses are employed. If this is true, then an externality exists where WLB measures are provided for male workers, and the level of WLB measures provided by individual firms may not be socially optimal.

To explore this point more in detail, the next section examines whether the WLB measures for male workers reduce the wives' probability of leaving their jobs. I then present a theoretical model of WLB measures offered by firms and discuss the efficiency of the WLB measures offered by individual firms.

8.1.1. The effect of male work-life balance measures on the female turnover rate

The data I used for this study come from the Japanese Panel Survey of Consumers, conducted annually by the Institute for Research on Household Economics. The survey began in 1993 and contains data on 1500 women aged 25–35 in that year. Another 500 women aged 25–29 were added to the sample in 1997. I used four panels from the years 1997 to 2000.

I was interested in the effect of WLB measures offered by the firms where the husbands were working. Because the variables that capture WLB measures are limited, I used a dummy variable of a childcare leave system as a proxy measure of the level of overall WLB measures in a firm. Firms that have a childcare leave system are thought to be more concerned about the work-life balance of their employees than firms that do not have such a system in place. It is reasonable to assume that a childcare leave system and the level of other WLB measures are positively correlated. Therefore, male workers in firms with a childcare leave system are more likely to enjoy other types of WLB measures even if they do not take childcare leave.

This assumption is supported by Wakisaka (2001). He estimated the existence of WLB measures in firms using the 1996 Female Employment Management Survey and found that a childcare leave system was positively and significantly correlated with the following WLB measures: a short-time employment system for parents, a flexitime system for parents, exemption from overtime work for parents, an on-site childcare center, a subsidy for childcare expense, a nursing leave system, and a reemployment system. Only a family-care leave system was significantly negatively correlated with a childcare leave system.

My criteria for sample selection were as follows: women who were married, who were working, whose husbands were working full-time, whose husbands were not self-employed, and who had children 12 years old or younger. Table 8.1 lists the dependent and independent variables used in the analysis. The dependent variable is a dummy variable that takes on a value of 1 if a woman quit her job in the next 12 months, and 0 otherwise. For explanatory variables, I used a dummy variable of a childcare leave system in the wife's firm, the dummy variable of a childcare leave system in husband's firm, the dummy variable of part-time work by the wife, the logarithm of the wife's wage, the logarithm of the husband's annual income, a dummy variable having a value of 1 if a baby was born by the time of the next survey, a dummy variable having a value of 1 if a couple lived with the mother of the husband or the wife, dummy variables for the educational level of the wife, dummy variables for the year of the

Table 8.1. Definition of variables

Variable	Definition
quit_f	dummy variable: 1 if wife quits in the next twelve months
childcare_leave_f	dummy variable: 1 if wife's firm has a childcare leave system
childcare_leave_m	dummy variable: 1 if husband's firm has a childcare leave system
part_time_f	dummy variable: 1 if wife is a part-time worker
ln_wages_f	log of wife's real wages per hour
ln_income_m	annual income of husband (mil. yen)
number_children	number of children
childbirth	dummy variable: 1 if baby is born in the next twelve months
live_with_mother	dummy variable: 1 if couple lives with mother of husband or wife
junior_high_f	dummy variable: 1 if wife's education level is junior high school
high_f	dummy variable: 1 if wife's education level is high school
vocational_f	dummy variable: 1 if wife's education level is vocational school
junior_col_f	dummy variable: 1 if wife's education level is junior college
uni_f	dummy variable: 1 if wife's education level is university or higher
year_1997	dummy variable: 1 for year 1997
year_1998	dummy variable: 1 for year 1998
year_1999	dummy variable: 1 for year 1999
year_2000	dummy variable: 1 for year 2000
manufacture_f	dummy variable: 1 if wife is working in manufacturing industry
wholesale_retail_f	dummy variable: 1 if wife is working in wholesale and retail industry
finance_f	dummy variable: 1 if wife is working in banking, insurance or real estate
service_f	dummy variable: 1 if wife is working in service industry
government_f	dummy variable: 1 if wife is working in government sector
other_industry_f	dummy variable: 1 if wife is working in other industries
size_1_4_f	dummy variable: 1 if wife is working for a firm with 1–4 workers
size_5_9_f	dummy variable: 1 if wife is working for a firm with 5–9 workers
size_10_29_f	dummy variable: 1 if wife is working for a firm with 10–29 workers
size_30_99_f	dummy variable: 1 if wife is working for a firm with 30–99 workers
size_100_499_f	dummy variable: 1 if wife is working for a firm with 100–499 workers
size_500_999_f	dummy variable: 1 if wife is working for a firm with 500–999 workers
size_1000_f	dummy variable: 1 if wife is working for a firm with 1000 or more workers

survey, dummy variables for the industry in which the wife was working, and dummy variables for the size of the wife's firm.

Table 8.2 presents the sample means and standard errors of the means. The sample was divided into two groups: women who were still working for the same firm at the time of the next survey and women who had quit

Table 8.2. Descriptive statistics

Variable	All Women		Not Quit		Quit	
	Mean	Std. Error	Mean	Std. Error	Mean	Std. Error
quit_f	0.1845	0.0161	0	0	1	0
childcare_leave_f	0.6690	0.0196	0.7125	0.0208***	0.4766	0.0485
childcare_leave_m	0.6724	0.0195	0.7209	0.0206***	0.4579	0.0484
part_time_f	0.4466	0.0207	0.4038	0.0226***	0.6355	0.0467
ln_wages_f	6.9807	0.0180	7.0174	0.0203***	6.8185	0.0344
ln_income_m	1.6135	0.0130	1.6281	0.0140***	1.5487	0.0329
number_children	1.9862	0.0304	1.9852	0.0330	1.9907	0.0769
childbirth	0.0483	0.0089	0.0465	0.0097	0.0561	0.0223
live_with_mother	0.4672	0.0207	0.4947	0.0230***	0.3458	0.0462
junior_high_f	0.0241	0.0064	0.0169	0.0059	0.0561	0.0223
high_f	0.4259	0.0205	0.4165	0.0227	0.4673	0.0485
vocational_f	0.1948	0.0165	0.1924	0.0181	0.2056	0.0393
junior_col_f	0.2086	0.0169	0.2135	0.0189	0.1869	0.0379
uni_f	0.1466	0.0147	0.1607	0.0169**	0.0841	0.0270
year_1997	0.2534	0.0181	0.2579	0.0201	0.2336	0.0411
year_1998	0.2483	0.0180	0.2389	0.0196	0.2897	0.0441
year_1999	0.2621	0.0183	0.2685	0.0204	0.2336	0.0411
year_2000	0.2362	0.0177	0.2347	0.0195	0.2430	0.0417
manufacture_f	0.1741	0.0158	0.1797	0.0177	0.1495	0.0346
wholesale_retail_f	0.1741	0.0158	0.1649	0.0171	0.2150	0.0399
finance_f	0.0914	0.0120	0.0761	0.0122***	0.1589	0.0355
service_f	0.2603	0.0182	0.2537	0.0200	0.2897	0.0441
government_f	0.2500	0.0180	0.2812	0.0207***	0.1121	0.0306
other_industry_f	0.0103	0.0042	0.0085	0.0042	0.0187	0.0132
size_1_4_f	0.1086	0.0129	0.0994	0.0138*	0.1495	0.0346
size_5_9_f	0.0448	0.0086	0.0381	0.0088**	0.0748	0.0255
size_10_29_f	0.1431	0.0146	0.1374	0.0158	0.1682	0.0363
size_30_99_f	0.1224	0.0136	0.1184	0.0149	0.1402	0.0337
size_100_499_f	0.1707	0.0156	0.1734	0.0174	0.1589	0.0355
size_500_999_f	0.0586	0.0098	0.0634	0.0112	0.0374	0.0184
size_1000_f	0.1017	0.0126	0.0888	0.0131**	0.1589	0.0355
Observations	580		473		107	

Note: *, **, and *** imply that the mean difference between the two samples is significant at the 10% level, 5% level, and 1% level, respectively.

working for their firm by the next survey. Asterisks indicate whether sample means were significantly different between the workers who did not quit and those who did.

The table shows that the variables having significantly higher mean values for the sample of women who did not quit their jobs were a childcare leave system for the wife, a childcare leave system for the husband, the wife's wage rate, the husband's income, living with the mother or mother-in-law, university education for the wife, and government-sector employ-ment for the wife. The variables having significantly larger mean values for the sample of women who quit working were part-time work by the wife, employment by the wife in the finance industry, and the wife's working in a firm that employed 1–4 workers, 5–9 workers, or 1000 or more workers.

The fraction of women whose husbands were employed by firms having a childcare leave system was 72% among women who did not quit their jobs but only 46% among women who did quit. Thus, women who remained in their jobs were 26% more likely than those who did not to have husbands who worked for firms with a childcare leave system.

The estimation results are summarized in Table 8.3. Models 1, 3, and 5 are probit models; and models 2, 4, and 6 are random-effect probit models. Coefficients for the education dummies, year dummies, industry dummies, and firm-size dummies are omitted.

The coefficients for the childcare leave system of the husband's firm are stable, while those for the childcare leave system of the wife's firm vary according to the other explanatory variables. Models 5 and 6 seem to be fitted well. Since rho in Model 6 is not significantly different from zero at the 5% level, I selected the probit model. Model 5 shows that the childcare leave system for the wife, a childcare leave system for the husband, and living with the mother or mother-in-law had significantly negative effects on the probability of quitting. The existence of a childcare leave system in the wife's firm reduced the probability of her quitting by 14 percentage points, whereas a childcare leave system in the husband's firm reduced the probability of the wife's quitting by 9 percentage points.

Thus, the estimation result shows that the WLB measures in the hus-band's firm had a negative effect on the probability that the wife would quit her job. This is an important finding related to the efficiency of WLB measures. Firms that employ female workers may be able to reduce their turnover rate if firms that employ their spouses increase their level of WLB measures. This point is addressed more precisely in the next section.

8.2. Theoretical discussion

Here I present a simple model of WLB measures. Since it is the incentive for firms to offer male workers WLB measures that is of interest, I assume that firms absorb the whole cost of WLB measures and that they can set the level of WLB measures for male workers and that for female workers separately.

Table 8.3. Estimation of probability that wife quits job

Explanatory Variable	Probit Model 1			Random-effect Probit Model 2		
	Coefficient	Standard Error	Marginal Effect	Coefficient	Standard Error	Marginal Effect
childcare_leave_f	-0.2557*	0.1470	-0.0673	-0.3084*	0.1751	-0.0754
childcare_leave_m	-0.3918***	0.1331	-0.1048	-0.4211***	0.1600	-0.1046
part_time_f	0.3415**	0.1375	0.0878	0.3897**	0.1655	0.0925
ln_wages_f	–			–		
ln_income_m	–			–		
number_children	–			–		
childbirth	–			–		
live_with_mother	–			–		
Dummy variables						
education of wife		no			no	
industry of wife's firm		no			no	
size of wife's firm		no			no	
Number of observations		580			580	
Number of groups		–			271	
pseudo R^2		0.0653			–	
rho		–			0.2266	
likelihood test of rho = 0 (Prob >= chibar2)		–			0.037	

(continued)

Table 8.3. Continued

Explanatory variable	Probit Model 3			Random-effect Probit Model 4		
	Coefficient	Standard Error	Marginal Effect	Coefficient	Standard Error	Marginal Effect
childcare_leave_f	−0.1646	0.1587	−0.0419	−0.2118	0.1870	−0.0499
childcare_leave_m	−0.4109***	0.1572	−0.1088	−0.4381**	0.1862	−0.1074
part_time_f	0.2023	0.1578	0.0507	0.2218	0.1864	0.0510
ln_wages_f	−0.2874	0.1951	−0.0713	−0.3352	0.2287	−0.7610
ln_income_m	−0.0681	0.2296	−0.0168	−0.1076	0.2699	−0.0244
number_children	−0.0076	0.0887	−0.0019	−0.0033	0.1067	−0.0008
childbirth	0.2280	0.2998	0.0622	0.2568	0.3363	0.0655
live_with_mother	−0.2578**	0.1314	−0.0634	−0.2964*	0.1599	−0.0666
Dummy variables						
education of wife	no			no		
industry of wife's firm	no			no		
size of wife's firm	no			no		
Number of observations	580			580		
Number of groups	–			271		
pseudo R^2	0.0810			–		
rho				0.2233		
likelihood test of rho = 0 (Prob > = chibar2)	–			0.050		

(continued)

Table 8.3. Continued

Explanatory variable	Probit Model 5			Random-effect Probit Model 6		
	Coefficient	Standard Error	Marginal Effect	Coefficient	Standard Error	Marginal Effect
childcare_leave_f	−0.5476**	0.2165	−0.1407	−0.6231**	0.2542	−0.1502
childcare_leave_m	−0.3722**	0.1669	−0.0932	−0.4030**	0.1938	−0.0937
part_time_f	0.2927*	0.1718	0.0699	0.3124	0.1980	0.0687
ln_wages_f	−0.3633*	0.2077	−0.0854	−0.4134*	0.2390	−0.0892
ln_income_m	−0.3115	0.2471	−0.0732	−0.3724	0.2863	−0.0803
number_children	−0.0329	0.0962	−0.0077	−0.0228	0.1134	−0.0049
childbirth	0.1805	0.3197	0.0460	0.2189	0.3536	0.0524
live_with_mother	−0.2812**	0.1429	−0.0655	−0.3065*	0.1679	−0.0654
Dummy variables						
education of wife		yes			yes	
industry of wife's firm		yes			yes	
size of wife's firm		yes			yes	
Number of observations		580			580	
Number of groups		–			271	
pseudo R^2		0.1311			–	
rho		–			0.1937	
likelihood test of rho = 0 (Prob $>$ = chibar2)		–			0.096	

Note: *, ** and *** imply that the coefficient is significantly different from zero at the 10% level, 5% level, and 1% level, respectively.

Akira Kawaguchi

In most advanced countries, it is illegal for firms to offer different WLB measures for male and female workers, except for maternity leave. There are, however, more barriers for male workers than for female workers to use WLB measures. Those barriers include a lack of information, social norms, a risk of unfavorable treatment for male users of WLB measures, workplace practices, a lack of understanding by colleagues and managers, and so on. Hence, it is possible that firms set an informal upper limit on WLB measures for male and female workers separately without violating a law.

8.2.1. Assumptions

The model has many firms and a mass of men and women. The population of each sex is normalized to unity. All people are married to persons of the opposite sex. The set of firms is denoted by K. Each firm has an identical production function, $y = X$, where y is output and X is the number of employees.

The timing of the game is summarized as follows:

Day 1: Each worker randomly meets a firm. Firms recruit all workers.
Day 2: Needs for housekeeping are randomly allocated to households.
Day 3: Each firm chooses the level of WLB measures for male workers and female workers separately.
Day 4: Couples choose their household division of labor. Some employees quit their jobs.
Day 5: Employees work. Firms pay wages.

On day 1, workers randomly apply for jobs at firms, and all of them are recruited. On day 2, the need for housekeeping, h_i, is randomly allocated to couples. The need is uniformly distributed such that $h_i \in [0, 1]$. Firms cannot know the need for housekeeping of employees, but know the distribution of the need. The need for housekeeping is large if, for example, there are small children or a family member suffers from an illness or disability. Firm $k \in K$ chooses the level of WLB measures for male workers, b_m^k, and that for female workers, b_f^k, separately. The cost of the WLB measures per worker is denoted by $c(b_j^k)$, $j = m, f$. It is assumed that $c' \geq 0$, $c'(0) = 0$ and $c'' > 0$. The firm pays the whole cost of the WLB measures.

Each couple decides the household division of labor on day 4. Either the husband or the wife quits if a couple can attain a higher utility level than when both of them work in the labor market. In such a case, a husband quits with probability γ, and a wife quits with probability $1 - \gamma$,

Table 8.4.   *Household division of labor and the couple's utility*

Husband	Wife	
	Labor Market	Home
Labor market	$2w - h_i + b_f^k + b_m^l$	w
Home	w	0

where $0 \leq \gamma < 0.5$. On day 5, employees work in the labor market, and receive wages, w. The wages are the same for all workers.

A couple has a risk-neutral utility function. The utility of the i-th couple is summarized in Table 8.4, where $b_f^k \geq 0$ ($b_m^l \geq 0$) is the level of WLB measures for female (male) workers offered by firm $k \in K$ ($l \in K$) that the wife (husband) is working for. Note that h_i, b_f^k, and b_m^l are included only in the utility of a double-earner couple. Although they affect the utility of a single-earner couple and non-earner couple, the effect is smaller than that of a double-earner couple. For the sake of simplicity, I assume that the effect of h_i, b_f^k, and b_m^l on the utility of a single-earner couple is zero. The utility of a double-earner couple increases as the WLB measures become richer, and it decreases as the needs for housekeeping increase.

8.2.2. Equilibrium: The optimal strategy of firms

The expected profit that a female worker yields for firm k is given as follows:

$$(1 - q_f^k)(1 - w) - d_f^k c(b_f^k)$$

where q_f^k is the probability that a female worker of firm k quits on day 4, and d_f^k is the probability that a female worker uses the WLB measures, which is equal to the probability that her husband works in the labor market on day 5. A female worker of couple i quits with probability $1 - \gamma$ if $2w - h_i + b_f^k + b_m^l < w$ or $h_i < w + b_f^k + b_m^l$. If all the other firms select the same level of WLB measures for male workers, b_m, the probability that a female worker of firm k uses the WLB measures and the probability that a female worker of firm k quits are given as follows:

$$d_f^k = \min(w + b_m + b_f^k, \ 1) \tag{8.1}$$

and

$$q_f^k = (1 - \gamma)(1 - d_f^k)$$

Note that the number of firms is large enough; hence one can ignore the case in which a husband and wife work for the same firm. Since the firm does not offer b_f^k such that $w + b_m + b_f^k$ exceeds unity, one can ignore the case in which $w + b_m + b_f^k > 1$. Hence, equation (8.1) is simplified as follows:

$$d_f^k = w + b_m + b_f^k$$

This implies that the number of double-earner couples increases and the probability of the wife's quitting decreases as male WLB measures increase. This implication is consistent with the estimation result of the previous section.

The expected profit yielded by a female worker is given by

$$\pi_f^k = \left\{ 1 - (1 - \gamma)(1 - w - b_m - b_f^k) \right\} (1 - w) - (w + b_m + b_f^k)c(b_f^k)$$

Firm k selects the optimal level of WLB measures, b_f^k, so that the expected profit is maximized. The first-order condition is as follows:

$$(1 - \gamma)(1 - w) - c(b_f^k) - (w + b_m + b_f^k)c'(b_f^k) \equiv F(b_f^k, b_m) = 0 \quad (8.2)$$

The second-order condition is given by

$$-2c'(b_f^k) - (w + b_m + b_f^k)c''(b_f^k) < 0$$

Thus, the second-order condition is satisfied.

The optimal level of WLB measures for male workers is obtained the same way. The first-order condition is given by

$$\gamma(1 - w) - c(b_m^k) - (w + b_m^k + b_f)c'(b_m^k) \equiv M(b_m^k, b_f) = 0 \quad (8.3)$$

Now, the following proposition holds:

Proposition 1. The individually optimal level of WLB measures for male (female) workers, when the level of WLB measures offered by other firms is given, increases as γ increases (decreases).

This proposition is derived directly from the first-order conditions (8.2) and (8.3). The intuitive interpretation of Proposition 1 is as follows. Parameter γ is the sensitivity of the male quit rate to the WLB measures.

The optimal level of WLB measures for male workers is lower if the probability of quitting is not sensitive to the measures. In the actual world, γ is close to zero; male workers seldom quit because of family matters. Hence the optimal level of WLB measures for male workers is close to zero.

A Nash equilibrium is the case in which all firms select the optimal strategies against strategies selected by other firms. It is given by $(b_{\mathrm{m}}^*, b_{\mathrm{f}}^*)$ that satisfies the following conditions:

$$F(b_{\mathrm{f}}^*, b_{\mathrm{m}}^*) = 0 \tag{8.4}$$

and

$$M(b_{\mathrm{m}}^*, b_{\mathrm{f}}^*) = 0 \tag{8.5}$$

Figure 8.5 illustrates the Nash equilibrium. The horizontal axis measures the level of WLB measures that are offered to female workers. The vertical axis measures the level offered to male workers. Curves DD and EE represent equations (8.4) and (8.5), respectively. Proposition 1 implies that curve DD shifts up and curve EE shifts rightward as γ increases.

Figure 8.5. Levels of WLB offered to male and female workers

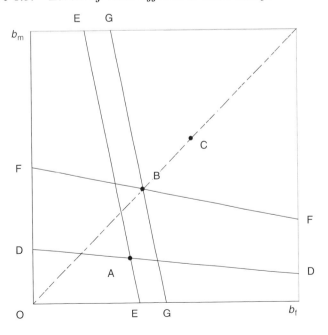

8.2.3. Externalities

As I have already mentioned, WLB measures create externalities. If firm k implements them, it benefits firms for which the spouses of firm k employees are working because the quit rate of those spouses declines. The externality of male WLB measures is larger as γ is smaller, and the externality of female WLB measures is larger as γ is larger. If γ is close to zero, a firm obtains little benefit by offering male employees WLB measures, but it benefits firms for which their wives are working. If externality exists, the Nash equilibrium is generally suboptimal. That is also true in this model.

Now it is possible to derive the condition for joint-profit maximization, rather than individual-profit maximization, and to compare the level of WLB measures. When firms jointly maximize profit, the optimization problem is as follows:

$$\max_{b_m, b_f} \pi = (1 + w + b_m + b_f)(1 - w) - (w + b_m + b_f)(c(b_m) + c(b_f))$$

where $1 + w + b_m + b_f$ is the number of workers who work on day 5 and $w + b_m + b_f$ is the number of double-earner couples. Note that parameter γ has disappeared from the maximization problem. This implies that it does not matter for joint-profit maximization whether a husband or a wife quits. The first-order condition is given by

$$(1 - w) - c(b_f) - c(b_m) - (w + b_m + b_f)c'(b_f) \equiv J(b_f, b_m) = 0 \quad (8.6)$$

and

$$(1 - w) - c(b_f) - c(b_m) - (w + b_m + b_f)c'(b_m) \equiv J(b_m, b_f) = 0 \quad (8.7)$$

where curves FF and GG in Figure 8.5 represent equations (8.6) and (8.7), respectively. The intersection of those curves, point B, gives the jointly profit-maximizing level of WLB measures. Since this joint profit-maximization model is symmetric in gender, $b_f = b_m$ at B.

The following proposition holds:

Proposition 2. The joint profit-maximizing level of male WLB measures is higher than the individual profit-maximizing level.

The proof is as follows: Equations (8.6) and (8.7) can be written as

$$J(b_f, b_m) = F(b_f, b_m) + M(b_m, b_f) + (w + b_m + b_f)c'(b_m) = 0$$

$$J(b_m, b_f) = F(b_f, b_m) + M(b_m, b_f) + (w + b_m + b_f)c'(b_f) = 0$$

At the Nash equilibrium, however, $F(b_f^*, b_m^*) = M(b_m^*, b_f^*) = 0$, hence $J(b_f^*, b_m^*) > 0$ and $J(b_m^*, b_f^*) > 0$. This implies that curve FF lies upward of curve DD, and curve GG lies rightward of curve EE. Therefore, the male WLB level at point B is higher than that at point A.

The socially optimal level of WLB measures is even larger, because WLB measures improve the utility of workers as well. The sum of utility of all households is given by

$$u = \int_0^{w+b_m+b_f} (2w - h + b_m + b_f)dh + \int_{w+b_m+b_f}^1 wdh = \frac{1}{2}(w + b_m + b_f)^2 + w$$

Let me define the social welfare as $s = \pi + u$. The first-order condition for social welfare maximization is given by

$$\frac{\partial s}{\partial b_f} = \frac{\partial \pi}{\partial b_f} + \frac{\partial u}{\partial b_f} = J(b_f, b_m) + (w + b_m + b_f) = 0 \tag{8.8}$$

and

$$\frac{\partial s}{\partial b_m} = \frac{\partial \pi}{\partial b_m} + \frac{\partial u}{\partial b_m} = J(b_m, b_f) + (w + b_m + b_f) = 0 \tag{8.9}$$

If firms jointly maximize their profit but do not take into account the utility of workers, $J(b_f, b_m) = J(b_m, b_f) = 0$. This implies that the left-hand sides of equations (8.8) and (8.9) are positive at point B. Therefore, the levels of WLB measures should increase in order to satisfy equations (8.8) and (8.9). Point C on Figure 8.5 shows the socially optimal level of the WLB measures.

The above discussion is valid even if firms and workers share the cost of WLB measures. Suppose firms bear fraction η of the cost of WLB measures, and workers bear fraction $1 - \eta$ of the cost. Parameter η is exogenously given. Firms set the upper limit of WLB measures for male and female workers separately. Each worker selects the level of WLB measures such that it does not exceed the upper limit set by his or her employer. With this assumption, one can show that double-earner couples always use the WLB measures up to the limit set by employers.

If there were no upper limit, all double-earner couples would demand the WLB measures, $\tilde{b}$, such that $(1 - \eta)c'(\tilde{b}) = 1$, of which the left-hand side is the marginal cost and the right-hand side is the marginal utility. The profit-maximization level of WLB measures never exceeds $\tilde{b}$, whatever the value of η is. The reason is as follows: If the level of WLB measures exceeded $\tilde{b}$, the utility of double-earner couples would decline and hence the quit rate would increase. That in turn would reduce the firms' profits. Therefore, the upper limit set by firms is always binding. It is firms, not workers, that select the level of WLB measures. This implies that most of the discussion in this section is valid under the assumption of cost sharing if the cost function of firms is slightly modified.

8.3. Conclusion

In discussing the reasons for and consequences of the low acceptance rates of WLB measures by male workers, I have argued that one of the most important reasons is that employers are reluctant to offer WLB measures to male workers. Since male workers place higher priority upon market work, and female workers on family care, male workers seldom quit or reduce their participation in the labor market because of family responsibilities. Female workers are more likely to reduce their labor force participation when the need for childcare or domestic duties increases. As family responsibilities do not normally reduce the labor force participation of male workers, there is little incentive for firms to offer male workers WLB measures.

I have also argued that there is a positive externality related to WLB measures for male workers. WLB measures that are provided for male workers are thought to have a positive effect on their wives and the firms for which their wives work by reducing the wives' quit rates. I examined this hypothesis through empirical testing. The existence of this externality implies that the level of WLB measures at Nash equilibrium is suboptimal. Therefore, actions taken to increase males' use of WLB measures will improve market efficiency.

References

Bureau of Statistics. 2005. *Survey on Employment Structure 2002 (Nippon no Shugyo Kozo: Heisei* 14-*nendo Shugyo Kozo Kihon-Chosa no Kaisetsu).* Tokyo: Nippon Tokei Kyokai.

Hammer, Leslie B., Margaret B. Neal, Jason T. Newton, Krista J. Brockwood, and Cari L. Colton 2005. "A longitudinal study of the effects of dual-earner couples' utilization of family friendly workplace supports on work and family outcomes". *Journal of Applied Psychology* 90(4): 799–810.

Ministry of Health, Labour and Welfare. 2005. *Survey on Female Employment Management, 2004 (Heisei* 16-*nendo Josei Koyo Kanri Chosa).* http://www.mhlw.go.jp/houdou/2005/08/h0808-2.html.

Netemeyer, Richard G., James S. Boles, and Robert McMurrian. 1996. "Development and validation of work-family conflict and family-work conflict scales". *Journal of Applied Psychology* 81(4): 400–410.

Organization for Economic Co-operation and Development (OECD). 2001. *Employment Outlook 2001*. Paris.

Sakamoto, Ariyoshi. 2002. *Does the Male Acceptance Rate for Childcare Leave Increase? (Dansei no ikuji kyugyo shutokuritsu wa josho suruka?)*. NLI Research Institute Report No.12. http://www.nli-research.co.jp/doc/li0212a.pdf.

Sato, Hiroki, and Emiko Takeishi 2004. *Childcare Leave of Men (Dansei no ikuji kyugyo)*. Tokyo: Chuokouronsha.

Wakisaka, Akira. 2001. "Analysis of family-friendly measures (Shigoto to katei no ryoritsu shien seido no bunseki)". In Takenori Inoki and Fumio Ohtake, (eds) *Economic Analysis of Employment Policy (Koyo seisaku no keizai bunseki)*, Tokyo: University of Tokyo Press, 195–224.

CHAPTER 9

Optimal Education Policies Under an Equity–Efficiency Trade-Off

Takashi Oshio

Education is widely considered to be a means for giving individuals an equal opportunity to improve their productivity and increase their future earnings, and the positive external effects of education are believed to justify its public provision. In fact, the government plays a significant role in providing and financing education in every country. Public education, however, has an ambiguous feature of income distribution: Higher-ability individuals can receive more gains in educational output and future income than lower-ability individuals from the same input of public education. If that occurs, the uniform provision of public education can widen income inequality even if average income rises among individuals.

Indeed, an extensive literature exists on the redistributive effects of public education, initiated by Arrow (1971), Bruno (1976), and Ulph (1977), who discuss under what conditions "input-regressive" educational policies, which direct more expenditure to higher-ability individuals, can be justified. Lommerud (1989) has shown that subsidies to the most able individuals are optimal, stressing that they can restore the individuals' incentive to receive higher education, which is blunted by progressive income taxation. De Fraja (2002) derives the optimality of an elitist education policy within a framework where households differ in their incomes and in their children's abilities.

The redistributive aspects of education have also been examined through other approaches. Among others, Hanushek, Leung, and Yilmaz (2003) compare a government subsidy for education with alternative redistribution devices in terms of both equity and efficiency, although they assume a uniform subsidy regardless of each individual's ability. Dur and Teulings (2003) show that a combination of education-system subsidy and progressive taxation increases social welfare.

I thank Keiji Hashiomo and other participants for helpful comments and suggestions. I also appreciate financial support from Kobe and Hitotsubashi Universities.

POPULATION CHANGE, LABOR MARKETS, AND SUSTAINABLE GROWTH
VOLUME 281   ISSN 0573-8555/DOI 10.1016/S0573-8555(07)81009-1

A comparison between public and private education is another issue that has been of great interest in designing education schemes. Using an overlapping-generations model, Glomm and Ravikumar (1992) show that public education reduces income inequality more quickly under private education, while private education yields greater per capita income. Saint-Paul and Verdier (1993), Fernández and Rogerson (1997), and Gradstein and Justman (1997) provide other examples that compare public and private education regimes in terms of income distribution and growth within a dynamic framework.

This chapter attempts to extend the literature by directly deriving optimal education policies that maximize social welfare, and by comparing them for equity and efficiency. The analysis is based on a simple model, which does not deal with important issues such as asymmetric information regarding innate ability, uncertainty of educational outcomes, and intergenerational effects of education policies. Instead, it focuses on the basic issue of public education—that is, how to strike a balance between equity and efficiency in its provision and finance. In addition, the approach has two features, both of which help us to assess the results obtained by preceding studies.

The first is that it considers education policies under different degrees of inequality aversion, or different social welfare functions. Most preceding studies have explicitly or implicitly assumed a utilitarian government, which aims to maximize an unweighted sum of the utility of all individuals. This assumption, while it is a good starting point, tends to justify regressive public education because it puts less importance on equity. If we assume that a government considers income inequality more seriously, we could have different results. It is, however, quite difficult to derive optimal education policies under general social welfare functions. So, my approach is to first take two extreme versions of social welfare functions, Rawlsian and Benthamian, and examine how optimal education policies are sensitive to a choice between these two. Next, I apply numerical simulations to illustrate how the outcomes are sensitive to different degrees of inequality aversion.

The second feature of the model is that it considers a wide variety of education policies. In addition to comparing uniform and biased provisions of public education corresponding to each individual's ability, it takes into account mixed systems of public and private education and whether they are superior to the government's monopolistic provision of education. For example, I consider a double-decker system, in which all individuals receive compulsory, public education, and some (high-ability) individuals receive additional, private education. I also extend the analysis to the case in which the government optimizes redistribution policies and education policies simultaneously. It seems plausible that progressive income redistribution, such as a combination of proportional income taxation and lump-sum subsidies, can make the regressive provision of education more acceptable.

Furthermore, I examine how sensitive optimal education policies are, to different parameter values, using numerical simulations. The optimal shape of an education policy appears to depend on the ability gap between individuals, the share of each type of individual in the total population, the input elasticity of education-output functions, and the wage elasticity of labor output. This sensitivity analysis can help assess the robustness of any optimal education policy.

The chapter is organized as follows. In the following section I present the basic model on which my theoretical analysis is constructed and compare several alternative education systems based on two extreme versions of social welfare functions, Rawlsian and Benthamian. Next, I conduct some numerical simulations to illustrate optimal education policies under different assumptions about the degree of inequality aversion, and include some sensitivity analyses. Then, I extend the analysis to the case in which other devices for income redistribution are available. Finally, I summarize the main results and suggest some topics for future research.

9.1. Theoretical analysis

9.1.1. Basic model

Society consists of two types of individual—that is, low-ability individuals ($i = 1$) and high-ability individuals ($i = 2$), who share p and $1 - p$ ($0 < p < 1$), respectively, of the total population. I assume that each individual as well as the government can distinguish each individual's innate ability before undertaking education. This assumption is crucial because education can be considered to be a device for screening individual abilities. I believe, however, that this prototype model can grasp the basic features of education as a trade-off between equity and efficiency. The analysis should be more applicable to higher education than to primary or secondary education, as more information about an individual's ability is available at each successive stage of education.

Each individual maximizes his or her utility, which is determined by consumption and labor supply. The utility function of each individual is generally given by

$$U_i = U(C_i, L_i) = C_i - \kappa \frac{L_i^{1+\nu}}{1 + \nu}$$

where U_i, C_i, and L_i are utility, consumption, and labor supply, respectively; v (>0) is the inverse of the wage elasticity of labor supply; and κ (>0) is a parameter related to the disutility of labor.[1] The budget constraint of an individual in a general form is given by

$$C_i \leq (1 - t)a_i(E_i)L_i - cE_i$$

where E_i, t, and c are level of education input, income tax rate, and unit cost of (private) education, respectively. And, $a_i(E_i)$ denotes an education output function for individuals of ability type i, indicating the wage rate that is obtained by education input E_i.[2] In a private education system each individual determines the level of education input and pays for it directly. In a public education system the government determines the level of education and finances it from income tax revenues, and an individual does not directly pay any tuition. (I shall discuss the budget constraint of the government later.)

In general, the optimal education system seems to depend heavily on society's judgment on a balance between equity and efficiency, and it is difficult to present any general feature of the optimal system. Hence, in this section I focus on two extreme social welfare functions:

Rawlsian: $W_R = \min[U_1, U_2]$

Benthamian: $W_B = pU_1 + (1 - p)U_2$

and investigate how the outcomes are sensitive to a choice between these two versions of social welfare functions. A Benthamian social welfare function assumes a utilitarian government, which aims to maximize an unweighted sum of the utility of all individuals, while not considering equity at all. A Rawlsian social welfare function, by contrast, is another extreme case, in which the government focuses solely on helping the worst-off. Society's inequality aversion is lowest in the former case and highest in the latter case. In my model, a Rawlsian function can, in general, be expressed as $W_R = U_1$, provided $U_2 \geq U_1$, meaning that the utility of lower-ability individuals determines the overall social welfare. I apply a more general type of social welfare function in the Section 9.1.2

---

[1] This type of utility function has been used by many researchers in theoretical and empirical studies, including that by Hanushek, Lueing, and Yilmaz (2003).

[2] An alternative type of utility function looks like $U_i = U(C_i, L_i, E_i) = C_i - \kappa \frac{L_i^{1+v}}{1+v} - \kappa' \frac{E_i^{1+v'}}{1+v'}$, v, κ, v', $\kappa' > 0$, where the disutility of learning and schooling is taken into account. I do not apply this utility function, but just to simplify algebraic calculations.

and, using numerical simulations, examine how the optimal education system depends on the degree of inequality aversion.

As for the education output function, I also assume $a'_i(E_i) > 0$, $a''_i(E_i) < 0$, taking into account decreasing returns on education. Specifically, I consider a particular type of education output function such as

$$a_i(E_i) = a_i E_i^\alpha, \quad 0 < a_1 < a_2, \quad 0 < \alpha < 1$$

where a_i and α denote the ability of each type of individual and the education input elasticity of education output, respectively.[3] Here, for simplicity I neglect the externality of education, which works only through spillover effects caused by reduced tax burdens due to education output by other individuals. The inequality $0 < \alpha < 1$ represents the declining marginal product of education, and for simplicity I assume that each individual has the same value. A high-ability individual obtains productivity gains (a_2/a_1) times as high as a low-ability one at any level of education input. I define $\theta \equiv a^2/a^1$ and call θ the "ability ratio" between the two types of individual. I assume that the quality and unit cost are the same with public and private education, respectively, and for simplicity ignore what is called peer-effect in education. Finally, I assume that $\kappa = 1$ and $c = 1$, provided that the unit of labor supply and the price of consumption goods are appropriately arranged.

9.1.2. Comparisons of Private vs. Public Education

I begin by comparing three education systems, based on two extreme social welfare functions: System I (*private*), in which there is no public education available and each type of individual receives private education; System II (*public-uniform*), in which the government provides each individual with the same level of public education; and System III (*public-biased*), in which the government adjusts levels of public education to the ability of each individual. In Systems II and III no private education is available for institutional reasons, and System III includes two variations: progressive and regressive education. I shall discuss mixed systems— combinations of private and private education—shortly.

I consider first System I, the entirely private system, using it as a benchmark for comparing alternative education systems. In this system, each type of individual determines the optimal combination of education and labor supply to maximize his or her utility. The government offers no

---

[3] This particular form was also used by Ulph (1977).

education, and so it levies no tax on individuals to finance it. Then, each individual solves

$$\max_{\{E_i, L_i\}}: \ U_i = a_i E_i^{\alpha} L_i - E_i - \frac{L_i^{1+\nu}}{1+\nu}$$

The first-order conditions for utility maximization for each individual is given by

$$E_i = \left(\alpha^{\nu} a_i^{1+\nu}\right)^{1/\Delta}, \quad L_i = \left(\alpha^{\alpha} a_i\right)^{1/\Delta}$$

where $\Delta \equiv \nu - (1+\nu)\alpha$ and I assume that $\Delta > 0$ so that the demand for education is an increasing function of ability. A simple calculation also shows that each individual spends $\alpha \times 100\%$ of wage income on education, reflecting the assumption of the same elasticity of educational output across individuals.

One can express the maximized utility (the indirect utility function) of each individual as

$$U_i = \frac{\Delta}{1+\nu} \left(\alpha^{\alpha} a_i\right)^{(1+\nu)/\Delta}$$

and show that $U_2 > U_1$, meaning that a higher-ability individual obtains higher utility. Accordingly, I obtain two types of social welfare:

$$W_R^I = U_1 = \frac{\Delta}{1+\nu} \alpha^{\alpha(1+\nu)/\Delta} \, a_1^{(1+\nu)/\Delta} \tag{9.1}$$

$$W_B^I = pU_1 + (1-p)U_2 = \frac{\Delta}{1+\nu} \alpha^{\alpha(1+\nu)/\Delta} \Gamma \tag{9.2}$$

where

$$\Gamma = pa_1^{(1+\nu)/\Delta} + (1-p)a_2^{(1+\nu)/\Delta} > 0$$

corresponding to two extreme social welfare functions. I investigate whether each alternative education system can raise the level of social welfare assessed in both social welfare functions.

9.1.2.3. System II (Public-uniform)

Let us now consider a public education system, starting with an egalitarian system in which the government provides an equal amount of education to both types of individual and finances education costs from proportional income tax. I assume that there is no chance for individuals to receive any private education to supplement public education, and also that public education is compulsory, in that each individual must receive education as directed by the government. No dropouts are allowed before students complete the public education programs.

In this scenario, each individual chooses the optimal labor supply to maximize his or her utility, given the public education, $\overline{E}$, and tax rate, t. So each individual solves

$$\max_{\{L_i\}}: U_i = (1 - t)a_i\overline{E}^\alpha L_i - \frac{L_i^{1+\nu}}{1 + \nu}$$

where that individual pays for his or her education cost indirectly through income tax rather than directly. The optimal labor supply is obtained from the first-order conditions for utility maximization:

$$L_i = \left[(1 - t)a_i\overline{E}^\alpha\right]^{1/\nu}$$

Given the labor supply of each individual, the government faces a budget constraint, which is expressed in per capita terms by

$$\overline{E} = t\left[pa_1\overline{E}^\alpha L_1 + (1 - p)a_2\overline{E}^\alpha L_2\right]$$

Plugging the labor supply, L_i, into this budget constraint and solving the supply level of public education yields

$$\overline{E} = \left[(1 - t)t^\nu\Pi^\nu\right]^{1/\Delta}$$

where

$$\Pi = pa_1^{(1+\nu)/\nu} + (1 - p)a_2^{(1+\nu)/\nu} > 0$$

meaning that the level of public education is determined solely by the tax rate, under the budget constraint of the government. With a certain tax rate and the corresponding level of public education, each individual maximizes his or her utility. The maximized utility of each individual is given by

$$U_i = \frac{\nu}{1 + \nu}a_i^{(1+\nu)/\nu}\left[(1 - t)\overline{E}^\alpha\right]^{(1+\nu)/\nu}$$

$$= \frac{\nu}{1 + \nu}a_i^{(1+\nu)/\nu}\Pi^{\alpha(1+\nu)/\Delta}\left[(1 - t)^{1-\alpha}t^\alpha\right]^{(1+\nu)/\Delta}$$

where $U_2 > U_1$. Hence, the optimal tax rate is calculated as α for both Rawlsian and Benthamian social welfare functions. As in System I with no public education, each individual spends $\alpha \times 100\%$ of his or her income on education in this system, but through income tax rather than directly in this system.

Next, we can check whether public education can enhance social welfare as compared with the private education system. The levels of social welfare are calculated as

$$W_R^{II} = U_1 = \frac{\nu}{1+\nu} a_1^{(1+\nu)/\nu} \Pi^{\alpha(1+\nu)/\Delta} \left[(1-\alpha)^{1-\alpha} \alpha^{\alpha} \right]^{(1+\nu)/\Delta} \qquad (9.3)$$

$$W_B^{II} = pU_1 + (1-p)U_2 = \frac{\nu}{1+\nu} \Pi^{\nu/\Delta} \left[(1-\alpha)^{1-\alpha} \alpha^{\alpha} \right]^{(1+\nu)/\Delta} \qquad (9.4)$$

In the case of a Rawlsian social welfare function, we can compare W_R^I and W_R^{II}:

$$W_R^{II} - W_R^I = \frac{1}{1+\nu} \alpha^{\alpha(1+\nu)/\Delta} a_1^{(1+\nu)/\Delta}$$
$$\left[\nu(1-\alpha)^{(1-\alpha)(1+\nu)/\Delta} \left[p + (1-p)\theta^{(1+\nu)/\nu} \right]^{\alpha(1+\nu)/\Delta} - \Delta \right]$$

If $W_R^{II} > W_R^I$, we can judge that this egalitarian public education system is superior to the private education system. The results seem to depend on the values of related parameters, because the sign of the above equation is indeterminate a priori. Still, one can qualitatively mention two things. First, the more inequality of innate ability there is—that is, with a higher θ—the more likely the inequality of $W_R^{II} > W_R^I$ is to hold, meaning that we can more easily justify this kind of public education. This makes sense intuitively: public education is financed by income tax paid by high-ability individuals as well low-ability ones, and the latter type of individuals can enjoy an indirect income transfer from the former through public education. Second, the lower the share of low-ability individuals is—that is, with lower p—the more likely it is that we can justify public education. It also sounds intuitive, because low-ability individuals can enjoy more financial support in per capita terms from this indirect income redistribution when they account for a smaller share of the total population.

As a numerical example, suppose that $\nu = 3$ and $\alpha = 0.1$, both of which look somewhat plausible. If we also tentatively set $p = 0.5$, θ can be as low as 1.027 to justify this uniform provision of public education. And, if we set $\theta = 1.5$, the share of high-ability individuals can be as high as 88.5% to make public education preferable to no public education. These examples imply that it is in general easy to justify egalitarian public education with a Rawlsian social welfare function, which puts most emphasis on equity.

How about the Benthamian case? Comparing the maximized levels of social welfare between public and private education yields

$$W_B^{II} - W_B^{I} = \frac{1}{1+\nu} \alpha^{\alpha(1+\nu)/\Delta} a_1^{(1+\nu)/\Delta}$$

$$\left\{ \nu(1-\alpha)^{(1-\alpha)(1+\nu)/\Delta} \left[p + (1-p)\theta^{(1+\nu)/\nu} \right]^{\nu/\Delta} \right.$$

$$\left. - \Delta \left[p + (1-p)\theta^{(1+\nu)/\Delta} \right] \right\}$$

Simple calculations show that $W_B^{II} < W_B^{I}$, meaning that private education is better than uniform public education from a Benthamian viewpoint.[4] In sharp contrast to the Rawlsian case, the government should not provide any public education, and instead should let each individual choose his or her optimal level of private education. This reflects the social assessment of a loss of economic efficiency caused by the negative impact of income tax on the incentive to work.

9.1.2.4. System III (Public-biased)

An important topic in public education has been how to allocate education resources among individuals of different abilities. In other words, should public education be progressive or regressive? On one hand, the government may want to provide lower-ability individuals with more education to reduce the potential income inequality that people would face after graduating from school. Egalitarian public education, which is described above, cannot reduce income inequality, even if it can give an equal opportunity to all individuals to receive an education and raise their productivity. On the other hand, the government may want to offer more

---

[4] First, define $f(\alpha) \equiv \nu(1-\alpha)^{(1-\alpha)(1+\nu)/\Delta} - \Delta$. Plugging $\nu = (\Delta+\alpha)/(1-\alpha)$ to it yields $f(\alpha) = (\Delta+\alpha)(1-\alpha)^{1/\Delta} - \Delta$. Then, $f'(\alpha) = -\alpha(1+\Delta)(1-\alpha)^{(1-\Delta)/\Delta}/\Delta < 0$, meaning that $f(\alpha)$ is a decreasing function of α. Given $f(0) = \Delta(1-0)^{1/\Delta} - \Delta = 0$, it concludes that for $0<\alpha<1, f(\alpha) < 0$, that is, $\nu(1-\alpha)^{(1-\alpha)(1+\nu)/\Delta} < \Delta$. ....(F1).
Second, define $g(\theta) \equiv \nu \ln\left\{ p + (1-p)\theta^{(1+\nu)/\nu} \right\} - \Delta \ln\left\{ p + (1-p)\theta^{(1+\nu)/\Delta} \right\}$. Then,

$$g'(\theta) = (1-p)(1+\nu)\left[p + (1-p)\theta^{(1+\nu)/\nu} \right]^{-1}$$

$$\left[p + (1-p)\theta^{(1+\nu)/\Delta} \right]^{-1} \left[1 - \theta^{\alpha(1+\nu)^2/\Delta \cdot \nu} \right] \theta^{1/\nu} < 0,$$

since $\theta > 1$, meaning that $g(\theta)$ is a decreasing function of θ. Given $g(0) = 0$, it concludes that for $\theta > 1$, $g(\theta) < 0$, that is, $\left[p + (1-p)\theta^{(1+\nu)/\nu} \right]^{\nu/\Delta}$ $< \left[p + (1-p)\theta^{(1+\nu)/\Delta} \right]$. ....(F2) Combining (F1) and (F2), we have $W_B^{II} < W_B^{I}$.

education to higher-ability individuals to raise the overall economic outcome most effectively. The latter type of education policy appears to favor high-ability individuals in general, but the possibility cannot be ruled out that it can also add to the utility of low-ability individuals. For example, low-ability individuals can enjoy the same level of public education with a lower tax rate if high-ability individuals get more education, obtain higher incomes, and pay more income tax to finance overall public education.

Consider the public education system in which the government can adjust the level of public education to each individual's ability. Each individual chooses the optimal level of labor supply to maximize his or her utility given the level of public education, $\overline{E}_i$, and tax rate, t. So each individual solves

$$\max_{\{L_i\}}: U_i = (1 - t)a_i\overline{E}_iL_i - \frac{L_i^{1+\nu}}{1 + \nu}$$

As in the case of uniform public education, each individual determines the labor supply such that

$$L_i = \left[(1 - t)a_i\overline{E}_i^{\alpha}\right]^{1/\nu}$$

Then, the budget constraint of the government is expressed in per capita terms as

$$p\overline{E}_1 + (1 - p)\overline{E}_2 = t\left[pa_1\overline{E}_1^{\alpha}L_1 + (1 - p)a_2\overline{E}_2^{\alpha}L_2\right]$$

Let us define λ as the "education ratio," which indicates the ratio of education offered to high-ability individuals to that offered to low-ability ones. If the optimal value of λ turns out to be greater (less) than one, regressive (progressive) public education can be justified. The level of public education provided to each type of individual is given by

$$\overline{E}_1 = \left[(1 - t)t^{\nu}\Omega^{\nu}\right]^{1/\Delta}, \quad \overline{E}_2 = \lambda\overline{E}_1$$

where

$$\Omega = \frac{pa_1^{(1+\nu)/\nu} + (1 - p)(a_2\lambda^{\alpha})^{(1+\nu)/\nu}}{p + (1 - p)\lambda} > 0$$

Then, the maximized utility of each type of individual is expressed as

$$
\begin{aligned}
U_1 &= \frac{\nu}{1+\nu} a_1^{(1+\nu)/\nu} \left[(1-t)\overline{E}_1^{\alpha} \right]^{(1+\nu)/\nu} \\
&= \frac{\nu}{1+\nu} a_1^{(1+\nu)/\nu} \Omega^{\alpha(1+\nu)/\Delta} \left[(1-t)^{1-\alpha} t^{\alpha} \right]^{(1+\nu)/\Delta} \\
U_2 &= \frac{\nu}{1+\nu} a_2^{(1+\nu)/\nu} \left[(1-t)\overline{E}_2^{\alpha} \right]^{(1+\nu)/\nu} \\
&= \frac{\nu}{1+\nu} \left(a_2 \lambda^{\alpha} \right)^{(1+\nu)/\nu} \Omega^{\alpha(1+\nu)/\Delta} \left[(1-t)^{1-\alpha} t^{\alpha} \right]^{(1+\nu)/\Delta}
\end{aligned}
$$

As can be seen from these social welfare functions, the government can separately choose the optimal value of the tax rate and that of education ratios. As for the tax rate, its optimal value is equal to α for both social welfare functions. This result reflects the assumption of the same elasticity of education output between the two ability types of individuals, as was the case for Systems I and II.

The task remaining for the government is to determine the optimal value of λ; that is, how to allocate tax revenues for public education to each type of individual. Assuming that $U_2 \geq U_1$, which requires $\lambda \geq \theta^{-1/\alpha}$,[5] the levels of social welfare are given by

$$
W_{\mathrm{R}}^{\mathrm{III}} = U_1 = \frac{\nu}{1+\nu} a_1^{(1+\nu)/\nu} \Omega^{\alpha(1+\nu)/\Delta} \left[(1-\alpha)^{1-\alpha} \alpha^{\alpha} \right]^{(1+\nu)/\Delta} \tag{9.5}
$$

$$
\begin{aligned}
W_{\mathrm{B}}^{\mathrm{III}} &= pU_1 + (1-p)U_2 \\
&= \frac{\nu}{1+\nu} [p + (1-p)\lambda] \Omega^{\nu/\Delta} \left[(1-\alpha)^{1-\alpha} \alpha^{\alpha} \right]^{(1+\nu)/\Delta}
\end{aligned} \tag{9.6}
$$

In the Rawlsian case, one can focus solely on maximizing Ω, as can be seen in equation (9.5). It is, however, impossible to algebraically solve the value of λ that satisfies the first-order condition: $d\Omega/d\lambda = 0$. Instead I assess $d\Omega/d\lambda$ at $\lambda = 1$ to obtain

$$
\left. \frac{d\Omega}{d\lambda} \right|_{\lambda=1} = \frac{1}{\nu}(1-p) a_1^{(1+\nu)/\nu} \left\{ [\alpha(1+\nu) - (1-p)\nu] \theta^{(1+\nu)/\nu} - p\nu \right\} \tag{9.7}
$$

The sign of this equation is ambiguous, but one can infer from its RHS that regressive public education is more likely to be justified where there is a wider gap of ability (higher θ) and a higher share of lower-ability

---

[5] This inequality can easily hold. For example, if $\alpha = 0.1$ and $\theta = 1.5$, $\lambda > \theta^{-1/\alpha} = 0.017$, implying that quite progressive education policy can be allowed.

individuals (higher p). These are intuitively understandable. With a wider gap of innate ability, low-ability individuals can expect more economic benefits from putting more weight on public education for high-ability individuals. Also, if high-ability individuals share a smaller part of society, there is more room for the government to offer them more education.

It is still unclear, however, to what extent such reasoning actually makes sense, so let us numerically check how realistic the conditions of θ and p that allow regressive public education look, compared with the egalitarian case. As in System II, let us assume that $v = 3$, $\alpha = 0.1$, and $p = 0.5$. Then, the RHS of equation (9.7) is negative regardless of the value of θ (> 1). This is generally the case for a combination of α that is not very low and p that is not very high, implying that it is difficult for the Rawlsian social welfare function to justify a regressive education policy.

By contrast, it is reasonable to expect that a regressive education policy is more acceptable in the Benthamian case, because it is likely to mitigate the distortional effects of public education and adds to economic efficiency. Indeed, differentiating W_B^{III} in equation (6) with respect to λ yields:

$$\frac{dW_B^{III}}{d\lambda} = \frac{vp(1-p)a_1^{(1+v)/v} \lambda^{\Delta/(1+v)}}{p + (1-p)\lambda} \Omega^{\alpha(1+v)/\Delta}$$
$$\left[(1-\alpha)^{1-\alpha}\alpha^\alpha\right]^{(1+v)/\Delta} \left[\theta^{(1+v)/v} - \lambda^{\Delta/v}\right]$$

Hence, the optimal value of λ is equal to $\theta^{(1+v)/\Delta}$, which is larger than one because $\theta > 1$, providing a rationale for regressive public education. As a numerical example where $v = 3$, $\alpha = 0.1$, and $\theta = 1.5$, the optimal value of λ is equal to 1.87. Moreover, the wider the gap of abilities is between the two types of individual, the more the government should spend on education for high-ability types. This is in line with the results of earlier studies that assumed a utilitarian government and justified a regressive education scheme.

Another question is whether this regressive system of public education is superior to the system in which only private education is available. Comparing W_B^{III} (with $\lambda = \theta^{(1+v)/\Delta}$) in equation (9.6) with W_B^I, we get

$$W_B^{III} - W_B^I = \frac{1}{1+v}\alpha^{\alpha(1+v)/\Delta} a_1^{(1+v)/\Delta}$$
$$\left[p + (1-p)\theta^{(1+v)/\Delta}\right]\left[v(1-\alpha)^{(1+\Delta)/\Delta} - \Delta\right]$$

Because a simple calculation shows that the sign of this inequality is negative,[6] we can conclude that the public education system, even if it is regressive, cannot exceed the private education system in the Benthamian case.

To sum up the comparisons made thus far, we can generally rank education systems in terms of social welfare:

Rawlsian case: System III (progressive) $\succ$ System II $\succ$ System I,
Benthamian case: System I $\succ$ System III (regressive) $\succ$ System II.

Of course, the real world lies between these two extreme cases, and the optimal education system relies heavily on society's judgment about a balance between equity and efficiency.

9.1.3. Comparisons of mixed systems

For Systems II and III, I assume that the government offers public education in a monopolistic manner, and that no private education is available. This assumption is unrealistic, of course; there is usually a mixed system of public and private education, and so I shall try to investigate what the optimal system looks like. There can be various types of mixed-education system, and it is beyond the scope of this chapter to discuss them in general. Instead, I assume that individuals are first required to receive and complete public education, which is uniformly or not uniformly offered according to their ability, and then receive additional, private education if they desire. The government aims to establish the optimal shape of this double-decker education system, given individuals' behaviors of utility maximization. An extreme case could be such that the government offers public education only to low-ability individuals and makes high-ability ones receive private education from the beginning. For simplicity, I also assume that the quality and unit cost are the same, respectively, between public and private education, and that each individual cannot receive *negative* private education; that is, there is a non-negative constraint on private education.

In this mixed education system, each individual solves

$$\max_{\{E_i, L_i\}} : U_i = (1-t)a_i\left(\overline{E_i} + E_i\right)^\alpha L_i - E_i - \frac{L_i^{1+\nu}}{1+\nu}$$

---

[6] Let us define $h(\alpha) \equiv \nu(1-\alpha)^{(1+\Delta)/\Delta} - \Delta = (\Delta+\alpha)(1-\alpha)^{1/\Delta} - \Delta$. Since $h'(\alpha) = -(1+\Delta)\alpha(1-\alpha)^{1/\Delta}/\Delta < 0$ and $h(0) = 0$, we have $h(\alpha) < 0$ and hence $W_B^{III} - W_B^I < 0$ for $0 < \alpha < 1$.

given the level of public education applied to his or her ability, $\overline{E}_i$, and the tax rate, t. Ignoring the non-negative constraint on private education, the optimal levels of private education and labor supply are given by

$$E_i = \left[\alpha^{\nu}(1-t)^{1+\nu}a_i^{1+\nu}\right]^{1/\Delta} - \overline{E}_i \tag{9.8}$$

$$L_i = \left[\alpha^{\alpha}(1-t)a_i\right]^{1/\Delta}$$

The former equation is derived from the condition that each individual should adjust the level of his or her private education to make the marginal product of total education he or she receives equal to its marginal cost. The per capita budget constraint of the government is expressed as

$$p\overline{E}_1 + (1-p)\overline{E}_2 = t\left[pa_1\left(\overline{E}_1 + E_1\right)^{\alpha}L_1 + (1-p)a_2\left(\overline{E}_2 + E_2\right)^{\alpha}L_2\right]$$

Defining λ as the education ratio, as before, which indicates the size of education for high-ability individuals in relation to that for high-ability individuals, we find that the optimal levels of public education and levels of maximized utility for each individual are given by

$$\overline{E}_1 = t(1-t)^{[1+\alpha(1+\nu)]/\Delta}\,\alpha^{\alpha(1+\nu)/\Delta}\,\frac{\Gamma}{p+(1-p)\lambda} \tag{9.9}$$

$$\overline{E}_2 = \lambda\overline{E}_1 \tag{9.10}$$

$$U_1 = \frac{1}{1+\nu}\alpha^{\alpha(1+\nu)/\Delta}(1-t)^{[1+\alpha(1+\nu)]/\Delta}\left[\Delta\, a_1^{(1+\nu)/\Delta}(1-t)\right.$$
$$\left. + \frac{(1+\nu)\Gamma}{p+(1-p)\lambda}t\right]$$

$$U_2 = \frac{1}{1+\nu}\alpha^{\alpha(1+\nu)/\Delta}(1-t)^{[1+\alpha(1+\nu)]/\Delta}\left[\Delta a_2^{(1+\nu)/\Delta}(1-t)\right.$$
$$\left. + \frac{(1+\nu)\lambda\Gamma}{p+(1-p)\lambda}t\right]$$

To meet the non-negative constraints $E_1 \geq 0$ and $E_2 \geq 0$, the tax rate must satisfy

$$t \leq \frac{[p+(1-p)\lambda]\alpha}{[p+(1-p)\lambda]\alpha + \left[p+(1-p)\theta^{(1+\nu)/\Delta}\right]} \tag{9.11}$$

$$t \leq \frac{[p+(1-p)\lambda]\alpha\theta^{(1+\nu)/\Delta}}{[p+(1-p)\lambda]\alpha\theta^{(1+\nu)/\Delta} + \lambda\left[p+(1-p)\theta^{(1+\nu)/\Delta}\right]} \tag{9.12}$$

respectively, given equations (9.8), (9.9), and (9.10). Here let us assume $\lambda < \theta^{(1+\nu)/\Delta}$, the RHS of which is equal to the optimal value of λ in the Benthamian case of System III, meaning that the government does not offer quite regressive education. Then, equation (9.12) automatically holds if equation (9.11) is satisfied, so we need to consider only (9.11), meaning that the non-negative constraint is binding only for low-ability individuals. A simple calculation can confirm that the optimal tax rate—which maximizes the utility of low-ability individuals, ignoring the non-negative constraint and with a given λ—cannot meet the condition of equation (9.11) as far as:

$$\lambda \leq \frac{\Delta(1-p)\theta^{(1+\nu)/\Delta} - \alpha p[1 + \alpha(1+\nu)]}{(1-p)\{\Delta + \alpha[1 + \alpha(1+\nu)]\}}$$

This inequality can hold with a relatively wide range of λ; for example, assuming $p = 0.5$, $\theta = 1.5$, $\alpha = 0.1$, and $\nu = 3$, the upper limit of λ is calculated as 1.72. It implies that low-ability individuals tend to be unwilling to receive additional, private education, even if the government conducts quite regressive education policy and spend less on education of low-ability individuals.

Therefore, in what follows, I concentrate on asymmetric mixed systems in which low-ability individuals receive only public education, while high-ability individuals receive both public education and additional, private education if they desire. More specifically, I consider two versions of mixed systems for comparison: System IV (*mixed-uniform*), in which the government offers the same level of public education to both low- and high-ability individuals, and only high-ability individuals can receive additional, private education; and System V (*mixed-biased*), in which the government adjusts the level of public education to the ability of each individual, and high-ability individuals can receive additional, private education.[7] We can reasonably expect System V to be superior to System IV, because the government can adjust the level of education to each individual in System V. System IV, however, appears to be a somewhat realistic option for providing public education, and so it is worth considering. Unfortunately, it is not possible to directly compare Systems IV and V to Systems I, II, and III, and so I leave their comparisons to numerical simulations later in the chapter.

---

[7] As discussed in the section on numerical simulations, the optimal shape of System V turns out to be such that the government does not offer any public education to high-ability individuals.

9.1.3.1. System IV (mixed-uniform)

In System IV, the government offers uniform, compulsory education to all individuals. Low-ability individuals receive only this public education, whereas high-ability individuals receive additional, private education if they desire. Public education is financed by proportional income tax, which is levied on both types of individual. High-ability individuals must additionally and directly pay for their private education.

Utility-maximization problems differ between the two types of individual. Low-ability individuals adjust labor supply to maximize their utility:

$$\max_{\{L_1\}}: \; U_1 = (1-t)a_1\overline{E}^{\alpha}L_1 - \frac{L_1^{1+\nu}}{1+\nu}$$

given the level of public education, $\overline{E}$, and the tax rate, t. Their optimal levels of labor supply and maximized level of utility are given by

$$L_1 = \left[(1-t)a_1\overline{E}^{\alpha}\right]^{1/\nu}$$

and

$$U_1 = \frac{\nu}{1+\nu}a_1^{(1+\nu)/\nu}\left[(1-t)\overline{E}^{\alpha}\right]^{(1+\nu)/\nu}$$

respectively. High-ability individuals adjust the levels of both education and labor supply to maximize their utility:

$$\max_{\{E_2,L_2\}}: \; U_2 = (1-t)a_2\left(\overline{E}+E_2\right)^{\alpha}L_2 - E_2 - \frac{L_2^{1+\nu}}{1+\nu}$$

Hence, the first-order conditions and the maximized utility are calculated as

$$E_2 = \left[\alpha^{\nu}(1-t)^{1+\nu}a_2^{1+\nu}\right]^{1/\Delta} - \overline{E}$$

$$L_2 = \left[\alpha^{\nu}(1-t)a_2\right]^{1/\Delta}$$

$$U_2 = \frac{\Delta}{1+\nu}\left[\alpha^{\alpha}(1-t)a_2\right]^{(1+\nu)/\Delta} + \overline{E}$$

The budget constraint of the government is given by

$$\overline{E} = t\left[pa_1\overline{E}^{\alpha}L_1 + (1-p)a_2\left(\overline{E}+E_2\right)^{\alpha}L_2\right]$$

Plugging each individual's labor supply and demand for education of high-ability individuals into this budget constraint leads to the level of public education:

$$\overline{E} = t\left[pa_1^{(1+\nu)/\nu}(1-t)^{1/\nu}\,\overline{E}^{\alpha(1+\nu)/\nu}\right.$$
$$\left. + (1-p)\alpha^{\alpha(1+\nu)/\Delta}\,(1-t)^{[1+\alpha(1+\nu)]/\Delta}\,a_2^{(1+\nu)/\Delta}\right] \tag{9.13}$$

Given the tax rate, t, one can implicitly derive the level of public education, $\overline{E}$, by solving (9.13).

The levels of social welfare are calculated as

$$W_{\mathrm{R}}^{\mathrm{IV}} = U_1 = \frac{\nu}{1+\nu}a_1^{(1+\nu)/\nu}\left[(1-t)\overline{E}^{\alpha}\right]^{(1+\nu)/\nu} \tag{9.14}$$

$$W_{\mathrm{B}}^{\mathrm{IV}} = pU_1 + (1-p)U_2 = \frac{p\nu}{1+\nu}a_1^{(1+\nu)/\nu}\left[(1-t)\overline{E}^{\alpha}\right]^{(1+\nu)/\nu}$$
$$+ \frac{(1-p)\Delta}{1+\nu}\left[\alpha^{\alpha}(1-t)a_2\right]^{(1+\nu)/\Delta} + (1-p)\overline{E} \tag{9.15}$$

assuming that $U_2 \geq U_1$.[8] This assumption holds with a wide variety of plausible parameter value sets, as well as under the numerical simulations presented in the section on numerical simulations below. Because one cannot algebraically obtain the optimal values for tax rate and public education, I instead search for them with the help of a computer in the next section. Conceptually, I first put a certain small number for t in equation (9.13), and derive the value of $\overline{E}$ that satisfies (9.13); second, I put those values of t and $\overline{E}$ into equations (9.14) or (9.15) for social welfare; third, I iterate the same calculation with all $t \in [0, 1]$ having a certain ridge to find the optimal value of t that maximizes social welfare. I present the results of this procedure in the section on numerical simulations.

9.1.3.2. System V (mixed-biased)

Finally, let us consider System V, in which the government adjusts the level of public education to each individual. As in System IV, low-ability individuals receive only public education, and high-ability individuals can receive private education in addition to public education. Utility-maximization problems for each type of individual, which are almost the same as in System IV, are expressed as

$$\max_{\{L_1\}}: \ U_1 = (1-t)a_1\overline{E}_1\,L_1 - \frac{L_1^{1+\nu}}{1+\nu}$$

---

[8] This assumption holds with a wide variety of plausible parameter value sets, as well as under our numerical simulations.

$$\max_{\{E_2, L_2\}} : U_2 = (1 - t)a_2\left(\overline{E}_2 + E_2\right)^\alpha L_2 - E_2 - \frac{L_2^{1+\nu}}{1 + \nu}$$

The maximized levels of their maximized utility are calculated as

$$U_1 = \frac{\nu}{1 + \nu}a_1^{(1+\nu)/\nu}\left[(1 - t)\overline{E}_1^\alpha\right]^{(1+\nu)/\nu}$$

$$U_2 = \frac{\Delta}{1 + \nu}\left[a^\alpha(1 - t)a_2\right]^{(1+\nu)/\Delta} + \lambda\overline{E}_1$$

where λ indicates the education ratio as in System III. The budget constraint of the government in per capita terms is expressed as

$$p\overline{E}_1 + (1 - p)\overline{E}_2 = t\left[pa_1 E_1^\alpha L_1 + (1 - p)a_2\left(\overline{E}_2 + E_2\right)^\alpha L_2\right]$$

which is rewritten as

$$\begin{aligned}\overline{E}_1 = t\Big[&pa_1^{(1+\nu)/\nu}(1 - t)^{1/\nu}\overline{E}_1^{\alpha(1+\nu)/\nu} + (1 - p)\alpha^{\alpha(1+\nu)/\Delta}\\ &(1 - t)^{[1+\alpha(1+\nu)]/\Delta}\, a_2^{(1+\nu)/\Delta}\Big]/[p + (1 - p)\lambda]\end{aligned} \tag{9.16}$$

The levels of social welfare are given by

$$W_R^V = U_1 = \frac{\nu}{1 + \nu}a_1^{(1+\nu)/\nu}\left[(1 - t)\overline{E}_1^\alpha\right]^{(1+\nu)/\nu} \tag{9.17}$$

$$\begin{aligned}W_B^V = pU_1 + (1 - p)U_2 = &\frac{p\nu}{1 + \nu}a_1^{(1+\nu)/\nu}\left[(1 - t)\overline{E}_1^\alpha\right]^{(1+\nu)/\nu}\\ &+ \frac{(1 - p)\Delta}{1 + \nu}\left[\alpha^\alpha(1 - t)a_2\right]^{(1+\nu)/\Delta} + (1 - p)\lambda\overline{E}_1\end{aligned} \tag{9.18}$$

assuming that $U_2 \geq U_1$.[9] As in System IV, one cannot algebraically solve the optimal values of the tax rate, t, and the education weight, λ, and so I apply an iterative method to obtain them. In the Rawlsian case, however, equations (9.16) and (9.17) imply that the government should reduce λ to zero, suggesting that it should establish a progressive education scheme with higher inequality aversion. In the Benthamian case, a higher λ per se raises the public education for high-ability individuals and their utility. As implied by equation (9.18), however, that effect is likely to be at least partly offset by the negative effect of lower education offered to low-ability

---

[9] This assumption holds with a wide variety of plausible parameter value sets, as well as under the numerical simulations presented below.

individuals. If the optimal tax rate is low, the possibility that the optimal value of λ is equal to zero as in the Rawlsian case cannot be ruled out.

9.2. Numerical simulations

This section presents some numerical simulations to compare the above-mentioned alternative education systems, which are illustrated in Figure 9.1, and to examine how the results are sensitive to related parameters. It is particularly interesting to compare Systems I, II, and III with Systems IV and V, because it is difficult to do so algebraically.

9.2.1. Method and parameters

I assume a general social welfare function:

$$W(\varepsilon) = p\frac{U_1^{1-\varepsilon} - 1}{1 - \varepsilon} + (1 - p)\frac{U_2^{1-\varepsilon} - 1}{1 - \varepsilon}, \ 0 \le \varepsilon, \varepsilon \neq 1$$

$$W(1) = p\log U_1 + (1 - p)\log U_2,$$

where ε is a parameter of inequality aversion. $W(0)$ corresponds to the Benthamian social welfare function, and $W(+\infty)$ corresponds to the Rawlsian function. I apply five values to ε: 0 (Benthamian), 0.5, 1, 1.5, and $+\infty$ (Rawlsian), and examine how the relative weight put on economic equity or efficiency affects the shape of the optimal education system. Numerical calculations are straightforward in Systems I and II, because I have already algebraically obtained the optimal values of policy variables (regardless of the social welfare function). For the remaining three systems, it is necessary to conduct iterative calculations to find them.

For the parameters, I set up the benchmark $\alpha = 0.1$, $v = 3$, $\theta = 1.5$ and $p = 0.5$. As discussed in Systems I–III, the value of α roughly corresponds to the share of spending on education in total wage income. According to the OECD's *Education at a Glance* (2004), the average share of spending on education (both public and private) was 5.6% of nominal GDP. Given that national income is about 85% of nominal GDP on average among OECD countries, and that the share of wage income in national income is about 70%, the share of spending on education in wage income is nearly 10%. There is a wide range of estimates for labor-supply elasticity, which is an inverse of v, but I assume that $v = 3$ as a base case, as did Hanushek, Leung, and Yilmaz (2003). Assumptions about θ and p are

Figure 9.1. **Alternative education systems**

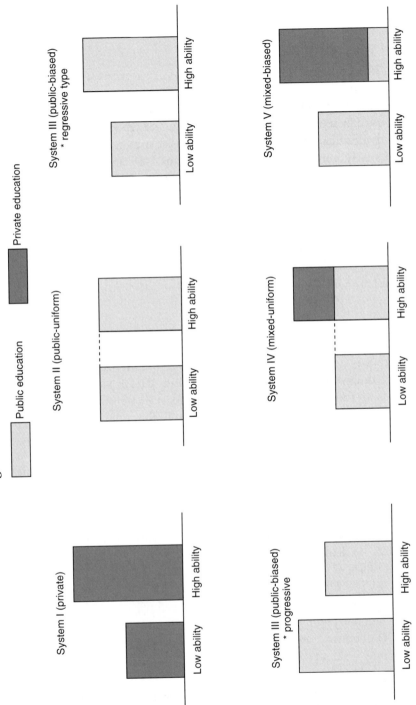

tentative, but I shall check how sensitive the results are to a change in their values later.

9.2.1.1. Results

Table 9.1 summarizes the simulation results using different values of inequality aversion, ε, in terms of social welfare, tax rate, and relative weight on education of high-ability individuals. Four points are worth mentioning.

First, in System III, where there is no private education and the government adjusts the level of public education according to the individual's ability, λ is more likely to exceed one with a lower ε; that is, regressive education tends to be justified with a lower inequality aversion. It should be emphasized, however, that the rationale for regressive education depends greatly on how much importance society puts on inequality

Table 9.1.   Social welfare under alternative education systems

Education System	Inequality Aversion (ε)				
	$+\infty$ (Rawlsian)	1.5	1	0.5	0 (Benthamian)
Social welfare: level (W)					
I. Private	0.4561	−0.5647	−0.4731	−0.4021	0.6536
II. Public-uniform	0.4768	−0.5534	−0.4704	−0.4047	0.6477
III. Public-biased	0.5084	−0.5528	−0.4703	−0.4032	0.6518
IV. Mixed-uniform	0.4780	−0.5474	−0.4650	−0.3997	0.6524
V. Mixed-biased	0.5268	−0.5208	−0.4514	−0.3942	0.6533
Social welfare: ranking order					
I. Private	5	5	5	3	1
II. Public-uniform	4	4	4	5	5
III. Public-biased	2	3	3	4	4
IV. Mixed-uniform	3	2	2	2	3
V. Mixed-biased	1	1	1	1	2
Optimal education ratio (λ)					
III. Public-biased	0.08	0.86	1.07	1.39	1.87
V. Mixed-biased	0.00	0.00	0.00	0.00	0.00
Optimal tax rate (t)					
I. Private	–	–	–	–	–
II. Public-uniform	0.100	0.100	0.100	0.100	0.100
III. Public-biased	0.100	0.100	0.100	0.100	0.100
IV. Mixed-uniform	0.091	0.079	0.076	0.072	0.067
V. Mixed-biased	0.091	0.050	0.046	0.040	0.035

Note: $\alpha = 0.1$, $p = 0.5$, $\theta = 1.5$, $v = 3$.
   Levels of social welfare cannot be compared under different values of inequality aversion.
   "Optimal education ratio" means the ratio of public education offered to high-ability individuals to that offered to low-ability individuals.

Figure 9.2.   Education ratio and social welfare

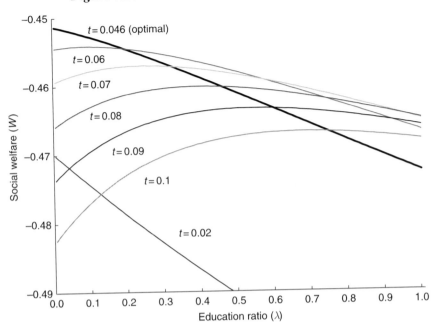

Note: $\alpha = 0.1$, $p = 0.5$, $\upsilon = 3$, $\varepsilon = 1$.
"Education ratio" means the ratio of public education offered to high-ability individuals to that offered to low-ability individuals.

aversion. With a higher ε, λ is more likely to fall below one, indicating the optimality of progressive rather than regressive education.

Second, in System V, where the government adjusts the level of public education to each individual and high-ability individuals can receive private education, λ turns out to be equal to zero in all cases, meaning that the government should spend all tax revenues on education for low-ability individuals. This result is somewhat surprising, even though it is reasonable to expect that higher inequality aversion requires the government to reduce the relative weight of education for high-ability individuals. To explain the reason, Figure 9.2 depicts how the value of λ affects social welfare at a given tax rate in the case of $\varepsilon = 1$.[10] As can be seen from this figure, the higher the tax rate is, the higher the relative weight of education for high-ability individuals should be. The level of social welfare is, however, maximized with a relatively low tax rate—0.046 in

[10] We can depict the same pattern of this figure in the cases of $\varepsilon = 1.5$ and $\varepsilon = +\infty$ (Benthamian).

this case—which makes the optimal value of λ equal to zero. This result appears to depend on model specifications and parameter values but implies the rationale for progressive education if additional, private education is available.

Third, the ranking order of social welfare is somewhat sensitive to the degree of inequality aversion. In a benchmark case with $\varepsilon = 1$, we recognize that System V $\succ$ System IV $\succ$ System III $\succ$ System II $\succ$ System I. The order differs with degrees of inequality aversion, ε; a lower ε tends to prefer System I, whereas a higher ε can make System III more preferable. It should also be stressed that System V is most preferable, except in the Benthamian case. Finally, Systems IV and V, in which private education is available (to high-ability individuals), are superior to Systems II and III, in which the government monopolizes the provision of education, except in the Rawlsian case.

Fourth, the tax rate is lower in Systems IV and V than in Systems II and III, since the government can at least partly save public education costs to high-ability individuals in the former mixed systems. Lower taxes tend to alleviate the loss of efficiency and add to the advantage of that system.

Table 9.2 summarizes education levels, both publicly provided and privately demanded, in each system. Low-ability individuals receive more education in Systems II–VI than in System I, confirming that public education systems are effective for raising their education level. Together with results in Table 9.1, this suggests that public education can raise utility levels of low-ability individuals. By contrast, any commitment to education by the government lowers the education level of high-ability individuals. It implies that the government needs to explain why it offers public education at the sacrifice of the utility of high-ability individuals. The most reasonable rationale is income transfer from high-ability individuals to low-ability ones from a viewpoint of equity.

9.2.1.2. Sensitivity Analysis

The assessment of education systems appears to rely heavily on other parameters, as well as inequality aversion. In what follows, I present some results of a sensitivity analysis. I change one of the key parameters from the benchmark, while keeping the other parameters unchanged and assuming that the inequality aversion is equal to one, and see how the outcome is affected. Table 9.3 summarizes the results.

We notice, first, that the ranking order is somewhat sensitive to the ability ratio, θ. The smaller the gap in ability, the fewer benefits individuals receive from the government's provision of public education. Second, the higher education output elasticity, α, is—in other words, the less concave the education output function is—the less attractive public education becomes. These two results seem reasonable because public education

Table 9.2. Education levels under alternative education systems

Education System	Inequality Aversion (ε)									
	+∞ (Rawlsian)		1.5		1		0.5		0 (Benthamian)	
	Public	Private	Public	Private	Public	Private	Public	Private	Public	Private
Low-ability individuals										
I. Private	0	0.070	0	0.070	0	0.070	0	0.070	0	0.070
II. Public-uniform	0.096	0	0.096	0	0.096	0	0.096	0	0.096	0
III. Public-biased	0.155	0	0.103	0	0.093	0	0.081	0	0.067	0
IV. Mixed-uniform	0.088	0	0.077	0	0.074	0	0.070	0	0.065	0
V. Mixed-biased	0.184	0	0.100	0	0.092	0	0.079	0	0.069	0
High-ability individuals										
I. Private	0	0.131	0	0.131	0	0.131	0	0.131	0	0.131
II. Public-uniform	0.096	0	0.096	0	0.096	0	0.096	0	0.096	0
III. Public-biased	0.012	0	0.088	0	0.099	0	0.112	0	0.126	0
IV. Mixed-uniform	0.088	0.025	0.077	0.039	0.074	0.042	0.070	0.047	0.065	0.053
V. Mixed-biased	0	0.113	0	0.121	0	0.122	0	0.123	0	0.124

Note: $\alpha = 0.1$, $p = 0.5$, $\theta = 1.5$, $v = 3$.

Table 9.3.   *Sensitivity analysis of social welfare ranks*

Ability ratio (θ)	1.1	1.25	1.5	2	2.5
I. Private	2	3	5	5	5
II. Public-uniform	5	5	4	4	4
III. Public-biased	4	4	3	3	3
IV. Mixed-uniform	3	2	2	2	2
V. Mixed-biased	1	1	1	1	1

Education elasticity (α)	0.025	0.05	0.1	0.2	0.3
I. Private	5	5	5	2	2
II. Public-uniform	4	4	4	5	5
III. Public-biased	3	3	3	4	4
IV. Mixed-uniform	2	2	2	3	3
V. Mixed-biased	1	1	1	1	1

Share of low-ability individuals (p)	0.1	0.25	0.5	0.75	0.9
I. Private	3	5	5	5	3
II. Public-uniform	5	4	4	4	5
III. Public-biased	4	3	3	3	4
IV. Mixed-uniform	2	2	2	2	2
V. Mixed-biased	1	1	1	1	1

Inverse of labor supply elasticity (v)	1	2	3	4	5
I. Private	5	5	5	5	5
II. Public-uniform	4	4	4	4	4
III. Public-biased	3	3	3	3	3
IV. Mixed-uniform	2	2	2	2	2
V. Mixed-biased	1	1	1	1	1

Note: Inequality aversion: $\varepsilon = 1$. Benchmark: $\theta = 1.5$, $\alpha = 0.1$, $p = 0.5$, $v = 3$.

works as a device for income redistribution within my framework: The smaller ability gap and lower concavity of the education output function make income redistribution through public education less effective. Third, if the relative share of the total population, p, is significantly different between the two ability types, a biased allocation of public education tends to be less effective in providing overall social welfare. Finally, the inverse of labor supply elasticity, v, does not affect the ranking order of the education systems.

Looking through these variations, we can conclude from this table that a combination of public and private education tends to be generally superior to a monopolistic provision of education by the government. The table also suggests that the government should put more emphasis on offering public education to low-ability individuals and allow high-ability individuals to receive private education. If no private education is available, however, we can justify both regressive and progressive public education, depending on the degree of inequality aversion.

9.3. Extension: Public education plus income redistribution

It is easy to extend the analysis to another case. One of the interesting issues is how introducing other devices for income redistribution affects the optimal structure of the education system. In fact, Ulph (1977) examined education policies when both education and income redistribution policies were optimized simultaneously and showed the possibility that regressive educational policies were justified. As implied by Lommerud (1989), another rationale for regressive education is that it can restore the incentive of high-ability individuals to seek higher education, which is blunted by redistribution policies. Let us deal with this issue here, based on the framework in System III, in which the government adjusts education inputs to an individual's ability and no private education is available.

It is plausible to suspect that the results depend on the shape of the social welfare function. On one hand, income redistribution in general tends to be more desirable in a society with stronger inequality aversion. On the other hand, I have already shown that progressive education is more likely to be justified in such a society. As suggested by Ulph and Lommerud, however, income-redistribution policies are expected to allow the government to provide less progressive education, and a combination of these two policies could raise net social welfare.

Let us consider a very simple policy of income redistribution: to give a lump-sum subsidy to all individuals, regardless of their income and ability levels, and finance it with a proportional income tax. The government uses tax revenues to provide both (biased) public education and the subsidy. Then, each individual solves

$$\max_{\{L_i\}}: \ U_i = a_i(1-t)\overline{E}_iL_i + S - \frac{L_i^{1+\nu}}{1+\nu}$$

where S is a lump-sum subsidy. The optimal level of labor supply is given in the same way as in System III:

$$L_i = \left[(1-t)a_i\overline{E}_i^{\alpha}\right]^{1/\nu}$$

and the budget constraint in per capita terms of the government is given by

$$p\overline{E}_1 + (1-p)\overline{E}_2 + S = t\left[pa_1\overline{E}_1^{\alpha}L_1 + (1-p)a_2\overline{E}_2^{\alpha}L_2\right]$$

If we set $\overline{E}_2 = \lambda\overline{E}_1$ and $S = \eta\overline{E}_1$ $(\eta \geq 0)$, then the levels of public education and subsidy are expressed as

$$\overline{E}_1 = \left[(1-t)t^{\nu}\tilde{\Omega}^{\nu}\right]^{1/\Delta}, \quad \overline{E}_2 = \lambda\overline{E}_1, \quad S = \eta\overline{E}_1$$

where

$$\tilde{\Omega} = \frac{pa_1^{(1+\nu)/\nu} + (1-p)(a_2\lambda^{\alpha})^{(1+\nu)/\nu}}{p + (1-p)\lambda + \eta} > 0$$

Each individual's maximized utility is given by

$$U_1 = \frac{\nu}{1+\nu}a_1^{(1+\nu)/\nu}\tilde{\Omega}^{\alpha(1+\nu)/\Delta}\left[(1-t)^{1-\alpha}t^{\alpha}\right]^{(1+\nu)/\Delta}$$
$$+ \eta\tilde{\Omega}^{\nu/\Delta}\left[(1-t)^{\nu}t^{\nu}\right]^{1/\Delta}$$

$$U_2 = \frac{\nu}{1+\nu}(a_2\lambda^{a})^{(1+\nu)/\nu}\tilde{\Omega}^{\alpha(1+\nu)/\Delta}\left[(1-t)^{1-\alpha}t^{\alpha}\right]^{(1+\nu)/\Delta}$$
$$+ \eta\tilde{\Omega}^{\nu/\Delta}\left[(1-t)^{\nu}t^{\nu}\right]^{1/\Delta}$$

And the levels of social welfare are given by

$$W_R^{III'} = U_1 = \frac{\nu}{1+\nu}a_1^{(1+\nu)/\nu}\tilde{\Omega}^{\alpha(1+\nu)/\Delta}\left[(1-t)^{1-\alpha}t^{\alpha}\right]^{(1+\nu)/\Delta}$$
$$+ \eta\tilde{\Omega}^{\nu/\Delta}\left[(1-t)^{\nu}t^{\nu}\right]^{1/\Delta}$$

$$W_B^{III'} = \frac{\nu}{1+\nu}\left[pa_1^{(1+\nu)/\nu} + (1-p)(a_2\lambda^{\alpha})^{(1+\nu)/\nu}\right]\tilde{\Omega}^{\alpha(1+\nu)/\Delta}$$
$$\left[(1-t)^{1-\alpha}t^{\alpha}\right]^{(1+\nu)/\Delta} + \eta\tilde{\Omega}^{\nu/\Delta}\left[(1-t)^{\nu}t^{\nu}\right]^{1/\Delta}$$

on the assumption that $U_2 \geq U_1$, which requires $\lambda \geq \theta^{-1/\alpha}$.

The government searches for an optimal set comprising tax rate, t, education ratio, λ, and subsidy ratio, η, to maximize social welfare, which is determined by these two utilities based on the degree of inequality aversion. We cannot algebraically solve this. In the Benthamian case, however, it is possible to show $dW_B^{III'}/d\eta|_{\eta=0} < 0$ with the tax and education ratio being equal to their optimal values in the case of no subsidy

(System III), meaning that the government should not enact any subsidy.[11] In the cases with positive inequality aversion, however, we cannot rule out a positive subsidy; indeed, we can easily confirm the optimality of a positive subsidy in the Rawlsian case.[12] Furthermore, assuming a positive value of the optimal subsidy ($\eta > 0$), the government should raise both the education ratio and the tax rate more than otherwise.[13]

Table 9.4 summarizes the simulation results, comparing the cases with and without a lump-sum subsidy under the different values of inequality aversion (the without case corresponds to the original System III). As anticipated, the Benthamian case does not allow the government to enact a subsidy: It should instead keep the regressive structure of public education ($\lambda = 1.87$) and the tax rate ($\lambda = 0.1$) unchanged from the case without. As the degree of inequality aversion increases, however, the government can both introduce the subsidy and raise the regressivity (or lower progressivity) of public education; for example, in the case of $\varepsilon = 1$, the optimal education ratio rises from 1.18 to 1.07. At the same time, the optimal tax rate rises and social welfare improves. Figure 9.3, which illustrates the main results in Table 4, shows an upward shift of the optimal education ratio curve with a lump-sum subsidy at each value of inequality aversion. These results imply that additional redistribution

---

[11] A simple calculation yields

$$\left.\frac{dW_B^{III'}}{d\eta}\right|_{\eta=0} = \Omega^{\nu/\Delta}\left\{\left[(1-\alpha)^{\nu}\alpha^{\nu}\right]^{1/\Delta} - \frac{\alpha\nu}{\Delta}\left[(1-\alpha)^{(1-\alpha)}\alpha^{\alpha}\right]^{(1+\nu)/\Delta}\right\}, \text{ and also confirm}$$

$$\left[(1-\alpha)^{\nu}\alpha^{\nu}\right] \div \left(\frac{\alpha\nu}{\Delta}\right)^{\Delta}\left[(1-\alpha)^{(1-\alpha)}\alpha^{\alpha}\right]^{(1+\nu)} = (1-\alpha)^{\nu-(1-\alpha)(1+\nu)}\left[1-\frac{\alpha(1+\nu)}{\nu}\right]^{\nu-\alpha(1+\nu)}$$

$$< (1-\alpha)^{\nu-1} < 1, \text{ provided } \nu > 1. \text{ So, we have } \left.\frac{dW_B^{III'}}{d\eta}\right|_{\eta=0} < 0.$$

[12] As in note 10, we have $\left.\dfrac{dW_R^{III'}}{d\eta}\right|_{\eta=0} = \Omega^{\nu/\Delta}\left\{\left[(1-\alpha)^{\nu}\alpha^{\nu}\right]^{1/\Delta} - \right.$

$\left.\dfrac{\phi\alpha\nu}{\Delta}\left[(1-\alpha)^{(1-\alpha)}\alpha^{\alpha}\right]^{(1+\nu)/\Delta}\right\}$, where $\phi \equiv \left[p+(1-p)(\theta\lambda^{\alpha})^{(1+\nu)/\nu}\right]^{-1}$ (≤ 1 for $\lambda \geq \theta^{-1/\alpha}$).

If ϕ is not very large, we can have: $\left.\dfrac{dW_R^{III'}}{d\eta}\right|_{\eta=0} > 0$ from note 10. We can confirm that it holds with $p=0.5$, $\theta=1.5$, $\alpha=0.1$, $t=0.1$, and $\lambda=0.08$, which correspond to the Rawlsian case in System III.

[13] We have $\tilde{\Omega} = \dfrac{p+(1-p)\lambda}{p+(1-p)\lambda+\eta}\Omega$, and can assume that Ω is maximized at Ω^* with

$\lambda=\lambda^*$. Then, we have $\left.\dfrac{d\tilde{\Omega}}{d\eta}\right|_{\lambda=\lambda^*} = \dfrac{(1-p)\eta}{[p+(1-p)\lambda+\eta]^2}\Omega^* > 0$, if $\eta>0$. Hence, if $\eta>0$, both U_1 and U_2 are maximized with $\lambda > \lambda^*$. Moreover, for both U_1 and U_2, the first term of the RHS is maximized with $t=\alpha$ and the second term is maximized with $t = \nu/(1+\nu)(>\alpha)$, so that the optimal tax rate lies between the two provided that $\eta > 0$.

Table 9.4.   **Lump-sum subsidy and biased education**

Condition	Inequality Aversion (ε)				
	$+\infty$ (Rawlsian)	1.5	1	0.5	0 (Benthamian)
Without lump-sum subsidy					
Social welfare level (W)	0.5084	−0.5528	−0.4703	−0.4032	0.6518
Optimal education ratio (λ)	0.08	0.86	1.07	1.39	1.87
Optimal tax rate (t)	0.100	0.100	0.100	0.100	0.100
With lump-sum subsidy					
Social welfare level (W)	0.5528	−0.5458	−0.4682	−0.4031	0.6518
Optimal education ratio (λ)	0.47	1.05	1.18	1.40	1.87
Optimal tax rare (t)	0.394	0.209	0.169	0.109	0.100
Optimal subsidy rate (η)	2.16	1.12	0.75	0.11	0.00

Note: $\alpha = 0.1$, $p = 0.5$, $\theta = 1.5$, $v = 3$. System III is assumed.

"Optimal subsidy ratio" means the optimal ratio of a lump-sum subsidy to public education offered to low-ability individuals.

"Optimal education ratio" means the optimal ratio of public education offered to high-ability individuals to that offered to low-ability individuals.

Levels of social welfare cannot be compared under different values of inequality aversion.

Figure 9.3.   *Optimal education ratio*

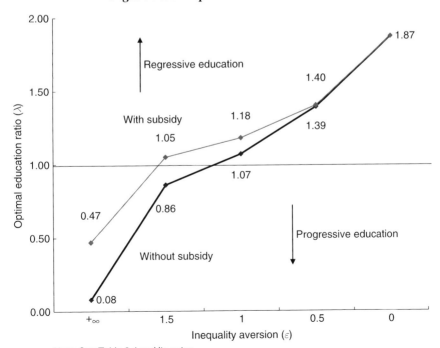

Note: See Table 9.4 and its notes.

policy can make regressive (or less progressive) public education more acceptable.

9.4. Summary and Conclusion

Using a simplified model and numerical simulations, this chapter has shown what optimal education policies look like under a trade-off between equity and efficiency. The analysis has covered a wide variety of social welfare functions, including Benthamian (utilitarian) and Rawlsian functions as two opposite extremes. It has also examined cases in which private education is available in addition to public education, as well as the cases in which other redistribution policies are enacted simultaneously with public education. The key results can be summarized as follows.

First, a mixed system of public and private education tends to be superior to the monopolistic provision of public education by the government. The government should put more emphasis on offering public education to low-ability individuals, and give high-ability individuals a chance to receive private education. High-ability individuals can contribute to public education by paying income tax to finance its costs.

Second, if there is no private education available for institutional reasons, the government should adjust the level of public education to the ability of each individual, rather than offer uniform public education. A regressive structure of public education tends to be more acceptable if the degree of inequality aversion is low or if there are other redistributional devices. But this does not mean that progressive education is inferior, as it tends to be desirable under high inequality aversion.

Third, these results depend on certain parameters, especially the ability gap between individuals and a higher elasticity of education. A wider gap in individuals' ability tends to raise the superiority of regressive public education, and a higher input elasticity of education output tends to make public education less attractive as a device for income redistribution.

The analysis has several limitations because it is based on an extremely simplified framework, which aims to concentrate on a trade-off between equity and efficiency in education. The first is that the assumption that both each individual and the government have full information about an individual's ability before education is unrealistic. As suggested by Stiglitz's (1975) pioneering work, the role of education as a device for screening each individual's ability affects the optimal shape of education policy.

A second limitation is that education costs, whether paid directly or through taxes, are often paid by parents rather than children. Hence, the impact of education policy on social welfare, which is likely to be transmitted across generations, can be more precisely investigated in an overlapping-generations framework.

A third limitation is that the scope of externality of education discussed in this chapter is limited. It considers only the case in which an individual's taxes can be reduced by higher education output by other individuals. However, an individual is likely to enjoy more direct externality from others' human capital accumulation. If we take into account this sort of externality, the assessment of education policy will be more mixed.

Finally, another consideration is the type of education system that people choose, as many researchers, including Stiglitz (1974) and Epple and Romano (1996, 1998), have discussed. The relation between a design for optimal education regimes and the public choosing them presents another important issue to be addressed.

References

Arrow, Kenneth. J. 1971. "A utilitarian approach to the concept of equality of public expenditures". *Quarterly Journal of Economics* 85(3): 175–208.

Bruno, Michael. 1976. "Equality, complementarity and the incidence of public expenditures". *Journal of Public Economics* 6(4): 395–407.

De Fraja, Gianni. 2002. "The design of optimal education policies". *Review of Economic Studies* 69(2): 436–66.

Dur, Robert A. J. and Coen N. Teulings. 2003. Are education subsidies an efficient redistributive device? Tinbergen Institute Discussion Paper 03-024/3. Amsterdam.

Epple, Dennis, and Richard E. Romano. 1996. "Ends against the middle: Determining public service provision when there are private alternatives". *Journal of Public Economics* 62(3): 297–325.

———.1998. "Competition between private and public schools, vouchers, and peer-group effects". *American Economic Review* 88(1): 33–62.

Fernández, Raquel and Richard Rogerson. 1997. "Education finance reform: A dynamic perspective". *Journal of Policy Analysis and Management* 16(1): 67–84.

Glomm, Gerhard and B. Ravikumar. 1992. "Public versus private investment in human capital: Endogenous growth and income inequality". *Journal of Political Economy* 100(4): 818–34.

Gradstein, Mark and Moshe Justman. 1997. "Democratic choice of an education system: Implications for growth and income distribution". *Journal of Economic Growth* 2(2): 169–83.

Hanushek, Eric A., Charles Ka Yui Leung and Kuzey Yilmaz. 2003. "Redistribution through education and other transfer mechanisms". *Journal of Monetary Economics* 50(8): 1719–50.

Lommerud, Kjell Erik. 1989. "Educational subsidies when relative income matters". *Oxford Economic Papers* 41(3): 640–52.

Organization for Economic Co-operation and Development (OECD). *Education at a Glance*. Paris.

Saint-Paul, Gilles, and Thierry Verdier. 1993. "Education, democracy and growth". *Journal of Development Economics* 42(2): 399–407.

Stiglitz, Joseph E. 1974. "The demand for education in public and private school systems". *Journal of Public Economics* 3(3): 349–85.

———. 1975. "The theory of 'screening,' education and the distribution of income". *American Economic Review* 65(3): 283–300.

Ulph, David. 1977. "On the optimal distribution and educational expenditure". *Journal of Public Economics* 8(3): 341–56.

CHAPTER 10

Why Are Japanese Refusing to Pay the National Pension Tax? A Simultaneous Equation Analysis

Mitoshi Yamaguchi and Noriko Aoki

The average rate of payment into the Japanese National Pension is very low, at about 60% of the amount expected to be paid into the system, and it is likely to decrease further. One reason is that as the Japanese birth rate decreased drastically, many pensioners have been afraid of not receiving benefits after paying into the system. In 2001 the number of unpaid pensioners was 3,267,000. This situation has caused people to have doubts about the system. Problems associated with the pension system are therefore a topic of general concern in Japan. The rate of payment into the National Pension varies widely by prefecture, however. This chapter attempts to clarify the payment structure of the pension system, giving due consideration to regional perspectives, by using a simultaneous equation.

The Japanese Pension Insurance System was established in 1942. Initially it provided pension insurance for workers who paid into the system, but in 1944 it was expanded to provide employees' pension insurance to others. A legislative change called the Japanese Pension Act came into effect in 1959, forcing all Japanese to join the pension system. Currently the system divides policyholders into three groups. The first consists of the self-employed, farmers, and students. The second group comprises all other workers (those who belong to the employees' pension system) and civil servants (who belong to the mutual pension system). The spouses of those in the second group belong to the third group. The first and third groups are entitled to receive only a basic pension. The second group can receive both the basic pension and earnings-related benefits.

The payers of rational pension have to pay 202, 800 yen per year which increases 3,360 yen each year. The Japanese government began granting an

I thank Kazuki Taketoshi and other participants for helpful comments and suggestions. I also appreciate financial support from COE fund to Kobe University.

POPULATION CHANGE, LABOR MARKETS, AND SUSTAINABLE GROWTH
VOLUME 281   ISSN 0573-8555/DOI 10.1016/S0573-8555(07)81010-8

exemption from paying into the national pension system for university students in 2000 and a partial exemption for the poor in 2002. The payers of employees' pension must pay 14.288% (in 2006) of their annual income into the employees' pension system. The amount of benefits the system delivers is about 50% of the annual disposable per capita income for a person who reaches retirement age. In 2001, the eligible age for receiving the pension was raised from 60 to 61 (65 in 2013). Because the Japanese total fertility rate has declined to a low level of 1.25 children per woman (in 2005), however, people have been expressing concern about the sustainability of the pension system, particularly as the rate of payments into the system has fallen to about 60% (see Akimoto 2002, Oshio 2001, and Suzuki and Zhou 2001 for details).

10.1. Hypotheses

Abe (2001) describes three factors that influence the rate of payment into the National Pension as follows. The first is the pension-holder's liquidity condition. This is a relative value consisting of income in relation to the burden of payment. The second is the community factor. It implies that individuals who live in large cities lose their sense of belonging to a community and for that reason are more likely to refuse to pay into the pension system. The third factor is the substitutability between the national pension and other forms of old-age security, such as insurance and savings.

Our analysis tests three slightly different hypotheses. In the process of constructing them, we consider economic, social, and other factors that are expected to influence the rate of payment into the pension system. Our first hypothesis is that good economic conditions should raise the rate of payment and poor economic conditions should lower it. Specifically, a high birth rate, which decreases per capita income, should decrease the rate of payment. At the household level, large family size puts strong pressure on family income and should cause the rate of payment to decline. It is also obvious that a high unemployment rate should decrease the rate of payment. The second hypothesis is that the substitutability between other economic resources and the pension should decrease the rate of payment into the system. Specifically, a large amount of savings should decrease the rate of payment. The third hypothesis is that people who live in urban areas tend to be autonomous and not to care about their neighbors' welfare as much as do people who live in rural areas. Therefore, they should feel less obligated to pay the pension fee, and the rate of payment should be lower in urban than in rural areas. We can call this a community factor. We shall attempt to test the validity of these three hypotheses.

For that purpose, we use cross-sectional data from 47 prefectures during the period 1997–2002 and both Ordinary (OLS) and Two-Stage

Least-Square (2SLS) methods to estimate simultaneous relationships between the rate of payment into the pension system and other economic factors. The model is described below. In Appendix 10.1, we present several other models that consider the effects of pension fees, the share of young people in the population, the government's policy of exempting students and the poor from paying into the system, and other variables.

10.1.1. The model

1. a. Rate of payment $=f$(university student enrollment, death index, amount of money invested in life insurance contracts, amount of money on deposit in savings)
   b. Rate of payment $=f$(university student enrollment, amount of money invested in life insurance contracts, family size, unemployment rate)
   c. Rate of payment $=f$(death index, amount of money invested in life insurance contracts, amount of money on deposit in savings, population density)
   d. Rate of payment $=f$(family size, amount of money on deposit in savings, birth rate, unemployment rate)
   e. Rate of payment $=f$(family size, amount of money on deposit in savings, unemployment rate, population density)
2. a. Enrollment of university students $=f$(family size, amount of money on deposit in savings, population density)
   b. Enrollment of university students $=f$(amount of money invested in life insurance contracts, family size, population density)
3. Death index $=f$(family size, amount of money on deposit in savings, population density)
4. Amount of money invested in life insurance contracts $=f$(rate of payment, family size, amount of money on deposit in savings, population density)
5. a. Family size $=f$(university student enrollment, birth rate, unemployment rate)
   b. Family size $=f$(death index, the amount of money on deposit in savings, population density)

The model also has five endogenous variables and four exogenous variables. The five *endogenous variables* are the rate of payment (Pay:-payment), university student enrollment (unv), the death index (DI), the amount of money invested in life insurance contracts (LI), and family size (NF). The four *exogenous variables* are the amount of money on deposit in savings (s), the birth rate (B), the unemployment rate (ue), and population density (pop).

We checked the identification problem and estimated the model using both OLS and the 2SLS methods.

10.1.2. Data

Most of the econometric studies of the National Pension have used data on individuals. Our analysis relies instead on macro data. Both approaches are necessary to a full understanding of the National Pension system in Japan. Furthermore, aggregated behavioral data are required for the simulation model we use to clarify the structure of the pension. Our data are defined as follows and the sources of those data identified in parentheses.

For the endogenous variables, we use the following:

rate of payment (Pay:payment), defined as the total number of pension holders minus the number of pension holders who did not pay the pension fee at all for two years divided by the total number of pension holders (Social Insurance Agency 1998, 2001, 2003).

university student enrollment (unv), defined as the number of university students in each prefecture divided by the total population of each prefecture (Ministry of Education, Culture, Sports, Science, and Technology, Department of Investigation and Statistics, 1997–2002).

death index (DI), defined as the number of people who die of natural causes in a particular year divided by the population size in the same year (Asahi Newspaper Company 1998–2003).

life insurance contracts (LI), defined as the amount of money invested in life insurance contracts divided by the population of each prefecture (Life Insurance Association 1997– 2002).

family size (NF), defined as the number of people in families of each prefecture (Shibouta 1997–2002).

For the exogenous variables, we use the following:

money on deposit (s), defined as the amount of money in savings divided by the total population of each prefecture (Cabinet Office of the Economic, Social and General Research Institute 1997–2002).

birth rate (B), defined as the total fertility rate in each prefecture (Shibouta 1997–2002).

unemployment rate (ue), defined as usual (Yano Kota Memorial Society 1997–2002).

population density (pop), defined as usual.

10.1.3. Amplification of the hypotheses

Having described the data and their uses, we can now restate the hypothesis to be tested with our model. We begin by describing the expected effects of the five endogenous variables in our model.

1. For the rate of payment into the National Pension system
   - A higher birth rate and a higher rate of unemployment lead to a decrease in per capita income. Therefore, these two variables are classified as the liquidity factor, and the rate of payment decreases when they increase. The family size should decrease the rate of payment.
   - The rate of university student enrollment and population density are classified as a community factor. Therefore, they should decrease the rate of payment.
   - The rate of payment should increase when the amount of money invested in life insurance contracts increases. This comes from the liquidity factor. The substitutability between payments into the Nation Pension and money in savings should decrease the rate of payment.
   - As for the death index, the hypothesized result is ambiguous. The rate of payment may increase or decrease when the death index increases. Families react both ways, some paying into the National Pension when a family member dies, others not.
2. For the rate of university student enrollment
   - The amount of money invested in life insurance contracts and the amount of money on deposit in savings, which indicate solvency, should increase the rate of enrollment. Conversely, a larger family size, creating financial difficulty in sending children to institutions of higher education, should decrease the enrollment rate.
   - The rate of university enrollment should increase if families live in a city, especially in a large city in which there is high population density.
3. For the death index
   - Population density, which makes it easier to select better hospitals and medical facilities, should decrease the death index.
   - The amount of money on deposit in savings, which enables families to avail themselves of better health facilities, should decrease the death index.
   - Family size may have both effects. On the one hand, the pressure of a large family on a fixed income may increase the death index. On the other, the experience of a large family in preventing illness and caring for an ill member may decrease the death index. We hypothesize the latter—that is, that the death index should decrease in a large family.

4. For the amount of money invested in life insurance contracts
   - An increase of money in savings and a higher rate of payment into the National Pension should increase the amount of money invested in life insurance contracts.
   - An increase of population density should also increase the amount of money invested in life insurance because of greater access to prospective customers by insurance companies.
   - An increase in family size should decrease the amount of money invested in life insurance.
5. For family size
   - An increase in the birth rate and a decrease in the death index should increase family size.
   - An increase of money in savings should increase family size. In contrast, an increase in unemployment should decrease family size.
   - An increase of population density in which the nuclear family prevails should decrease family size. A family desiring higher education for its children is likely to have fewer members.

We can summarize the hypotheses by putting a plus or minus sign above each variable's symbol.

$$\text{Pay} = f(\overset{(-)}{\text{unv}}, \overset{(+,-)}{\text{DI}}, \overset{(+)}{\text{LI}}, \overset{(-)}{s}) \tag{10.1a}$$

$$\text{Pay} = f(\overset{(-)}{\text{unv}}, \overset{(+)}{\text{LI}}, \overset{(-)}{\text{NF}}, \overset{(-)}{\text{ue}}) \tag{10.1b}$$

$$\text{Pay} = f(\overset{(+,-)}{\text{DI}}, \overset{(+)}{\text{LI}}, \overset{(-)}{s}, \overset{(-)}{\text{pop}}) \tag{10.1c}$$

$$\text{Pay} = f(\overset{(-)}{\text{NF}}, \overset{(-)}{s}, \overset{(-)}{B}, \overset{(-)}{\text{ue}}) \tag{10.1d}$$

$$\text{Pay} = f(\overset{(-)}{\text{NF}}, \overset{(-)}{s}, \overset{(-)}{\text{ue}}, \overset{(-)}{\text{pop}}) \tag{10.1e}$$

$$\text{unv} = f(\overset{(-)}{\text{NF}}, \overset{(+)}{s}, \overset{(+)}{\text{pop}}) \tag{10.2a}$$

$$\text{unv} = f(\overset{(+)}{\text{LI}}, \overset{(-)}{\text{NF}}, \overset{(+)}{\text{pop}}) \tag{10.2b}$$

$$\text{DI} = f(\overset{(+,-)}{\text{NF}}, \overset{(-)}{s}, \overset{(-)}{\text{pop}}) \tag{10.3}$$

$$\text{LI} = f(\overset{(+)}{\text{Pay}}, \overset{(+,-)}{\text{NF}}, \overset{(+)}{s}, \overset{(+)}{\text{pop}}) \tag{10.4}$$

$$NF = f(\overset{(-)}{unv}, \overset{(+)}{B}, \overset{(-)}{ue}) \tag{10.5a}$$

$$NF = f(\overset{(-)}{DI}, \overset{(+)}{s}, \overset{(-)}{pop}) \tag{10.5b}$$

10.2. Estimation results for 47 prefectures

Next, we estimate our pension models. As there are so many combinations, we summarize them in Appendix 10.2.

10.2.1. Estimation results using cross-sectional data

As already stated, we use cross-sectional data from 47 Japanese prefectures for the period 1997–2002. and estimate our model by using both OLS and 2SLS (Table 10.1). The results are highly satisfactory in both estimation methods.

The estimated results of 2SLS (Table 10.1) are as follows:

First, the rate of payment into the National Pension decreases when the university enrollment rate, the amount of money deposited in savings, the birth rate, the unemployment rate, and population density respectively increase. Conversely, the rate of payment increases when the death index or the amount of money invested in life insurance increases. Family size has both signs in relation to the rate of payment. Two out of three of them are negative (i.e., the rate of payment decreases when family size increases) and significant.

Second, the university enrollment rate increases when the amount of money invested in life insurance, the amount of money deposited in savings, and population density increases, respectively. Conversely, the enrollment rate decreases when family size increases.

Third, the death index increases when the amount of money deposited in savings increases, an outcome not predicted by our hypothesis. One explanation may be that wealthy people who eat a lot of expensive, fatty foods may die earlier than others. Conversely, the death index decreases when family size and population density increase.

Fourth, the amount of money invested in life insurance increases when the rate of payment into the National Pension, the amount of money deposited in savings, and population density increase. Conversely, the amount of money invested in life insurance decreases when family size increases (although the *t*-statistics value is not significant).

Fifth, family size has a positive association with the amount of money deposited in savings and the birth rate. Conversely, family size is negatively associated with the university enrollment rate, the death index, the unemployment rate, and population density.

In short, we conclude that almost all the results are consistent with our hypotheses.

Table 10.1. Estimated results for the rate of payment, university student enrollment, death index, life insurance, and family size: 47 prefectures of Japan (2SLS simultaneous equation)

Dependent Variable		(10.1) Pay (Rate of Payment)					(10.2) unv (University Student Enrollment)		(10.3) DI (Death Index)	(10.4) ln LI (Life Insurance)	(10.5) ln NF (Family Size)	
Independent Variable		10.1a	10.1b	10.1c	10.1d	10.1e	10.2a	10.2b	10.3	10.4	10.5a	10.5b
Pay %										0.0061*** (9.8408)		
unv %											−0.0234*** (−7.4465)	
DI				−0.0078 (−0.1146)								−0.0026*** (−6.1627)
ln LI		137.6374*** (15.6424)	21.0506 (0.8559)	164.4616*** (17.6081)				2.4001*** (1.9381)				
ln NF			−92.1192*** (−3.9189)		57.9227*** (3.0302)	−47.5217*** (−2.5147)	−7.4575*** (−3.4264)	−9.2567*** (−3.6700)	−124.513*** (−4.6888)	−0.0118 (−0.0726)		
ln s (Money on deposit)		−39.0292*** (−6.9101)		−51.6986*** (−11.742)	−17.167*** (−5.9975)	−7.8269** (−2.335)	1.7551*** (3.3668)		33.3297*** (5.2402)	0.3161*** (9.7759)		0.1008*** (3.9085)
B % (Birth rate)					−27.0158*** (−5.6558)						0.1429*** (5.8435)	
ue % (Unemployment rate)			−4.8172*** (−4.9428)		−4.4796*** (−10.9485)	−5.7273*** (−15.4653)					−0.0110*** (−6.3461)	
ln pop (Population density)				−12.5818*** (−5.6966)		−6.1347*** (−5.6558)	0.9002*** (5.3629)	0.9655*** (5.1263)	−34.1181*** (−16.6581)	0.0750*** (7.0150)		−0.1183*** (−8.6584)
Constant		−353.846*** (−12.8975)	67.0579 (0.7036)	−379.396*** (−13.4657)	151.807*** (10.4738)	164.0296*** (11.2944)	−3.0605* (−1.6408)	−6.2708* (−1.4646)	140.9632*** (6.1940)	2.3121*** (19.6866)	0.4004*** (17.0890)	0.7024*** (9.5689)
$\bar{R}^2$		0.6715	0.6715	0.6715	0.6715	0.6715	0.3990	0.3828	0.5488	0.5137	0.4124	0.2669
No. of observations		282	282	282	282	282	282	282	282	282	282	282

Source: Calculated from data in various tables from Asahi Newspaper Company, Social Insurance Agency, Life Insurance Association, General Affairs Statistical Bureau, Toyo–keizai shinbosha, Cabinet Office of the Economic, Social and General Research Institute, Department of Investigation and Statistics in Ministry of Education, Culture, Sports, Science and Technology, Yano Kota Memorial Society. See the text for details.
*** Significant at 1%, ** Significant at 5%, * Significant at 10%. Values in parenthesis are *t* values.

10.3. Estimation results for the seven regions of Japan

As stated at the outset, we divided the whole of Japan into seven regions and estimated the regional differences. The prefectures belonging to each region are as follows:

Region 1 *Hokkaido and Tohoku Districts*: Hokkaido, Aomori, Iwate, Miyagi, Akita, Yamagata, Fukushima prefectures

Region 2 *Kanto District*: Ibaragi, Tochigi, Gunma, Saitama, Chiba, Tokyo, Kanagawa prefectures

Region 3 *Chubu District*: Niigata, Toyama, Ishikawa, Fukui, Yamagata, Nagano, Gifu, Shizuoka, Aichi prefectures.

Region 4 *Kinki District*: Mie, Shiga, Kyoto, Osaka, Hyogo, Nara, Wakayama prefectures

Region 5 *Shikoku District*: Tokushima, Kagawa, Ehime, Kouchi prefectures

Region 6 *Chugoku District*: Tottori, Shimane, Okayama, Hiroshima, Yamaguchi prefectures

Region 7 *Kyusyu District*: Fukuoka, Saga, Nagasaki, Kumamoto, Ooita, Miyazaki, Kagoshima, Okinawa prefectures

Figure 10.1 shows how the rate of payment into the National Pension system varied among regions over the period from 1997 to 2002. The rate was highest in Chubu and also high in Chugoku and Shikoku. Throughout most of the period, the rate was lowest in Kanto and Kinki, but in 2002 Kyushu had the lowest rate. The region that includes Hokkaido and Tohoku districts began the period with one of the highest rates but in 2002 joined the group with low rates.

We calculated these regional differences by using our simultaneous equation model, the results of which are given in Tables 10.2–8. We draw the following inferences from the results.

For the rate of payment,

1. All seven regions have a negative association (as does the whole of Japan) to the amount of money deposited in savings (all seven relationships are significant) and to the unemployment rate (six of those relationships are significant).

2. Six regions have a positive association (the same as for the whole of Japan) to life insurance (in five regions the association is significant) and to the death index (in only one region is the association significant).

3. Six regions have a negative association (the same as for the whole of Japan) to university student enrollment (in three regions the association is significant).

4. Five regions have a negative association (as does the whole of Japan) to the family size (in three regions the association is significant).

**Figure 10.1.   Regional differences in the rate of payment
into the National Pension**

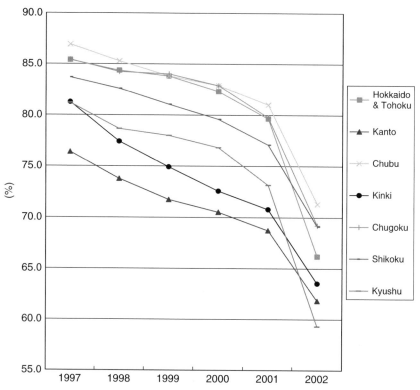

Source: Calculated by using data from various tables from Social Insurance Agency, *Outline of the Social Insure System* (1997–2002).

5. Only three regions have a negative association (as does the whole
   of Japan) to population density (in three regions the association is
   significant) and to the birth rate (in two regions, however, is the
   association significant).

For Hokkaido and Tohoku, an increase in the university student enrollment rate, the death index, and population density, respectively, increases
(not decreases as in the case of entire Japan) the rate of payment. Kanto
and Chubu have similar results. For Kinki, the enrollment rate, the death
index, family size, the amount of money deposited in savings, the unemployment rate, and population density have a negative sign. This is almost
the same result that we obtained for the whole of Japan. For Shikoku,
Chugoku, and Kyushu, the amount of money deposited in savings and the
unemployment rate have negative signs. This result is similar to that for
the whole of Japan. Almost all other variables are not significant.

Table 10.2. Estimated results for Hokkaido and Tohoku (2 SLS)

Dependent Variable	(10.1) Pay (Rate of Payment)					(10.2) unv (University Student Enrollment)		(10.3) DI (Death Index)	(10.4) ln LI (Life Insurance)	(10.5) ln NF (Family Size)	
Independent Variable	10.1a	10.1b	10.1c	10.1d	10.1e	10.2a	10.2b	10.3	10.4	10.5a	10.5b
Pay %									-0.0037*** (-2.8455)		
unv %		28.9176** (1.9289)								0.0744* (1.4568)	
DI			1.3788*** (7.6584)								0.0043*** (3.5752)
ln LI	-138.802* (-1.6247)	-358.226*** (-2.5600)	86.4260*** (2.9337)				2.8297 (1.1689)				
ln NF		-13.8714 (-0.4079)		2913.655 (1.2121)	-497.387*** (-3.3595)	-2.9093* (-1.3063)	-4.0306** (-2.0350)	84.5590** (1.8882)	1.4030*** (5.0308)		
ln s (Money on deposit)	-1347.41*** (-3.3707)		-108.644*** (-4.0708)	-1523.64 (-1.2028)	261.8238*** (3.6746)	-0.3549 (-0.2189)		73.0311** (2.2400)	-0.7955*** (-5.9750)		-0.0700 (-0.4210)
B % (Birth rate)				-388.77* (-1.3675)						-0.2853* (-1.3059)	
ue % (Unemployment rate)		-15.5631*** (-3.2445)		65.0939 (1.0992)	-19.4776*** (-4.6418)			-24.0177*** (-4.0538)	0.0463** (2.1152)	-0.0396*** (-3.0849)	
ln pop (Population density)			19.8029*** (3.2750)		5.8956* (1.3675)	1.0122*** (3.4353)	0.8789*** (3.0077)				0.1004*** (2.6750)
Constant	2262.17*** (2.7447)	1548.501*** (2.7198)	-116.313 (-0.7517)	3627.515 (1.2507)	-446.963*** (-3.0317)	1.5487 (0.3428)	-10.0479 (-1.0986)	-107.784 (-1.1865)	6.0622*** (15.2269)	0.8071*** (4.2051)	-0.0186 (-0.0487)
$\bar{R}^2$	0.6510	0.6510	0.6510	0.6510	0.6510	0.2120	0.2384	0.3780	0.5179	0.3466	0.3804
No. of observations	42	42	42	42	42	42	42	42	42	42	42

Note: See the source note and explanatory notes for Table 10.1.

Table 10.3. Estimated results for Kanto (2 SLS)

Dependent Variable	(10.1) Pay (Rate of Payment)					(10.2) unv (University Student Enrollment)		(10.3) DI (Death Index)	(10.4) ln LI (Life Insurance)	(10.5) ln NF (Family Size)	
Independent Variable	10.1a	10.1b	10.1c	10.1d	10.1e	10.2a	10.2b			10.5a	10.5b
Pay %									0.0096*** (2.5240)		
unv %	−3.1446 (−0.3600)	−0.2179 (−0.0519)								−0.0356*** (−19.7749)	
DI			0.2323 (0.5856)								−0.0002 (−0.2933)
ln LI	121.5395* (1.5977)	−41.6298 (−0.7245)	85.4614*** (2.8032)				7.2757*** (5.1072)				
ln NF		−60.1701 (−0.9910)		−22.2485 (−0.6632)	−96.9266 (−0.3656)	79.6475*** (3.3039)	−26.2667*** (−6.0927)	−300.142 (−0.8718)	1.5136 (0.2433)	−0.3824*** (−6.0265)	
ln s (Money on deposit)	−60.5217 (−0.8102)		−94.091*** (−4.3069)	−17.986 (−0.8598)	−38.0907 (−0.6387)	28.1538*** (5.1547)		17.1420 (0.2197)	1.1579 (0.8320)		−0.2086*** (−3.4660)
B % (Birth rate)				8.3626 (0.2618)							
ue % (Unemployment rate)		−7.4347*** (−3.6801)		−5.1016*** (−5.5023)	−5.2635*** (−6.2237)					−0.0164*** (−6.7943)	
ln pop (Population density)			4.1327 (0.3600)		−4.2455 (−0.2618)	5.9552*** (3.9987)	−0.5537* (−1.6357)	−46.9553** (−2.2077)	0.1176 (0.3075)		−0.0671*** (−3.4140)
Constant	−207.033 (−0.4113)	297.6522* (1.3562)	9.2289 (0.0875)	155.208* (1.3817)	277.1146 (0.7568)	−145.706*** (−4.3642)	−14.1218** (−1.7421)	306.7842 (0.6434)	−1.5678 (−0.1843)	0.9441*** (14.2820)	1.3618*** (14.5610)
$\bar{R}^2$	0.6822	0.6822	0.6822	0.6822	0.6822	0.9599	0.9596	0.8360	0.4246	0.9566	0.9553
No. of observations	42	42	42	42	42	42	42	42	42	42	42

Note: See the source note and explanatory notes for Table 10.1.

Table 10.4. Estimated results for Chubu (2 SLS)

Independent Variable	(10.1) Pay (Rate of Payment)					(10.2) unv (University Student Enrollment)		(10.3) DI (Death Index)	(10.4) ln LI (Life Insurance)	(10.5) ln NF (Family Size)	
	10.1a	10.1b	10.1c	10.1d	10.1e	10.2a	10.2b	10.3	10.4	10.5a	10.5b
Pay %									0.0190*** (3.4378)	0.0389** (1.7766)	
unv %	−1.1479 (−0.2219)	−3.2773 (−0.6384)									0.0035*** (3.1086)
DI	0.2616 (1.1892)		0.3829 (1.0897)								
ln LI	89.9924*** (4.1341)	−13.8194 (−0.2913)	87.0705*** (3.6447)				12.354*** (2.4398)			−0.5151*** (−3.0835)	−0.0352 (−0.5169)
ln NF		0.7777 (0.0078)		48.8719 (0.3762)	157.5099 (1.0012)	−10.9222* (−1.3868)	−39.7392*** (−2.4684)	172.4237*** (3.4059)	−3.1431** (−1.7444)		
ln s (Money on deposit)	−71.9323*** (−3.0823)		−78.293*** (−4.0509)	−22.4568 (−0.9277)	−40.2587* (−1.3271)	3.2826** (1.8316)		21.6345** (1.8780)	1.3269*** (3.3513)		
B % (Birth rate)				−14.1411 (−0.4057)							
ue % (Unemployment rate)		−5.7074*** (−3.2089)		−4.8591* (−1.4623)	−2.8288 (−1.1233)					−0.0329*** (−3.9261)	
ln pop (Population density)			2.5491 (0.2219)		3.3293 (0.4057)	0.5012 (0.9315)	−1.3202 (−1.2477)	−21.2486*** (−6.1440)	−0.0172 (−0.2585)		0.0532* (1.4458)
Constant	−71.2369 (−0.8115)	161.3261 (1.0246)	−59.1902 (−0.7436)	162.1954*** (2.5571)	139.7548*** (2.7904)	−5.3346 (−0.9718)	−26.1012** (−2.2039)	3.3793 (0.0957)	−0.3246 (−0.4123)	1.0332*** (6.6254)	0.0927 (0.5409)
$\bar{R}^2$	0.4064	0.4064	0.4064	0.4064	0.4064	0.2762	0.3098	0.8444	0.5652	0.4280	0.4605
No. of observations	54	54	54	54	54	54	54	54	54	54	54

Note: See the source note and explanatory notes for Table 10.1.

Table 10.5. Estimated results for Kinki (2 SLS)

Dependent Variable	(10.1) Pay (Rate of Payment)					(10.2) unv (University Student Enrollment)		(10.3) DI (Death Index)	(10.4) ln LI (Life Insurance)	(10.5) ln NF (Family Size)	
Independent Variable	10.1a	10.1b	10.1c	10.1d	10.1e	10.2a	10.2b			10.5a	10.5b
Pay %									0.0256 (1.1763)		
unv %	-8.5976*** (-9.2484)	0.4741 (0.7028)								-0.0485*** (-4.019)	
DI	-1.7941*** (-6.5159)		-0.2434* (-1.5706)								-0.0006 (-0.6766)
ln LI	-32.015** (-1.9237)		195.1427*** (8.5605)			12.2832 (1.0144)					
ln NF		-225.777** (-2.0498)		26.4640 (0.5461)	172.2253 (0.4506)	-34.797*** (-2.6461)	-59.3839*** (-2.8689)	-39.6465 (-0.4378)	-6.6125 (-0.9476)		
ln s (Money on deposit)	-203.73*** (-11.2581)		-20.9032** (-1.7884)	-33.2396*** (-2.8867)	-56.9816 (-1.0309)	-9.4253*** (-2.4790)		-19.2791 (-0.7364)	1.6848 (0.9889)		0.0613 (0.8541)
B % (Birth rate)				4.6337 (0.3919)						0.8306*** (3.6992)	
ue % (Unemployment rate)		-10.0441*** (-5.3933)		-4.3693*** (-4.1210)	-2.1830 (-0.3871)					0.0041 (0.6975)	
ln pop (Population density)			-32.4745*** (-9.2484)			0.2465 (0.2330)	-3.2697* (-1.4925)	-11.8439** (-1.6255)	-0.1002 (-0.3731)		-0.0706*** (-4.6605)
Constant	1091.026*** (8.1729)	512.4166** *(3.2114)	-525.744*** (-4.8998)	190.0989*** *(3.7753)	182.7901*** (2.8220)	48.7587*** (3.9650)	-11.8303 (-0.3185)	216.6933*** (2.5590)	-0.3555 (-0.1004)	-0.2670 (-1.2395)	0.4984** (1.6882)
$\bar{R}^2$	0.8272	0.8272	0.8272	0.8272	0.8272	0.3329	0.2454	0.1890	0.6801	0.6854	0.4613
No. of observations	42	42	42	42	42	42	42	42	42	42	42

Note: See the source note and explanatory notes for Table 10.1.

Table 10.6. Estimated results for Shikoku (2 SLS)

Dependent Variable	(10.1) Pay (Rate of Payment)					(10.2) unv (University Student Enrollment)		(10.3) DI (Death Index)	(10.4) ln LI (Life Insurance)	(10.5) ln NF (Family Size)	
Independent Variable	10.1a	10.1b	10.1c	10.1d	10.1e	10.2a	10.2b	10.3	10.4	10.5a	10.5b
Pay %											
unv %	−3.1063 (−0.1348)	−23.6964*** (−3.2469)							0.0079 (0.5884)	0.0710*** (8.2377)	
DI	−0.3968 (−1.1368)		0.9935 (0.0934)								0.0798*** (4.4116)
ln LI	117.8218** (1.7493)	47.8260 (0.5076)	101.9591* (1.5901)				−7.5943*** (−4.3563)				
ln NF		146.5896* (1.5120)		−928.875* (−1.5611)	322.639 (1.3553)	4.8203*** (2.4463)	17.5280*** (8.2550)	8.2132 (0.2228)	0.2525 (0.1037)		
ln s (Money on deposit)	−41.5046 (−0.6033)		−56.7838 (−1.2314)	192.2199* (1.3092)	−121.41** (−1.9248)	2.1910*** (4.2542)		2.8434 (0.2952)	0.3739 (0.3324)		−0.1651** (−1.9272)
B % (Birth rate)				136.7705*** (2.4685)						0.2111*** (3.7083)	
ue % (Unemployment rate)		−1.3473 (−0.5515)		−16.5843** (−1.7524)	2.9629 (0.6221)					−0.0066** (−1.8889)	
ln pop (Population density)			35.0204 (0.1348)		8.5864*** (2.4685)	−0.4088*** (−2.9739)	−0.5572*** (−4.1476)	−24.4962*** (−9.5279)	−0.0884 (−0.7313)		1.9701*** (4.4963)
Constant	−200.044 (−0.3990)	−139.809 (−0.3810)	−345.315 (−0.2202)	−224.952 (−0.9064)	318.4124*** (3.3456)	−7.2298*** (−5.5077)	25.5705*** (4.0208)	169.8202*** (6.9174)	2.2237 (0.6251)	0.1775*** (2.9146)	−13.6625*** (−4.4987)
$\bar{R}^2$	0.6933	0.6933	0.6933	0.6933	0.6933	0.7557	0.7612	0.8523	0.4105	0.8588	0.7631
No. of observations	24	24	24	24	24	24	24	24	24	24	24

Note: See the source note and explanatory notes for Table 10.1.

Table 10.7. Estimated results for Chugoku (2 SLS)

Dependent Variable	(10.1) Pay (Rate of Payment)					(10.2) unv (University Student Enrollment)		(10.3) DI (Death Index)	(10.4) ln LI (Life Insurance)	(10.5) ln NF (Family Size)	
Independent Variable	10.1a	10.1b	10.1c	10.1d	10.1e	10.2a	10.2b			10.5a	10.5b
Pay %									0.0083** (1.7077)		
unv %										-0.1073*** (-9.0916)	
DI	-24.0265 (-0.7292)										-0.0036*** (-5.6575)
ln LI	-1853.81 (-0.7287)	-137.719** (-2.3816)	38.7113 (0.8775)				-16.468*** (-5.2039)				
ln NF		156.1235** (1.9194)		11.2058 (0.2403)	-58.1121 (-0.8432)	4.4493* (1.6149)	37.7626*** (5.7273)	-225.44*** (-3.6753)	2.2204*** (5.8581)		
ln s (Money on deposit)	-622.162 (-0.8335)		-77.6935*** (-3.2979)	-64.1575** (-2.1144)	-51.6996* (-1.5174)	-1.0503 (-1.0078)		-8.7338 (-0.3764)	0.7096** (1.7081)		-0.0444 (-0.7489)
B % (Birth rate)				-27.1762* (-1.3483)						0.7433*** (7.5881)	
ue % (Unemployment rate)		-7.1310*** (-3.6031)		-2.2134 (-0.9716)	-2.8238 (-1.1657)					0.0135*** (2.6194)	
ln pop (Population density)			14.4094 (0.7355)		-16.2649* (-1.3483)	3.5666*** (7.3632)	7.6533*** (8.6953)	-76.1981*** (-7.0658)	0.3409*** (4.1739)	-0.2970*** (-7.9588)	
Constant	13005.64 (0.7484)	585.0876*** (2.8613)	89.3975 (0.3413)	317.2777*** (3.1808)	322.7207*** (3.2420)	-5.3893* (-1.3971)	32.8743*** (4.0489)	426.8602*** (4.9707)	-0.7550 (-0.3944)	-0.1284* (-1.4615)	1.7157*** (8.0585)
$\bar{R}^2$	0.4878	0.4878	0.4878	0.4878	0.4878	0.7908	0.8935	0.7273	0.5172	0.8118	0.7944
No. of observations	30	30	30	30	30	30	30	30	30	30	30

Note: See the source note and explanatory notes for Table 10.1.

Table 10.8. Estimated results for Kyushu (2 SLS)

Dependent Variable	(10.1) Pay (Rate of Payment)					(10.2) unv (University Student Enrollment)		(10.3) DI (Death Index)	(10.4) ln LI (Life Insurance)	(10.5) ln NF (Family Size)	
Independent Variable	10.1a	10.1b	10.1c	10.1d	10.1e	10.2a	10.2b			10.5a	10.5b
Pay %								0.0065*** (14.0991)			
unv %	−7.0789** (−1.8618)	1.7886 (0.2940)								0.0120 (1.1024)	
DI			−0.2986 (−1.0503)								−0.008* (−1.3266)
ln LI	153.4574*** (5.9695)	−1.2362 (−0.0233)	193.9209*** (4.7798)				1.6030** (2.1366)				
ln NF		10.0788 (0.2569)				−6.7414*** (−3.0314)	−7.4140*** (−3.4999)	−95.5026* (−1.4852)	−0.2734* (−1.5918)		
ln s (Money on deposit)	−52.331*** (−2.9847)		−45.8982** (−2.3166)	21.5409 (0.6875)	1.1072 (0.0784)	1.1819*** (1.5404)		105.7447*** (4.7661)	0.3493*** (5.8376)		0.0171 (0.1697)
B % (Birth rate)				23.9773 (0.5341)						0.2315*** (4.6408)	
ue % (Unemployment rate)		−6.7278*** (−2.8633)		−7.8863*** (−3.0476)	−6.7830*** (−9.1031)					−0.0127*** (−3.0064)	
ln pop (Population density)			−25.1397** (−1.8618)		2.9572 (0.5341)	1.4500*** (5.8479)	1.6458*** (8.5337)	−51.1311*** (−7.1313)	0.0895*** (3.9621)		−0.0028 (−0.0685)
Constant	−362.2*** (−3.9056)	105.9534 (0.5128)	−448.092*** (−3.4507)	49.2335 (0.6341)	98.6361** (2.2052)	−3.0712 (−1.2607)	−5.8520** (−1.9108)	−53.0439 (−0.7530)	2.2414*** (12.2822)	0.2563*** (6.0572)	0.4810** (2.2890)
$\bar{R}^2$	0.7204	0.7204	0.7204	0.7204	0.7204	0.6089	0.6265	0.5961	0.8649	0.2872	0.0541
No. of observations	48	48	48	48	48	48	48	48	48	48	48

Note: See the source note and explanatory notes for Table 10.1.

10.4. Conclusion

Our results can be summarized as follows: The rate of payment into the National Pension *decreases* when the university enrollment rate, the amount of money deposited in savings, the birth rate, the unemployment rate, or population density increases. Conversely, the rate of payment into the system *increases* when the death index or the amount of money invested in life insurance increases. Family size has both negative and positive signs in relation to the rate of payment. However, two out of three are negative and significant.

From these regional analyses, we can extrapolate consistent results for the case of Japan as a whole—except for the birth rate, for which we did not obtain a significant result. On the basis of all those results, we can draw the following conclusions: First, an increase in the unemployment rate decreases the rate of payment into the National Pension. That is as expected, since the unemployed are unlikely to have excess income to invest in the system. An increase in private savings also decreases the rate of payment into the system, indicating the substitutability between the National Pension and private savings. If people have a large amount of money saved (i.e., they can afford to support themselves during retirement), they do not have to depend on the National Pension. Third, and paradoxically, an increase in life insurance coverage increases the rate of payment into the National Pension, suggesting a complimentary relationship between the two forms of insurance. In other words, people who worry about their own, as well as their family's lives, pay for life insurance to supplement their pension benefits.

As hypothesized, the greater the university enrollment and the larger the average family size, the lower were the payments into the pension system in most of the regions, although in only three regions were the negative associations significant. Because having children enrolled at a university or having a large family to support increases pressure on a family's income, it is not surprising that payments into the pension system decline.

However, the hypothesized associations between payments into the system and the birth rate (negative), population density (negative), and the death index (positive) did not obtain in the regional analysis, although they were confirmed for Japan as a whole.

Japan's total fertility rate decreased to 1.25 children per woman in 2005. From the negative significant association between the amount of money on deposit in savings and the rate of payment into the National Pension system in almost all regions, we can conclude that people try to save money and avoid paying into the system if the government increases the payments required of income earners and decreases the benefits it pays to retirees as a result of the low fertility rate.

Appendix 10.1.

Our model did not include the effects of certain pension policies. Therefore, here we develop the model to include those effects. The Japanese government began granting an exemption from paying into the system for university students in 2000 and a partial exemption for the poor in 2002. In the case of the partial exemption for the poor, the central government transferred the administration of their pension fees to local governments, which strictly monitored their eligibility.

To estimate these effects, we constructed several models. Appendix Table 10.A1 summarizes the 2SLS results. We show only the result for the rate of payment, although we also obtained good results for four other

Table 10.A1. Estimated results of the dummy variables "Student" and "Poor" for the rate of payment (2SLS)

Variable	Equation Number				
	(10.1)	(10.2)	(10.3)	(10.4)	(10.5)
Constant	−283.0180 (−10.4426)	−318.0550 (−4.4577)	−349.7260 (−12.3060)	125.9118 (11.1251)	147.8198 (13.2704)
Unv%	−5.0923 (−6.8979)	−16.1261 (−10.0007)			
DI	0.2247 (7.4976)		0.0372 (0.7051)		
(ln)LI	109.1263 (11.0032)	121.5168 (6.5994)	151.0492 (14.4622)		
(ln)NF		−141.3150 (−8.0678)		97.7871 (6.4361)	−71.0606 (−5.0752)
(ln)s	−27.9339 (−4.9980)		−46.5507 (−10.3607)	−11.7463 (−5.3162)	2.2651 (0.8440)
B%				−43.7857 (−11.2118)	
Ue%		0.1818 (0.2343)		−2.5740 (−6.9831)	−4.7195 (−15.4350)
(ln)Pop			−11.5230 (−6.8979)		9.5729 −11.2118
StudentD	−0.7529 (−1.1856)	−2.9006 (−4.4843)	0.6453 (1.0351)	−0.9823 (−1.6732)	−0.6656 (−1.1487)
PoorD	−6.2925 (−7.3626)	−7.6668 (−9.9910)	−4.2694 (−5.0470)	−10.2497 (−4.3398)	−9.6016 (−13.6252)

endogenous variables (university student enrollment, death index, life insurance, and family size). Although we obtained good results for all five equations, equation (10.4) may be the best, judging from the t-value. In equation (10.4) all the dummy variables for the exemption of the poor have negative signs and are significant at 1 or 5 percent; and almost all the variables for the student exemption are negative, but only two are significant at 1% and 10%. This means that monitoring of the exemption for the poor is very severe, and as it increases many people cannot pay their pension fees. That is the reason why this dummy has a negative and significant sign. In the case of the student-exemption dummy, the sign is negative, but there were many nonsignificant estimates. People envy students, and some people who are not students do not want to pay the students' pension fees, believing that having to do so is unfair.

We also constructed other models that include the effects of the pension-fee payment (P) and young people—that is, the share of people between the ages of 20 and 29 (Young). The estimated result follows. Here we show only the result for the rate of nonpayment, although we obtained results for the other endogenous variables.

$$\text{Nonpay} = 2.0272P + 3.4522\text{Young} + 4.5746\ln\text{Pop} - 1527.89\text{Longevity}$$
$$(2.0553) \quad (10.3000) \quad\quad (4.0611) \quad\quad\quad (-5.4540)$$
$$-57.2262(\ln)\text{LI} + 7.9187\text{StudentD} + 1.2287\text{PoorD} + 3091.216$$
$$(-4.9936) \quad\quad (7.5006) \quad\quad\quad (15.1263) \quad\quad (5.5764),$$

where, Nonpay is the rate of nonpayment, Longevity is life expectancy, and other variables remain same as before. The signs for payment of the pension fee (P) and the share of the young (Young) are positive and significant at 1%. This shows that people avoid paying into the pension when the fee is high and they are young.

Appendix 10.2.

1. ①-a Pay $= f(\text{unv}, \text{DI}, \text{LI}, s)$
②-a unv $= f(\text{NF}, s, \text{pop})$
③   DI $= f(\text{NF}, s, \text{pop})$
④   LI $= f(\text{Pay}, \text{NF}, s, \text{pop})$
⑤-a NF $= f(\text{unv}, B, \text{ue})$

2. ①-a Pay $= f(\text{unv}, \text{DI}, \text{LI}, s)$
②-b unv $= f(\text{LI}, \text{NF}, \text{pop})$
③   DI $= f(\text{NF}, s, \text{pop})$
④   LI $= f(\text{Pay}, \text{NF}, s, \text{pop})$
⑤-a NF $= f(\text{unv}, B, \text{ue})$

3. ①-b $\text{Pay} = f(\text{unv}, \text{LI}, \text{NF}, \text{ue})$

    ②-a $\text{unv} = f(\text{NF}, s, \text{pop})$

    ③ $\text{DI} = f(\text{NF}, s, \text{pop})$

    ④ $\text{LI} = f(\text{Pay}, \text{NF}, s, \text{pop})$

    ⑤-a $\text{NF} = f(\text{unv}, B, \text{ue})$

4. ①-b $\text{Pay} = f(\text{unv}, \text{LI}, \text{NF}, \text{ue})$

    ②-b $\text{unv} = f(\text{LI}, \text{NF}, \text{pop})$

    ③ $\text{DI} = f(\text{NF}, s, \text{pop})$

    ④ $\text{LI} = f(\text{Ev}, \text{NF}, s, \text{pop})$

    ⑤-a $\text{NF} = f(\text{unv}, B, \text{ue})$

5. ①-c $\text{Pay} = f(\text{DI}, \text{LI}, s, \text{pop})$

    ②-a $\text{unv} = f(\text{NF}, s, \text{pop})$

    ③ $\text{DI} = f(\text{NF}, s, \text{pop})$

    ④ $\text{LI} = f(\text{Pay}, \text{NF}, s, \text{pop})$

    ⑤-a $\text{NF} = f(\text{unv}, B, \text{ue})$

6. ①-c $\text{Pay} = f(\text{DI}, \text{LI}, s, \text{pop})$

    ②-b $\text{unv} = f(\text{LI}, \text{NF}, \text{pop})$

    ③ $\text{DI} = f(\text{NF}, s, \text{pop})$

    ④ $\text{LI} = f(\text{Pay}, \text{NF}, s, \text{pop})$

    ⑤-a $\text{NF} = f(\text{unv}, B, \text{ue})$

7. ①-d $\text{Pay} = f(\text{NF}, s, B, \text{ue})$

    ②-a $\text{unv} = f(\text{NF}, s, \text{pop})$

    ③ $\text{DI} = f(\text{NF}, s, \text{pop})$

    ④ $\text{LI} = f(\text{Pay}, \text{NF}, s, \text{pop})$

    ⑤-a $\text{NF} = f(\text{unv}, B, \text{ue})$

8. ①-d $\text{Pay} = f(\text{NF}, s, B, \text{ue})$

    ②-b $\text{unv} = f(\text{LI}, \text{NF}, \text{pop})$

    ③ $\text{DI} = f(\text{NF}, s, \text{pop})$

    ④ $\text{LI} = f(\text{Pay}, \text{NF}, s, \text{pop})$

    ⑤-a $\text{NF} = f(\text{unv}, B, \text{ue})$

9. ①-d $\text{Pay} = f(\text{NF}, s, B, \text{ue})$

    ②-a $\text{unv} = f(\text{NF}, s, \text{pop})$

    ③ $\text{DI} = f(\text{NF}, s, \text{pop})$

    ④ $\text{LI} = f(\text{Pay}, \text{NF}, s, \text{pop})$

    ⑤-b $\text{NF} = f(\text{DI}, s, \text{pop})$

10. ①-d $\text{Pay} = f(\text{NF}, s, B, \text{ue})$

    ②-b $\text{unv} = f(\text{LI}, \text{NF}, \text{pop})$

    ③ $\text{DI} = f(\text{NF}, s, \text{pop})$

    ④ $\text{LI} = f(\text{Pay}, \text{NF}, s, \text{pop})$

    ⑤-b $\text{NF} = f(\text{DI}, s, \text{pop})$

11. ①-e $\text{Pay} = f(\text{NF}, s, \text{ue}, \text{pop})$

    ②-a $\text{unv} = f(\text{NF}, s, \text{pop})$

    ③ $\text{DI} = f(\text{NF}, s, \text{pop})$

    ④ $\text{LI} = f(\text{Pay}, \text{NF}, s, \text{pop})$

    ⑤-a $\text{NF} = f(\text{unv}, B, \text{ue})$

12. ①-e $\text{Pay} = f(\text{NF}, s, \text{ue}, \text{pop})$

    ②-b $\text{unv} = f(\text{LI}, \text{NF}, \text{pop})$

    ③ $\text{DI} = f(\text{NF}, s, \text{pop})$

    ④ $\text{LI} = f(\text{Pay}, \text{NF}, s, \text{pop})$

    ⑤-a $\text{NF} = f(\text{unv}, B, \text{ue})$

References

Abe, Aya. 2001. "The premium exempt structure reform of the National Pension: Its impact on the noncompliance rate and progressivity [Kokumin-Nenkin hokenryo menjyo-seido kaisei—Mikanyu, minouritsu to gyakusinsei he no eikyo]". *JCER Economic Journal* [*Nihon Keizai Kenkyu*]. Japan Center for Economic Research [Nihon Keizai Kenkyu Senta] 43: 34–54.

Akimoto, Miyo, ed. 2002. *Institutional administration and the Financial Implication of Social Insurance* [Syakai-hosho no seido to gyo-zaisei]. Tokyo: Yuhikaku.

Asahi Newspaper Company [Asahi-Shinbun-sha]. 1998–2003. *Nation's Power* [*Minryoku*]. Tokyo.

Cabinet Office of the Economic, Social and General Research Institute [Naikaku-Fu Keizai-Shakai Sougo-Kenkyu-Sho]. 1997–2002. *Annual report: Prefectural Economic Analysis* [*Kenmin keizai-keisan nenpo*]. Tokyo.

General Affairs Statistical Bureau (Somu-cho Toukei-kyoku). 1995, 2000. *Census report* [*Kokusei-Chosa-houkoku*]. Tokyo.

Life Insurance Association [Seimei-Hoken Kyoukai]. 1997–2002. *Outline of Life Insurance Work* [*Seimei-hoken jigyo-gaikyo*]. Tokyo.

Ministry of Education, Culture, Sports, Science, and Technology, Department of Investigation and Statistics [Monbu-Sho Chousa-Toukei-Ka]. 1997–2002. *Basic School Evaluation* [*Gakko kihon chosa houkoku*]. Tokyo.

Oshio, Takashi, 2001. *Economics of Social Security* [*Shakai hosho no keizaigaku*]. 2nd ed. Tokyo: Nihon Hyoron-sha.

Shibouta, Seishi, ed. 1997–2002. *General Outline of Regional Economies* [*Chiiki keizai souran*]. Tokyo: Toyo-Keizai–Shinbosha.

Social Insurance Agency [Shakai-Hoken-Cho]. 1998. *Evaluation of Membership and Others of the National Pension: Year of Heisei 10* [*Heisei 10 nen Kouteki-Nenkin kanyu-jyoukyo-tou chousa*]. Tokyo. http://www.sia.go.jp/infom/tokei/gaikyo1998/sanko/index.htm.

———. 2001. *Evaluation of the Membership and Others of the National Pension: Year of Heisei 13* [*Heisei 13 nen Kouteki-Nenkin kanyu-jyoukyo-tou chousa*]. Tokyo. http://www.sia.go.jp/infom/tokei/gaikyo1998/sanko/index.htm.

———. 2003. *Situation of the Number of Members and Payers into the National Pension: Year of Heisei 15* [*Heisei 15 nen no Kokumin-Nenkin no kanyu-nouhu jyoukyo*]. Tokyo. http://www.sia.go.jp/infom/tokei/gaikyo1998/sanko/index.htm.

———. 2000. *Insurance Fee Exemption System of the National Pension* [*Kokumin Nenkin no hoken-ryo menjo seido*]. Tokyo. http://www.sia.go.jp/infom/tokei/gaikyo1998/sanko/index.htm.

———. 1997–2002. *Outline of the Social Insurance System* [*Shakai-Hoken jigyo no gaiyo*]. Tokyo.

Social Insurance Agency, Administration [Shakai-Hoken-Cho, Gyousei], ed. 1990. *30-year History of the National Pension* [*Kokumin Nenkin sanjyu-nen no Ayumi*]. Tokyo.

Suzuki, Wataru, and Yanfei Zhou. 2001. "An economic analysis of the uninsured of the National Pension system in Japan [*Kokumin-Nenkin mikanyu-sha no keizai bunseki*]". JCER Economic Journal [*Nihon Keizai Kenkyu*]. 42: 44–60.

Yano Kota Memorial Society [Yano Kota Kinen-Kai]. 1997–2002. *Situation of Prefectures by Data Investigation* [*Deita de miru kensei*]. Tokyo: Kokusei-Sha.

AUTHOR INDEX

AARP 156
Abe, Aya 244
Ahlburg, Dennis A. 76, 96
Akimoto, Miyo 244
Aoki, Masahiko 142, 158
Aoki, Noriko 4, 243
Arrow, Kenneth J. 211, 241
Asahi Newspaper Company 246
Aten, Bettina 57

Baker, George 138, 158
Barro, Robert J. 5, 35, 39, 43, 73, 100, 101, 130
Becker, Gary S. 164, 185
Berger, Mark C. 137, 138, 158, 159
Binswanger, Hans P. 119, 131
Bloom, David E. 5, 7, 11, 13, 15, 16, 22, 35, 36, 42, 75, 96, 101, 103, 109, 130, 131
Boles, James S. 190, 208
Brander, J.A. 35, 36
Brockwood, Krista J. 208
Bruno, Michael 211, 241
Bureau of Statistics 191
Burtless, Gary 134, 158

Cabinet Office of the Economic 246
Cai, Fang 100, 131
Canning, David 5, 11, 15, 23, 35, 36, 39, 42, 75, 96, 102, 130
Chan, Sewin 133, 158
Chan, William 141, 158
Chen, Kong-Pin 158
Chen, Jian 100, 131
Coale, Ansley 40, 56, 73
Colton, Cari L. 208

Committee for Economic Development 134
Cutler, David M. 76, 79, 96

De Fraja, Gianni 211, 241
Deaton, Angus 75, 96
Doeringer, Peter B. 165, 185
Dowrick, Steven 35, 36
Du, Yang 100
Dur, Robert A. 211, 241

Epple, Dennis 241

Fernández, Raquel 212, 241
Fleisher, Belton M. 100, 131

Garen, John E. 137, 138, 158, 159
Gastil, Raymond, D. 36
Genda, Yuji 165, 185
General Affairs Statistical Bureau 250
Gibbons, Robert 164, 185
Gibbs, Michael 138
Glomm, Gerhard 212, 241
Grace-Martin, Karen 144, 159
Gradstein, Mark 212, 241
Graham, Bryan 16, 36, 75, 96

Hammer, Leslie B. 190, 208
Hanushek, Eric A. 211, 229, 241
Hardy, Melissa A. 133, 137, 158
Heston, Alan 37, 57, 73
Heywood, John S. 136, 137, 138, 158
Higgins, Matthew 11, 13, 24, 59, 61, 70, 73, 75, 98
Hirsch, Barry T. 133, 137, 158
Ho, Lok-Sang 136, 137, 158
Holmstrom, Bengt 138

Hoover, Edgar M. 40, 56, 73
Hu, Luojia 137, 138, 159
Huang, Wei 131
Hutchens, Robert M. 133, 136, 138, 141, 143, 144, 159

Idson, Todd L. 142, 159

Japan Institute for Labour Policy and Training 158, 165
Japan National Institute of Population and Social Security Research 103
Jensen, Eric R. 76, 96
Justman, Moshe 212, 241

Kalleberg, Arne 144, 159
Kawaguchi, Akira 4, 189
Kelley, Allen C. 5, 11, 36, 39, 56, 58, 74, 96, 97, 131
Kennedy, George 106, 119, 131
Kinugasa, Tomoko 3, 17, 36, 75, 97, 99, 131

Lai, Mun Sim 97
Lazear, Edward P. 138, 141, 143, 155, 159, 163, 185
Lee, Jong-Who 35, 36
Lee, Ronald D. 5, 10, 11, 12, 16, 24, 36, 84, 97
Lee, Sang-Hyop 76, 77, 95, 97
Leff, Nathaniel H. 58, 74
Leung, Charles Ka Yui 229, 241
Levine, Ross 11, 36, 55, 74
Life Insurance Association 246
Lloyd, B. 76, 98
Lommerud, Kjell Erik 211, 236, 241
Lueing 211, 229

McMurrian, Robert 190, 208
Macpherson, David A. 133, 137, 158
Maddison, Angus 97
Malaney, Pia N. 5, 11, 15, 23, 36, 102, 103, 130
Mason, Andrew 1, 2, 17, 24, 43, 36, 58, 74, 75, 76, 77, 78, 79, 80, 85, 95

Matsukura, Rikiya 75, 98
Merrick, Thomas 75, 98
Miller, Tim 16, 24, 36, 76, 97
Ministry of Education, Culture, Sports, Science, and Technology 246
Mitani, Naoki 134, 159, 165, 185
Montgomery, Mark R. 76, 98
Mulaney 2

Nakamura, Jiro 185
Neal, Margaret B. 208
Netemeyer, Richard G. 190, 208
Newton, Jason T. 208
Novos, Ian E. 141, 159

OECD 133, 134, 191, 229
Ogawa, Naohiro 75, 98
Ohashi, Isao 162, 177, 185
Okunishi, Yoshio 164, 185
Oshio, Takashi 4, 211, 244, 264
Oyer, Paul 138, 159

Paxson, H. 75, 96
Piore, J. 165, 185
Poterba, James M. 96
Prendergast, Canice 141, 159

Quinn, Joseph F. 134, 158

Radelet, Steven 5, 10, 11, 12, 36
Ravikumar, B. 212, 241
Renelt, David 11, 36, 55
Rogerson, Richard 212, 241
Romano, Richard E. 241

Sachs, Jeffery 5, 10, 11, 12, 36, 39
Saint-Paul, Gilles 212, 242
Sakamoto, Ariyoshi 189, 209
Sala-i-Martin, Xavier 100, 101, 130
Sato, Hiroki 193, 209
Schmidt, Robert M. 2, 5, 11, 13, 22, 36, 39, 56, 58, 72, 74, 75, 97, 99, 100, 102, 103, 104, 112, 131
Scott, Frank A. 137, 138, 158, 159

Sevilla, Jaypee 76, 96
Shaw, Paul R. 75, 98
Sheiner, Louise M. 96
Shibouta, Seishi 246, 264
Social Insurance Agency 246
Stevens, Ann Huff 133, 158
Stiglitz, Joseph E. 240, 241, 242
Summers, Lawrence H. 96
Summers, Robert 37, 57
Suzuki, Wataru 244, 264

Takeishi, Emiko 193, 209
Taylor, Alan M. 56, 57, 58, 70, 74
Teulings, Coen M. 211
Tung, An-Chi 97

Ulph, David 211, 236, 242
U.S. Census Bureau 134
U.S. Population Division 80, 81
U.S. Population Projections Branch 77
UN 57, 80, 81, 89
UNPD 80

Valsecchi, Irene 141
Verdier, Thierry 212, 242

Wakisaka, Akira 195, 209
Waldman, Michael 141, 159, 164, 185
Wang, Dewen 100
Wei, Huang 99
Wei, Xiangdong 158
Williamson, Jeffery G. 2, 5, 7, 11, 13, 22, 24, 36, 39, 42, 56, 57, 58, 73, 75, 96, 98, 101, 102, 109, 131
Williamson, Oliver E. 162, 185
World Bank 57, 83

Yamaguchi, Mitoshi 1, 3, 4, 99, 119, 128, 131, 243
Yano Kota Memorial Society 246, 264
Yao, Shujie 100, 131
Yilmaz, Kuzey 211, 229, 241

Zhang, Zongyi 100, 131

SUBJECT INDEX

Age discrimination 134, 157
Age structure 1, 56, 75, 76, 95
Age–skill profile 163, 166
Age–wage profile 164, 165, 170, 177, 180
Agriculture 14, 127, 144
Asymmetric information 140, 141, 155, 156
Awaji Yumebutai International Conference 1

Baby boom 77, 81, 83, 84, 93, 95, 117, 170, 175, 177
Baby-boom generation 170, 175, 177
Benthamian social welfare function 214, 217, 229
Birth rate 4, 39, 102, 103, 104, 117, 246, 247, 248

Capital 12–13, 55–58
Capital accumulation 3, 10, 76, 85, 101, 163
CATI 144
Childbirth 189, 193
Childcare leave 192–195
Childcare Leave Law 192
China 99
Chubu 251, 252
Chugoku 251, 252
Cluster analysis 175, 177
COE 1
Community factor 244, 247
Conditional convergence 10, 101, 109
Consideration age 167, 175
Continuous employment 161, 164
Convergence 10–12, 15, 42

Death Index 245, 246, 247
Declining-skill-profile 180
"Declining" 167
Deferred-payment system 162, 163
Delayed-payment contract 136, 142, 143, 155, 156, 157
Democracy 17, 18, 34
Demographic change 39, 45–46, 47–48, 49–53
Demographic core 16, 30–31
Demographic dividend 75, 77–80, 84–89
Demographic transition 30, 50, 78, 99
Demographic variable 5, 14, 17, 23, 24
Density 14–15
Dependency 12, 62–64
Dependency ratio 14, 17, 29, 43, 77
Deposit in saving 245, 247, 260
Desirable wage 162, 166, 170
Developed countries 46, 50, 191
Discrimination 134, 157
Displacement effects 180–183
Double-earner couple 203, 204, 206, 207, 208
Dynamic condition 87

East Asian "miracle" 75
Economic component 41, 43, 45
Economic condition 244
Economic core 16, 21
Economic growth 39, 99
Education 211, 236–240
Education and defense spending 17
Education at a Glance 229
Education output function 213, 214, 215, 233, 235

Effective number of consumer 79, 84, 85
Effective number of producer 78, 79
Elderly dependency 61–62, 63
Employer-sponsored training 143, 153, 155
Employment indices of older workers 165–177
Employment-protection legislation 161, 164, 165
Employment rate 9, 42, 244, 246
Employment/population ratio 162
Endogenous variable 245, 247, 262
Enriched 40, 54
Equity-efficiency trade-off 211
Exemption of the poor 262
Exogenous variable 31, 245, 246
Experience 39, 156
Externality 206–208

Factor-augmenting method 106
Family leave 191
Family size 246, 247, 248, 249, 260
Female Employment Management Survey 195
Fertility 1, 8, 52, 53, 99, 104
Fertility rate 189, 260
Firm-specific human capital 163, 164
First dividend 81–84
Fixed costs 135–137, 157, 163
"Flat" 167
Flexi-time system 189, 195
Flexi-time work 191

Gender 189
General equilibrium growth accounting 119
Golden-rule 87

Harvard 18, 22, 39, 40
Harvard model 8, 9, 22
Health 17, 150
Health insurance 137, 150
Hokkaido and Tohoku 251, 252

India 2, 24, 34, 76, 77, 80, 81, 82, 88, 89
Indices for the employment of older workers 170
Inflation 12, 17, 18, 34
Inside 3
Institute for Research on Household Economics 195
Internal labor market 164, 165
Internal wage structure 162, 180
Investment 55–63, 64

Japan 243, 251
Japanese Panel Survey of Consumers 195
Joint-profit maximization 206

Kanto 251, 252
Kinki 251, 252
Kyusyu 251

Labor 189
Labor force participation 8, 9, 118, 134, 157, 189, 190, 192, 194, 208
Labor market 133, 138, 162
Labor productivity 10, 12, 14, 39
Life-cycle motive 85
Life-cycle wealth 87–89
Life expectancy 1–3, 75, 82, 85
Life insurance contract 246, 247

Male Educ 16
Mandatory retirement 134, 136, 161–162, 164
Mandatory retirement age 161, 164, 175, 177
Maternity leave system 189
Maternity-pay entitlement 191
M-job 139, 140, 142
Mortality 1, 5, 16, 46, 52, 81, 82, 99, 117

Nash equilibrium 190, 205, 206, 207, 208
National Pension 243, 260

Neoclassical growth theory 9, 10, 42, 100, 101
New school leavers 180–183
"Normal age" 167

Old-age dependency 2, 77
Older worker 133, 161, 165, 180–183
On-site childcare center 189, 195
Optimal education policies 211
Ordered probit 152, 166
Outside worker 3, 135, 138, 139, 140, 142, 151, 155, 157

Parental-leave system 189
Part-time employment 133
Part-time work 191, 195, 198
Pay-for-performance dummy 180
Pay-for-performance systems 177, 180
"Peak age" 167
Pension 4, 133, 137, 142, 161, 162, 243–263
Pension fee 245, 246, 262
Performance-based wages 177
Population 5–8, 9–11, 12–14, 15–24, 21–23, 24–26, 27–28, 30, 53
Population density 102, 246, 247, 248, 249
Population growth 1, 21–22
Population size 14, 39–40, 43, 117
Population survey 137
Private education 215–223
Probit 198
Productivity component 12–15
Progressivity 238
Public education 215–223, 236–240
Public pension 4, 84, 95, 161, 162

Random-effect probit 198
Rate of payment 243, 244–245, 246
Rawlsian social welfare function 214, 218, 222

Regional economic growth 99
Regressivity 238
Residual method 128
Retirement 3–4, 162
Rising-profile occupation 170, 177
"Rising" 166, 167
R-job 139–140, 142

Saving 64–69
Schooling attainment 16
Second dividend 79, 87–94
Seniority-based wages 177
Shikoku 251, 252
Simple demography 18
Simulation 87–89
Single-earner couple 203
Size 3, 14, 22, 48, 100, 246
Skill profile 165–177
Social norm 202
Social security system 134
Steady state 12, 43, 87, 101
Student exemption 262
Substitutability 244, 247, 260
Substitution/complement relationship 180
Support ratio 80, 81–83

Technical change 14, 106, 119, 128, 129
Terms of trade 17, 28, 43
Tournament 141, 156
Training expense 135
Transaction costs 162, 163, 164, 177, 183
Translations 7–9, 21–23, 28–30, 48
Translations component 15
Translations demography 6, 18, 24, 30, 32, 40, 48, 54
Turning age 167, 175
Turnover rate 195–198
Two-Stage Least-Square 18

Unemployment rate 244, 245, 246

Unfavorable treatment 202
University student enrollment 246,
247, 251, 252, 262
US 78, 81, 83, 93, 134, 144

Value of marginal product 162, 164,
165
Verdoorn method 128

Wage gap 170, 180
Wage-skill gap 164, 165
Wealth 84, 87–89
White-collar 3, 137, 144, 145
Work-family reconciliation
policies 191

Work-life Balance (WLB) measures
189, 191–198
Wu-Hausman test 35, 70

Young 3, 77, 134, 136, 139,
161–162, 165
Young worker 4, 133, 180
Youth 7, 13, 23, 40, 43, 57, 62, 161,
165
Youth dependency 2, 29, 30, 40, 41,
48, 49, 52, 56, 57, 58, 61, 62, 63,
68, 70, 103
Youth dependency ratio 29, 48, 53

Zd impact 28, 29, 47, 49, 52